THE BEST TEST PREPARATION FOR THE
ADVANCED PLACEMENT
EXAMINATION *IN*

PHYSICS

Larry Dale Brown
Instructor of Physics
Lake Mary High School
Lake Mary, Florida

Steven Brehmer
Instructor of Physics
Mayo High School
Mayo, Minnesota

Michael L. Lemley
Instructor of Physics
Buckhannon–Upshur High School
Buckhannon, West Virginia

Research and Education Association
61 Ethel Road West
Piscataway, New Jersey 08854

The Best Test Preparation for the
ADVANCED PLACEMENT EXAMINATION
IN PHYSICS

Revised Printing, 1993

Printed in the United States of America

Library of Congress Catalog Card Number 92-80113

International Standard Book Number 0-87891-881-7

Research & Education Association
61 Ethel Road West
Piscataway, New Jersey 08854

REA supports the effort to conserve and
protect environmental resources by
printing on recycled papers.

ACKNOWLEDGMENTS

*We thank the following authors for their work on the
AP Physics Test Preparation Book:*

David K. Bross
Physics Teacher
Parkway West High School
Ballwin, Missouri

Michael H. Farmer
Physics Teacher
Greenville Technical College
Greenville, South Carolina

Joseph J. Molitoris, Ph.D.
Professor of Physics
Muhlenberg College
Allentown, Pennsylvania

Larry Weathers
Physics Teacher
The Bromfield School
Harvard, Massachusetts

* * *

In addition, special recognition is extended to the following persons:

Carl Fuchs, Director of Operations, for his overall guidance which
has brought this publication to completion.

Rochelle L. Stern, Managing Editor, for coordinating the editorial
staff throughout each phase of the project.

Judy Walters, Senior Editor, for her editorial contributions and
management of the project.

CONTENTS

About Research and Education Association vi
Preface vii
About the Test vii
Which Exam Should You Take viii
About the Review ix
Taking the Practice Exams xi
Scoring the Exam xi
AP Physics Study Schedules xii
AP Physics B Study Schedule xiii
AP Physics C Study Schedule xiv

AP PHYSICS B REVIEW

Chapter 1 — Vectors and Scalars 3

Chapter 2 — Mechanics 8

Chapter 3 — Electricity and Magnetism 27

Chapter 4 — Waves and Optics 42

Chapter 5 — Physical Optics 58

Chapter 6 — Heat, Kinetic Theory, and Thermodynamics 61

Chapter 7 — Modern Physics 72

AP PHYSICS C REVIEW

Chapter 8 — Classical Mechanics 80

Chapter 9 — Electricity and Magnetism 104

AP PHYSICS B TEST 1 125
 Test 1 127
 Answer Key 156
 Detailed Explanations of Answers 157

AP PHYSICS B TEST 2 175
 Test 2 177
 Answer Key 204
 Detailed Explanations of Answers 205

AP PHYSICS C TEST 3 227
 Mechanics 229
 Answer Key 244
 Detailed Explanations of Answers 245

 Electricity and Magnetism 264
 Answer Key 279
 Detailed Explanations of Answers 280

ANSWER SHEETS 301

About Research and Education Association

REA is an organization of educators, scientists, and engineers specializing in various academic fields. REA was founded in 1959 for the purpose of disseminating the most recently developed scientific information to groups in industry, government, universities, and high schools. Since then, REA has become a successful and highly respected publisher of study aids, test preps, handbooks, and reference works.

REA's Test Preparation series extensively prepares students and professionals for the Advanced Placement Exams (AP), SAT (Scholastic Aptitude Test), College Board Achievement Tests (CBAT), and Graduate Record Examinations (GRE). Whereas most Test Preparation books present a limited amount of practice exams, REA's series usually presents three or more exams which accurately depict the actual exams in both degree of difficulty and types of questions. REA's exams are always based on the most recently administered tests and include every type of question that can be expected on the actual tests.

REA's publications and educational materials are highly regarded for their significant contribution to the quest for excellence that characterizes today's educational goals. We continually receive an unprecedented amount of praise from professionals, instructors, librarians, parents, and students for our published books. Our authors are as diverse as their subjects and fields represented in the books we publish. They are well-known in their respective fields and serve on the faculties of prestigious universities and high schools throughout the United States.

PREFACE

This book provides an accurate and complete representation of the Advanced Placement Examination in Physics. Provided are three complete Advanced Placement Physics Exams: two AP Physics B and one AP Physics C exam. Each exam is composed of every type of question that can be expected on the AP Physics Exam. In addition, each exam is followed by an answer key and detailed explanations to every question. By completing the exams which correspond to the test you are taking (B or C) and by studying the explanations of answers and our AP Physics Review, you can discover your strengths and weaknesses and thereby become well prepared for the actual exam.

ABOUT THE TEST

The Advanced Placement (AP) Physics B and C Exams are given each May by the Educational Testing Service under the direction of the Advanced Placement Board. The Advanced Placement program is designed to allow high school students to pursue college-level studies while still attending high school. The AP exam is administered to high school students who have completed a year's study in a college-level physics course. The exam is taken by students in an attempt to earn college credit. At many colleges, if the student scores high enough on the exam, he/she will earn college credits, and will be granted appropriate academic placement. Thus the student may enter higher level classes while still a freshman.

There are two AP Physics examinations:

• the Physics B exam, and

• the Physics C exam

The Physics B exam primarily tests mechanics, heat, kinetic theory and thermodynamics, and electricity and magnetism. Knowledge of algebra and trigonometry is necessary. The Physics C exam consists of two tests. One concentrates on mechanics, and the other concentrates on electricity and magnetism. Both require a strong knowledge of calculus.

The Physics B exam consists of two sections.

- Section One   70 multiple-choice questions
                 90 minutes

- Section Two   6 free-response questions
                 90 minutes

The Physics C exam consists of two individual tests which are each divided into multiple-choice questions and free-response questions. The student may choose to take both tests, or, if it is preferred, the student can take either individual test which would consist of multiple-choice questions and free-response questions on one topic. Whether you choose to take one individual or both tests, you must take both the multiple-choice and the free-response questions for that test.

- Test One-Mechanics   35 multiple-choice questions dealing only
                        with mechanics
                        45 minutes

                        3 free-response questions
                        45 minutes

- Test Two-Electricity
  and Magnetism   35 multiple-choice questions dealing only
                        with electricity and magnetism
                        45 minutes

                        3 free-response questions
                        45 minutes

WHICH EXAM SHOULD YOU TAKE?

You can either take the Physics B or the Physics C exam, but you cannot take both. There are two ways to determine which exam you should take: 1. If your school is offering only the Physics B course, then take the B exam. If your school is offering only the Physics C course, then take the C exam. If you are taking the C exam, then you can choose to take only the mechanics section, or to take only the electricity and magnetism section, or to take both. It is your option depending on which subject areas you feel more comfortable. 2. If your school only offers a general AP Physics course and does not specify B or C, speak to your teacher regarding which exam you should take. Your teacher will be able to review your abilities and knowledge, and help you pick the appropriate exam.

The C exam is more difficult and requires more knowledge than the B exam; however, a good grade on either exam may earn you college credit. Keep in mind that you cannot take both exams, and that you cannot change your mind once you have signed-up to take one of the exams, so think carefully about which exam you wish to take.

ABOUT THE REVIEW

Our AP Physics B and C Reviews provide a comprehensive summary of the main areas tested on each of the AP Physics Exams, and are written to help you understand these topics. The review chapters have been developed based on the topical outline given by the test administrator and include the following subjects.

PHYSICS B REVIEW

Vectors and Scalars

Addition of Scalars, Subtraction of Vectors, The Components of a Vector, The Unit Vector, Adding Vectors Analytically, Multiplication of Vectors.

Mechanics

Kinematics, Dynamics, General Orbits of Planets and Satellites, Torque and Rotational Statistics, Energy and Momentum, Simple Harmonic Motion.

Electricity and Magnetism

Electrostatics, Electrostatics with Conductors, Electric Circuits, Parallel Plate Capacitors, Electromagnetism, Magnetostatics.

Waves and Optics

General Wave Properties, Properties of Standing Waves, Special Relativity, Mass and Energy Effects, Geometrical Properties.

Physical Optics

Heat, Kinetic Theory, and Thermodynamics

Thermal Properties, Kinetic Theory, Thermodynamics, First Law of Thermodynamics, The Second Law of Thermodynamics.

Modern Physics

Nuclear Structure and Transformation, Quantum Theory, and Atomic Structure.

PHYSICS C REVIEW

Classical Mechanics

Vectors, Linear Motion, Two-Dimensional Motion, Newton's Laws, Momentum, Energy and Work, Collisions, and Lagrangian Mechanics.

Electricity and Magnetism

Electric Fields, Capacitors, Current and Resistance, Circuits, The Magnetic Field, and Magnetic Fields and Currents.

By studying our review, your chances of scoring well on the actual exam will be greatly increased. After thoroughly studying the material presented in the Physics Review, you should go on to take the appropriate practice tests. Used in conjunction, the review and the practice tests will enhance your skills and give you the added confidence needed to obtain a high score.

TAKING THE PRACTICE EXAMS

Make sure to take the practice exam(s) which correspond(s) to the exam you are taking. When taking the practice exams, you should try to simulate your testing conditions.

- Work in a quiet place where you will not be interrupted.

- Time yourself!

- Do not use books, calculators, or similar articles, since these materials will not be permitted into the test center.

By following these tips, you will become accustomed to the time constraints you will face when taking the exam, and you will also be able to develop speed in answering the questions as the test format becomes more familiar.

SCORING THE EXAM

The multiple-choice section of the exam is scored by crediting each correct answer with one point, and by deducting one-fourth of a point for each incorrect answer. Questions omitted receive neither a credit nor a deduction, so it is to your advantage to utilize the process of elimination if you are unsure of an answer. The free-response section is scored by a group of "chief readers" who read your response and assign it a grade. Then both grades, the raw score on the multiple-choice section, and the grade on the free-response section, are combined and converted to the program's five-point scale:

5—extremely qualified

4—well-qualified

3—qualified

2—possibly qualified

1—no recommendation.

Colleges participating in the Advanced Placement Program usually recognize grades of three or higher.

AP PHYSICS STUDY SCHEDULES

It is important for you to discover the time and place for studying that works best for you. Some students may set aside a certain number of hours every morning to study, while others may choose to study at night before going to sleep. Other students may study during the day, while still others may study while waiting in line. Only you will be able to know when and where your studying is most effective. Use your time wisely. Work out a study routine and stick to it.

For those students taking only one part of the Physics C exam, either Magnetics or Electricity and Magnetism, you only have to study the appropriate chapter, 8 for Classical Mechanics, or 9 Electricity and Magnetism, and take that test. For those taking both parts, be sure to study both subjects.

AP PHYSICS B

You will find below a suggested four week study schedule. You may want to follow a schedule similar to this one. (Depending on the amount of study time before the exam, you may want to add to this schedule, condense it, or reorganize it.)

Week	Activity
1	Study chapters 1 through 4 of the Physics B review. As you study, notice that the bolded words are defined in the text. Because there are so many of them, you may want to design a flashcard study system. Write the word on one side and the definition on the other. You can test yourself or study with a friend. This will help you to remember key terms and refresh your memory as you learn more and more terms throughout the chapters.
2	Study chapters 5 through 7 of the Physics B review in the same manner. Draw up flashcards to test your retention of key definitions and concepts. Take the quiz at the end of each chapter.
3	Take Practice Test 1 and score yourself. Study the detailed explanations of answers to understand why you may have chosen incorrect answers. Go back and re-study any material with which you feel uncomfortable .
4	Take Practice Test 2 and score yourself. Has your score improved? If not, you may want to re-study the review once again in order to fully grasp the more difficult concepts. For extra confidence, you might want to re-work some of the problems of the test to make sure you fully grasp their concepts. You may also want to re-take test 1 or 2 to feel more comfortable with the time constraints of this test.

AP PHYSICS C

This is a suggested six week study schedule. If you have more time to prepare for the exam, you can add to the schedule, you can change which subject you study first, or, if your time is restricted, you can condense the schedule by combining two weeks into one.

Week	Activity
1	Begin to study chapter 8, Classical Mechanics. For those students who have opted to take only the Electricity and Magnetism section of the exam, you should begin to study chapter 9. If you are taking both parts of the exam, start with chapter 8, Classical Mechanics.
2	Complete your study of Chapter 8, Classical Mechanics, or, if you have opted not to take the Mechanics portion of the exam, complete your study of chapter 9, Electricity and Magnetism.
3	Take the appropriate part of test 3. If you are taking only Mechanics, take questions 1–35. If you are taking both the Mechanics and Electricity and Magnetism tests, take the Mechanics section, questions 1–35 now. If you are only taking the Electricity and Magnetism test, take questions 36–70 now. Score yourself and study the detailed explanations of answers to determine your strengths and weaknesses. If you are still weak in certain areas, re-study them.
4	If you are not satisfied with your score, you may want to re-study the appropriate material, and retake the exam. If you are taking both parts of the exam, you should now start studying the Electricity and Magnetism, chapter 9.
5	Finish studying the Electricity and Magnetism section.
6	Take the Electricity and Magnetism exam (Test 3, Questions 36–70). Score yourself and read the detailed explanations of answers. Re-study any area in which you still are weak.

ADVANCED PLACEMENT EXAMINATION IN
PHYSICS

B Course Review

CHAPTER 1

VECTORS AND SCALARS

BASIC DEFINITIONS OF VECTORS AND SCALARS

A **vector** is a quantity that has both magnitude and direction. Some typical vector quantities are displacement, velocity, force, acceleration, momentum, electric field strength, and magnetic field strength.

A **scalar** is a quantity that has magnitude but no direction. Some typical scalar quantities are mass, length, time, density, energy, and temperature.

Note: In this book, vectors are indicated by bold type.

ADDITION OF VECTORS (a + b) — GEOMETRIC METHODS

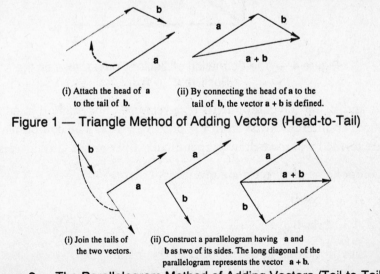

(i) Attach the head of **a** to the tail of **b**.

(ii) By connecting the head of **a** to the tail of **b**, the vector **a + b** is defined.

Figure 1 — Triangle Method of Adding Vectors (Head-to-Tail)

(i) Join the tails of the two vectors.

(ii) Construct a parallelogram having **a** and **b** as two of its sides. The long diagonal of the parallelogram represents the vector **a + b**.

Figure 2 — The Parallelogram Method of Adding Vectors (Tail-to-Tail)

SUBTRACTION OF VECTORS

The subtraction of a vector is defined as the addition of the corresponding negative vector. Therefore, the vector **P** – **F** is obtained by adding the vector (– **F**) to the vector **P**, i.e., **P** + (– **F**). See the following figure.

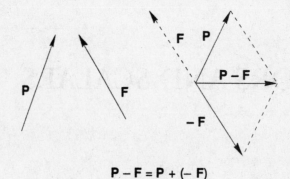

$$P - F = P + (- F)$$

Figure 3 — The Subtraction of a Vector

THE COMPONENTS OF A VECTOR

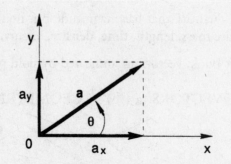

Figure 4 — The Formation of Vector Components on the Positive *x* – *y* Axis

a_x and a_y are the components of a vector **a**. The angle θ is measured counterclockwise from the positive *x*-axis. The components are formed when we draw perpendicular lines to the chosen axes.

The components of a vector are given by

$$A_x = A \cos \theta$$

$$A_y = A \sin \theta$$

A component is equal to the product of the magnitude of vector A and cosine of the angle between the positive axis and the vector.

The magnitude can be expressed in terms of the components:

$$A = \sqrt{A_x^2 + A_y^2}\,.$$

For the angle θ,

$$\tan\theta = \frac{A_y}{A_x}\,.$$

A vector **F** can be written in terms of its components F_x and F_y:

$$\mathbf{F} = \mathbf{i}F_x + \mathbf{j}F_y,$$

where **i** and **j** represent perpendicular unit vectors (magnitude = 1) along the x- and y-axis.

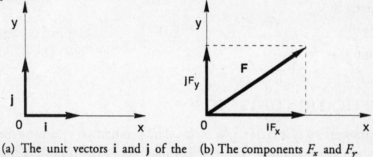

(a) The unit vectors **i** and **j** of the two-dimensional rectangular coordinate system.

(b) The components F_x and F_y.

Figure 5 — Vector Components and the Unit Vector

THE UNIT VECTOR

A **unit vector** in the direction of a vector **a** is given by

$$\mathbf{u} = \frac{\mathbf{a}}{|\mathbf{a}|} = \frac{\mathbf{a}}{a} = \left(\frac{a_x}{a}\mathbf{i} + \frac{a_y}{a}\mathbf{j}\right)\,.$$

ADDING VECTORS ANALYTICALLY

Analytical addition involves adding the components of the individual vectors to produce the sum, expressed in terms of its components.

To find **a** + **b** = **c** analytically:

i)   Resolve **a** in terms of its components:

$$\mathbf{a} = \mathbf{i}a_x + \mathbf{j}a_y.$$

ii) Resolve **b** in terms of its components:

$$b = ib_x + jb_y.$$

iii) The components of **c** equal the sum of the corresponding components of **a** and **b**:

$$c = i(a_x + b_x) + j(a_y + b_y)$$

and

$$c = ic_x + jc_y$$

and the magnitude

$$|c| = \sqrt{c_x^2 + c_y^2}$$

with θ given by

$$\tan \theta = \frac{c_y}{c_x}.$$

MULTIPLICATION OF VECTORS

Multiplication of a vector by a scalar. The product of a vector **a** and a scalar k, written as k**a**, is a new vector whose magnitude is k times the magnitude of **a**; if k is positive, the new vector has the same direction as **a**; if k is negative, the new vector has a direction opposite that of **a**.

The Scalar Product (Dot Product). The **dot product** of two vectors yields a scalar:

$$a \cdot b = ab \cos \theta.$$

The Vector Product (Cross Product). The **cross product** of two vectors yields a vector:

$$a \times b = c \quad \text{and} \quad |c| = ab \sin \theta.$$

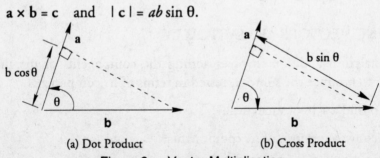

(a) Dot Product   (b) Cross Product

Figure 6 — Vector Multiplication

The direction of the Vector Product $\mathbf{a} \times \mathbf{b} = \mathbf{c}$ is given by the "Right-Hand Rule":

i)   With $\mathbf{a}$ and $\mathbf{b}$ tail-to-tail, draw the angle θ from $\mathbf{a}$ to $\mathbf{b}$.

ii) With your right hand, curl your fingers in the direction of the angle drawn. The extended thumb points in the direction of $\mathbf{c}$.

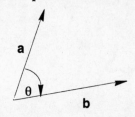

Figure 7 — The Direction of the Vector Product,

$\mathbf{c} = \mathbf{a} \times \mathbf{b}$ ($|\,\mathbf{c}\,|$ = $\mathbf{ab} \sin \theta$), is into the page.

CHAPTER 2

MECHANICS

KINEMATICS

Kinematics is a branch of mechanics in which motion along straight lines and curves is studied. The fundamental concepts described here are the basis for mechanical physics.

The concept of motion involves several important ideas, the first of which is speed. **Speed** is the time rate of motion, or simply, the distance traveled within a given time unit. To calculate a speed, the equation is

$$s = d/t$$

where s is the speed, d is the distance traveled, and t is the time to travel the distance. If, for example, a member of a track team were to run 100 meters in a time of 11.5 seconds, his speed would be 100 m/11.5s, which is 8.7 m/s.

The understanding of speed leads to a more complex concept known as velocity. **Velocity** is complex in that it consists of two parts, speed *and* direction. If a mass travels in a given direction, its time rate of motion is now considered a velocity. The numeric speed value is called the magnitude and the direction is specified. Examples of velocity values are 250 m/s south, or 50 m/s 10° north of west. When calculating velocity values, the equation is similar to the speed equation:

$$v = \Delta d/\Delta t$$

where v is the velocity, d is the distance, and t is the time. The magnitude of velocity can also be represented graphically.

Graph A shows the change in distance versus the travel time. The velocity is represented by the slope of the line. Since the slope of the line is constant, the magnitude of the velocity is constant. However, if the slope of the representative line changes during the time period, then the velocity is variable. Variable velocity is shown on Graph B.

Once again, the equation and graphs only represent the magnitude of the velocity, but the direction of the motion must be specified. This directional aspect makes velocity a vector quantity. Vectors are lines which can be used to graphically examine velocity. Because of their nature, vectors are more mathematically complex than numeric magnitudes. By examining the following velocity vector problem, the nature of vectors may be better understood.

An airplane flies east with a velocity of 150 km/hr. The wind at this time has a velocity of 45 km/hr south. What is the plane's resultant velocity? To solve the problem, a graphic representation is made using vectors. (See Figure 8.) By adding the wind vector to the plane vector, we find a resultant vector, v_r, at some angle south of east. In a scalar drawing, the resultant velocity, v_r, is equal to the length of v_r in centimeters times the 10 km/hr scale. For example, if v_r is 15 cm, then the velocity is 15×10 or 150 km/hr. The angle is measured with a protractor, and we find the direction of v_r to be some angle

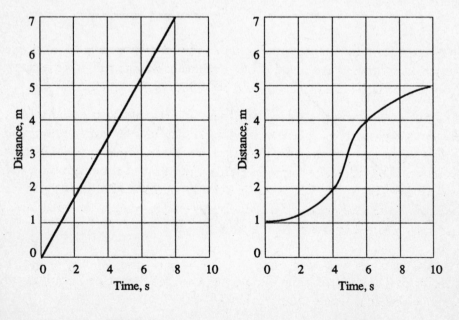

Graph A   Graph B

south of east. Directional angles should always be measured from the nearest horizontal or vertical reference, in this case, east.

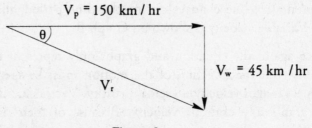

Figure 8

Without a scale drawing we solve the problem trigonometrically, beginning with the tangent function:

$$\tan \theta = 45/150 = 0.3$$
$$\theta = \arctan 0.3 = 16.7° \text{ S of E}$$
$$\sin \theta = 45/V_r$$
$$v_r = 45/\sin 16.7° = 156.6 \text{ km/hr}$$

When an object changes in velocity, it is accelerating. **Acceleration** is the rate of change of velocity within a given time period. Acceleration, *a*, is the

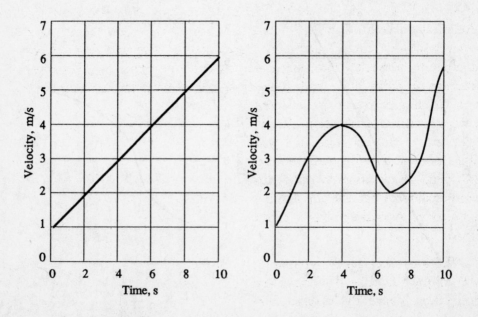

Graph C

Graph D

change in velocity divided by the time interval for the change. The equation is

$$a = \Delta v / \Delta t.$$

As with a velocity, acceleration can be represented graphically as the slope of a line for a velocity versus time graph. It can also be constant (Graph C) or variable (Graph D).

If a car is traveling at 20 km/hr, and then accelerates to 60 km/hr in 5 seconds, the acceleration would be $(60 - 20)/5 = 40/5 = 8$ km/hr/s. This means that for each of the 5 seconds, the velocity increases by 8 km/hr. The acceleration equation can be solved for a final velocity so that

$$v_f = v_i + a\Delta t.$$

Combining this equation with the velocity equation, $v = \Delta d/\Delta t$, we can produce an equation with which we may solve for the distance traveled by an accelerating object:

$$\Delta d = v_i \Delta t + {}^1/_2 a\Delta t^2.$$

Since acceleration is defined as a change in velocity, it is possible to accelerate by changing only the direction of the velocity and have the magnitude remain the same. An example of this idea is that if you were walking 3 m/s east, then turned and walked 3 m/s south, you have accelerated. If these directional changes were to occur constantly in equal amounts, then the resulting path of motion would be circular. Circular motion is the result of **centripetal acceleration**, which means acceleration towards a center point. Figure 9 shows a circular path and 2 positions for the same object. Upon examination, we see the direction of the velocity at any given time is perpendicular to the radius of the path. The velocity direction changes in such a way so as to move toward the center, hence, centripetal acceleration. Assuming θ and d are very small, the path will be circular. The force which causes centripetal acceleration is called the **centripetal force** because this force is also directed toward the center of the circular path.

Uniform circular motion has its own unique quantities of velocity and acceleration. Since the displacement

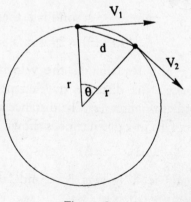

Figure 9

along a circle can be measured by angles, velocity about a circular path is known as **angular velocity**, ω, so that

$$\omega = \Delta\theta\ /\ \Delta t,$$

where $\Delta\theta$ is the change in angular displacement and Δt is the time interval for that change. **Angular acceleration**, α, relates to angular velocity by

$$\alpha = \Delta\omega\ /\ \Delta t,$$

where $\Delta\omega$ is the change in angular velocity, and Δt is the time interval for that change.

DYNAMICS

The foundation concept in the study of dynamics is the force. **Forces** are phenomena which pull or push on masses. **Gravity** is one such force. Gravity pulls masses toward the earth. Gravity accelerates all masses at 9.8 m/s². This means that small masses fall at the same rate as larger ones. However, the air around the earth can cause objects to fall more slowly. If we consider objects falling in a vacuum, then we can make predictions about their motion. Any equation involving acceleration, *a*, can be adapted for gravitation acceleration by replacing *a* with *g*; 9.8 m/s². Figure 10 shows the fall of a mass starting from rest. As the mass falls, it gains velocity at 9.8 m/s². The velocity after any given time of fall is

$$v = g\Delta t.$$

If we examine a 3 second fall, then

$$v = (9.8)\ (3) = 29.4 \text{ m/s.}$$

We also see that as the velocity increases, the distance traveled per second also increases. The distance an object falls in a given time is shown by

$$\Delta d = \tfrac{1}{2}\,g\,\Delta t^2.$$

Again looking at a 3 second fall, the distance fallen is

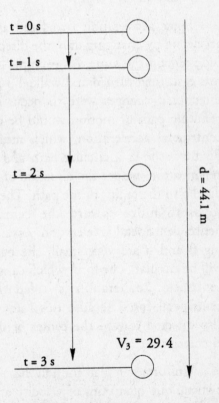

Figure 10

$\Delta d = \frac{1}{2} (9.8) (3^2) = 44.1$ meters.

An additional application of free falling objects is the parabolic motion of a projectile. Projectiles, such as a bullet, baseball, etc., have motion characteristics in two dimensions simultaneously. However, these horizontal and vertical motions are independent of one another. Figure 11 shows the path of a projectile with a velocity of 100 m/s at 30° above horizontal.

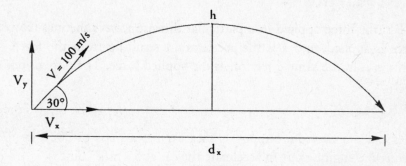

Figure 11

Since v is at an angle, the horizontal motion of the object is a result of the horizontal component of v, $v_x = v \cos 30°$. The vertical motion results from the vertical component $v_y = v \sin 30°$. Accordingly, the X motion is analyzed with a linear equation, and the Y motion is analyzed with falling object equations. The maximum height of a projectile, h, is the point at which $v_y = 0$. The time to reach maximum height is half the time of the total flight, and is given by

$t = v \sin \theta / g.$

For our example,

$t = (100) \sin 30°/9.8 = 5.1$ s.

By substitution,

$h = v^2 \sin^2 \theta / 2g.$

Thus, $h = (100)^2 \sin^2 30°/(2)(9.8) = 127.55$ m.

Since the total time is twice the time to maximum height or 10.2 s, the horizontal distance can be found by $d_x = v_x t$.

$d_x = v_x t = v \cos \theta\ t = (100) (\cos 30°) (10.2) = 883.3$ m

Masses tend to resist the effect of forces due to a characteristic known as **inertia**. Inertia is the platform for Newton's First Law of Motion. The first law states that if a mass is at rest, its inertia will act so as to keep the mass at rest. Also, if a mass is moving, its inertia acts to keep the mass moving with a constant velocity. This idea helps to explain orbiting satellites or planets. Once the motion is established, it will not change unless some external force acts to change the motion. The force is defined by Newton's Second Law of Motion. Mathematically,

$$F = m\mathbf{a},$$

where F is the force applied in a particular direction, m is the mass to which the force is applied, and **a** is the acceleration resulting from the force. The acceleration is in the same direction as the applied force. The dimensions of a force are

$$F = (kg)(m/s^2)$$

which is called a **newton**. Suppose a race car has a mass of 2000 kg. What force must the engine exert to accelerate the car at 50 m/s²? Since

$$F = m\mathbf{a},$$

$$F = (2000)(50) = 100,000$$

newtons of force. Newton's Third Law of Motion involves two forces. This law states that when one mass exerts a force on another, the second mass will exert a reaction force equal in magnitude and opposite in direction to the first. As stated earlier, the force of gravity pulls masses toward the earth. Newton developed a gravity relationship known as the Universal Law of Gravitation. The idea is that all masses exert a pulling force on all other masses. The attraction between two masses is directly proportional to the product of their masses, and inversely proportional to the square of the distance between their centers. The equation is

$$F = \frac{Gmm'}{d^2},$$

where G is the universal gravitational constant. The value of G is 6.67×10^{-11} Nm²/kg². The laws of motion and gravitation describe the basic ideas regarding forces. However, the study of forces requires a closer examination.

The motion of planets and satellites can be approximated by considering their orbits as circular. The gravitational force between the masses is the centripetal force which maintains circular motion. From the Law of Gravitation,

$$\mathbf{F} = Gmm'/d^2$$

and the centripetal force is given by

$$\mathbf{F}_c = m\omega^2 r.$$

Since $\mathbf{F} = \mathbf{F}_c$ and d can be considered the radius of the orbit,

$$Gmm' / r^2 = m\omega^2 r$$

$$\omega^2 = Gm' / r^3$$

This equation is the determination of the angular velocity for planetary or satellite orbits where m' is the larger mass which holds the planet or satellite. This equation also shows that the mass of the orbiting satellite, m, does not affect its velocity. If we wish to place a satellite in orbit 75,000 km above the earth, the velocity required to maintain this orbit is

$$\omega^2 = Gm' / r^3,$$

where G is 6.67×10^{-11} Nm^2/kg^2, m' is the mass of the earth, equal to 5.96 $\times 10^{24}$ kg, and r is the radius, 7.5×10^7 m.

$$\omega^2 = (6.67 \times 10^{-11}) (5.96 \times 10^{24}) / (7.5 \times 10^7)^3$$

$$\omega^2 = 3.97532 \times 10^{14} / 4.21875 \times 10^{23}$$

$$\omega^2 = 9.4229807 \times 10^{-10}$$

$$= 3.07 \times 10^{-5} \text{ rad/s}$$

Since one radian is the angle at which the circumference traveled equals the radius, the linear velocity is

$$v = (3.07 \times 10^{-5} \text{ rad/s}) (7.5 \times 10^7 \text{ m/rad})$$

$$= 2302.5 \text{ m/s} = 2.3 \text{ km/s}$$

GENERAL ORBITS OF PLANETS AND SATELLITES

Planets will always exhibit *elliptical* orbits, with the sun located at one focus of the ellipse.

A circle is a special case of an ellipse where both foci are located at the same (center) point. The potential energy of a planet moving along a *circular* orbit does *not* change, and neither does the kinetic energy. On an elliptical orbit, however, both the potential energy and the kinetic energy may continuously change with time, although the *total energy* remains *fixed*. ($E = E_p + E_k$, E remains constant. E_p and E_k can change.)

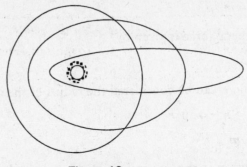

Figure 12

The total energy of an elliptical orbit depends on the distance between the farthest two points on the ellipse. To illustrate, all of the orbits below have the *same total energy*.

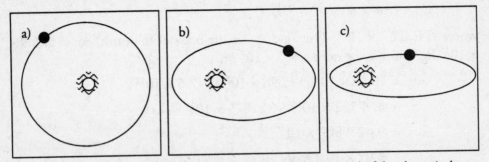

(Assume that in each of the three scenarios the mass of the sun, and of the planet, is the same.)

Figure 13

Forces are vector quantities, with magnitude and direction. This means they are added in the same manner as velocity vectors. When forces are added in this manner, they produce a **net force**, which is the final effect resulting from a force combination. If all forces counteract each other so that the net force is zero, then a translational equilibrium has been established. **Equilibrium** is the state of an object which is at rest. If a positive net force is applied to a mass, it will accelerate according to the second law of motion. Forces applied in the same or opposite directions add together arithmetically. For instance, a 20 N force east and a 13 N force east will result in a net force of 33 N east. Conversely, a 400 N force north added to a 150 N force south results in a net force of 250 N north. Once again, forces that combine at angles other than 0° or 180° require a vector diagram and trigonometric functions to calculate. The determination of net forces from force combinations is known as **force composition**.

PROBLEM

Two forces act on a point. One is 10 N east and the other is 30 N 30° south of west. What are the magnitude and direction of the resultant net force?

Solution

To solve, a diagram is needed. Figure 14 shows the proper position and proportion of the forces. If we now diagram the addition of the 30 N force to the 10 N force, we create a triangle which shows the resultant force, F_r. Since the F_r is opposite the known angle, the law of cosines is applied to find the magnitude of F_r.

$$F_r = \sqrt{F_1^2 + F_2^2 - 2(F_1)(F_2)(\cos \theta)}$$
$$F_r = \sqrt{10^2 + 30^2 - 2(10)(30)(\cos 30°)}$$
$$F_r = 21.9 \text{ N}$$

To find the direction of F_r, the law of sines is applied:

$$\frac{\sin \theta_1}{F_1} = \frac{\sin \theta_2}{F_2} = \frac{\sin \theta_r}{F_r}.$$

Solving for θ_2,

$$\sin \theta_2 = (\sin 30°)(30) / 21.9 = 0.685$$
$$\theta_2 = \arcsin 0.685 = 136.8°$$

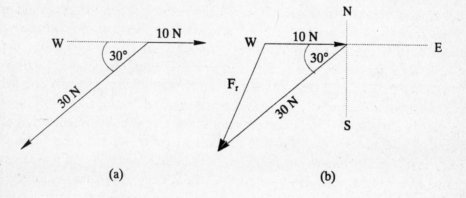

(a)   (b)

Figure 14

This is the angle in question but is not considered the proper direction for F_r. F_r is 136.8° from east, but the west reference is closer. In this case,

$$\theta = 180° - \theta_2 = 180° - 136.8° = 43.2° \text{ S of W}$$

$$F_r = 21.9 \text{ N} \quad 43.2° \text{ S of W}$$

Forces are not always combined into a composite force. Many situations involve a process known as force resolution. Resolving forces means to reduce a given force to its perpendicular components. Examine Figure 15 below.

Shown here is a force of 100 N 40° S of W. The question is what amount of the force is south and what amount is west. Adding the forces in triangular form, shown in Figure 15(b), shows F_s as the sine of 40° and F_w as the cosine of 40°.

$$\sin 40° = F_s / 100$$

$$F_s = \sin 40° (100) = 64.3 \text{ N south}$$

$$\cos 40° = F_w / 100$$

$$F_w = \cos 40° (100) = 76.6 \text{ N west}$$

Net forces applied to objects cause motion. Sometimes, one object must slide over another to move. When this occurs, a new force must be considered, **friction**. Frictional forces resist the sliding motion of objects by acting parallel to the sliding surfaces in the direction opposite the motion. The magnitude of friction depends upon certain situations. First, the nature of the surfaces which are in contact. Smoother surfaces have less friction than rough surfaces. Also, friction depends on the magnitude of the force pressing the

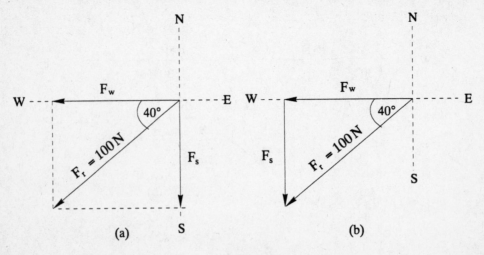

Figure 15

surfaces together. In looking at Figure 16, we see a block on an incline. The weight of the block is shown as force F_w. If F_w is resolved into its components, we see that the component F_p is parallel to the surface and could cause motion. Component F_N is the pressing force perpendicular to the surface. This force is known as the *normal* force, hence, F_N. Figures 17(a) and 17(b) show the friction force, F_f, which is parallel to the

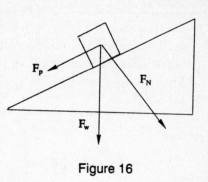

Figure 16

surface. In Figure 17(a), F_f is opposite F_p. If the block is at rest or sliding down the incline with a constant velocity, then F_f will equal F_p. If F_p is larger than F_f, then the block must accelerate down the incline because of the net force in that direction. If a force, F_a, is applied to the block, parallel to the surface and up the incline, as shown in Figure 17(b), then F_f will be in the direction of F_p. For F_a to cause upward motion, it must be at least as large as the sum of F_p and F_f:

$$F_a = F_p + F_f.$$

Once again, the amount of friction is determined by F_N and the contact surfaces. The surface factor can be incorporated using the ratio of F_f to F_N, which is unique to each case. This value is the coefficient of sliding friction, μ. In this ratio,

$$\mu = F_f / F_N,$$

where μ is the numeric value related to the types of surfaces in contact.

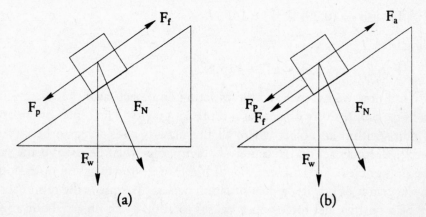

Figure 17

PROBLEM

The coefficient of friction between a metal block and an inclined surface over which it will slide is 0.20. If the surface makes a 20° angle with the horizontal, and the mass of the block is 80 kg, what force is required to slide the block up the incline at a constant velocity?

Solution

To solve, diagram the problem and identify all forces. The weight of the block, F_w, would be 80 kg times the gravitational acceleration for earth, $g = 9.8$ m/s².

$$F_w = (80)(9.8) = 784 \text{ N}$$

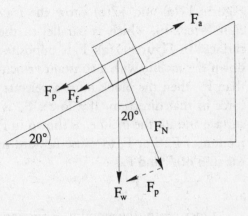

To resolve F_p and F_N,

$$F_p = \sin 20° (F_w)$$
$$= \sin 20° (784) = 268 \text{ N}$$
$$F_N = \cos 20° (F_w)$$
$$= \cos 20° (784) = 737 \text{ N}$$

Figure 18

Since the block is moving up the incline, F_f is in the direction of F_p. To produce constant velocity up the incline,

$$F_a = F_p + F_f.$$

Since μ is given as 0.20, $\mu = F_f / F_N$ becomes $F_f = \mu F_N$.

$$F_f = \mu F_N = (0.20)(737) = 147 \text{ N}.$$

Solving for F_a,

$$F_a = F_p + F_f = 268 + 147 = 415 \text{ N}.$$

Until now we have viewed forces acting on objects as if they were acting on a single point. Every object has a center of gravity. The center of gravity is that point within an object where all the mass is considered to be concentrated. If all forces act on the center of gravity, then their behavior is the same as the point objects we have examined. If, however, forces act on points other than the center of gravity, a new situation occurs. **Torque** is the term used to describe a positive net force which causes rotation of an object about a fixed pivot point.

TORQUE AND ROTATIONAL STATISTICS

Torque is defined as

$$\tau = r \times F,$$

the cross product of displacement, *r*, and force *F*. A force applied to a rigid body a distance *r* from a certain point will produce a torque at that point. (See Figure 19.)

The displacement vector *r* extends from the point where the torque appears to the point where the force *F* is being applied. The torque vector τ is perpendicular to *r* and *F*, since the cross product of the two vectors is always perpendicular to each one. The direction of τ is given by the right-hand rule. In the diagram below, the torque vector extends upward, out of the paper, from point O. The torques applied counteract each other, the net torque is zero. This condition is known as rotational equilibrium, and no rotation will occur. If a net torque is present, then the object will rotate. In examining Figure 20, we see a uniform bar, pivoted at the geometric center which is also the location of the center of gravity. The weight of the bar, 20 N, acts downward at the center of gravity. F_a is a force of 10 N up acting 5 cm left of pivot, and F_b is an 8 N force up acting 7 cm right of pivot. The torque, τ, provided by each force is found by $\tau = Fd$, where F is the force and *d* is the distance from the pivot.

τ for F_a is $\tau = 10(5) = 50$ N(cm)

τ for F_w is $\tau = 20(0) = 0$ N(cm)

τ for F_b is $\tau = 8(7) = 56$ N(cm)

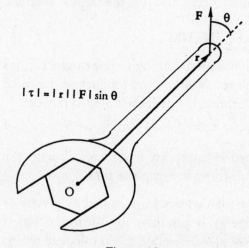

$$|\tau| = |r||F| \sin \theta$$

Figure 19

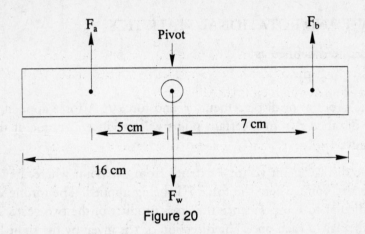

Figure 20

Rotation in the direction of F_a would be clockwise or positive torque. Rotation in the direction of F_b would be counterclockwise or negative torque.

τ net = τ clockwise + τ counterclockwise

τ net = 50 + (– 56) = – 6 N (cm)

This means the net torque is 6 N (cm) counterclockwise, and the bar will rotate counterclockwise. It is important to realize that forces applied at the pivot point *do not* create torque.

During rotational motion, the rotational inertia of the mass tends to resist motion changes according to the first law of motion. The amount of net torque is related to the inertial value by

$\tau = I\alpha,$

where I is the rotational inertia and α is the angular acceleration.

ENERGY AND MOMENTUM

When forces move objects through some distance, it is said that *work* has been done on the object. **Work** is the product of the force causing the motion and the distance through which the object is moved:

$W = F\Delta d.$

Energy is defined as the ability to do work. Energy can take a variety of forms, and can change forms at any given time.

Potential energy is an energy form caused by gravity or elasticity. Gravitational potential energy is produced by lifting an object to some height through which gravity may accelerate it. To calculate the gravitational potential energy for an object,

$$E_p = mgh,$$

where m is the mass, g is gravitational acceleration, and h is the height through which the object may be accelerated. Thus, a 100 kg boulder at the top of a 25 meter high cliff would have an

$$E_p = (100)\,(9.8)\,(25) = 24,500 \text{ joules.}$$

A second type of potential energy is produced by elasticity, such as the stretching or compression of a spring. When a spring is stretched or compressed beyond its equilibrium position, then it applies a force so as to return to equilibrium. The energy which applies the force is the elastic potential energy. To calculate the elastic potential energy,

$$E_p = \tfrac{1}{2}k(d^2),$$

where d is the distance from the equilibrium position and k is the force constant for the spring. The value of k depends upon the nature of the spring.

Elastic potential energy within a spring can provide a special type of repetitive motion known as *Simple Harmonic Motion*. Any object which moves over the same path repeatedly in equal time intervals has periodic motion. When the mass on the spring in Figure 21 is stretched and released, it is accelerated upward with a force proportional to the displacement from equilibrium. When the mass moves back towards equilibrium, it will accelerate past it. This causes compression of the spring which applies a force in the opposite direction with the same result. The motion of the mass will continue in a periodic oscillation. This linear oscillation is simple harmonic motion.

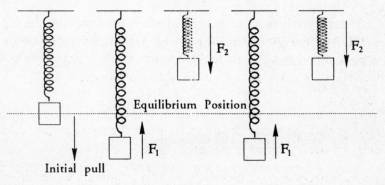

Figure 21

SIMPLE HARMONIC MOTION

For Simple Harmonic Motion to occur, the force on the mass must be a *linear restoring* force, linear with respect to the position, and acting to restore the mass to a certain equilibrium position.

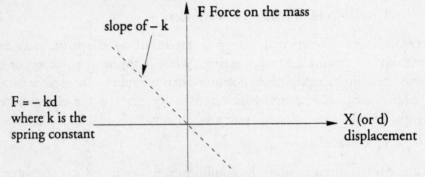

slope of – k

F Force on the mass

F = – kd
where k is the
spring constant

X (or d)
displacement

Figure 22

The potential energy of this system has a *quadratic* dependence on position.

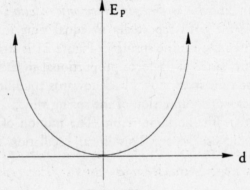

E_P

d

Figure 23

Kinetic energy is a form of energy which is produced by the motion of an object. Kinetic energy depends upon the mass and velocity of an object. To calculate kinetic energy,

$$E_k = \frac{1}{2} mv^2.$$

If a 2000 kg automobile is traveling at 12 m/s, then its kinetic energy is

$$E_k = \frac{1}{2} (2000) (12)^2 = 144{,}000 \text{ joules.}$$

The study of energy leads to a very important concept known as the Law of Conservation of Energy. This law states that the sum of all energy of all forms is equal to the total amount of energy within a system. Furthermore, the total energy in a system has a *constant* value. Figure 24 shows various amounts of different types of energy. The sum of those energies is also represented. At some point, some of the energy present may change form, as shown in Figure 25. Although the energy may change its form, *the sum of the energies will always equal the same constant total.*

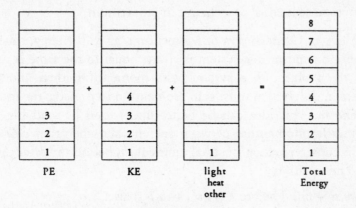

Figure 24

Laws of conservation also apply to other areas of motion study. The quantity of motion an object possesses is known as **momentum**. The momentum, **p**, is the product of an object's mass and velocity,

$$\mathbf{p} = m\mathbf{v}.$$

Momentum is also a vector quantity. For the motion of an object to change, its momentum must change. For example, a train and a car may be traveling with the same velocity, but the train will require a larger force to stop because its mass is much larger, thus it has a greater momentum to

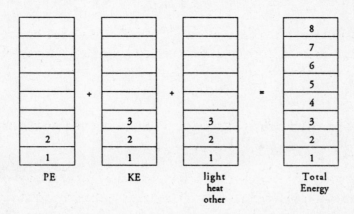

Figure 25

overcome. Momentum is involved in another idea regarding motion called impulse. **Impulse** is the product of a force and the time interval over which it acts. The impulse

$$F\Delta t = m\Delta v,$$

hence, an impulse is equal to a change in momentum.

The Law of Conservation of Momentum, as with energy, states that the sum of all momentum in a system is always equal to the same constant total amount. If an object in a system loses momentum, then another object somewhere in that system must gain momentum to preserve the total amount of momentum. This idea can be better understood by studying collisions. Objects transfer momentum between one another when they collide. If momentum is conserved, then the total momentum before and after the collision is equal. The equation

$$(m_1 v_1 + m_2 v_2) \text{ before} = (m_1 v'_1 + m_2 v'_2) \text{ after}$$

is used to calculate momentum magnitudes for a two object collision in one dimension. The sum of momentum before the collision is equal to the sum of momentum after the collision. Remember that momentum is a vector quantity and if collisions occur in two or three dimensions, then momentum must be calculated in the same manner as force and velocity vectors.

Angular momentum is the quantity of rotational motion. Angular momentum, in rotational terms, is $I\omega$, where I is the rotational inertia and ω is the angular velocity of the object.

CHAPTER 3

ELECTRICITY AND MAGNETISM

ELECTROSTATICS

Electrostatics is the study of stationary electrical charges. The Basic Law of Electrostatics states that charges which are alike repel one another, while charges which are opposite attract each other. Electric charge is measured in a unit known as a Coulomb. One **Coulomb** of charge is equivalent to 6.25×10^{18} electrons, which means that one electron holds a charge of 1.6×10^{-19} coulombs. The forces of repulsion and attraction acting on point charges are proportional in the same manner as gravitation between two masses. Figure 26 shows two sets of charges which are separated by a distance, d. In Figure 26(a), the opposite charges produce attraction forces, and in Figure 26(b), the similar charges produce repulsion forces.

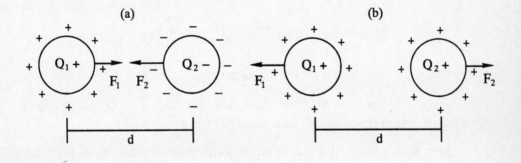

Figure 26

The magnitude of the forces is shown by

$$F = \frac{kQQ'}{d^2},$$

where F is the force, k is a constant, Q and Q' are the magnitudes of the charges, and d is the distance between the centers of Q and Q'. For calculating forces between charges in air,

$$k = 8.93 \times 10^9 \text{ Nm}^2/C^2.$$

In a vacuum,

$$k = 8.987 \times 10^9 \text{ Nm}^2/C^2.$$

To calculate the force between a $3C$ charge and a $7C$ charge which are 0.60 m apart in air, Coulomb's Law shows

$$F = kQQ'/d^2 = (8.93 \times 10^9)(3)(7)/(0.60)^2$$

$$F = 5.21 \times 10^{11} \text{ N}$$

Since both charges have the same sign, F is positive. This means that the force is repelling the charges. Opposite charges result in negative forces, which shows attraction.

Forces between charges occur because each charge generates an electric field. An **electric field** is that region in space in which a charge could experience an electric force. Electric fields are shown by lines of electric forces as in Figures 27 and 28.

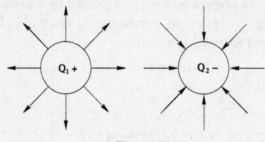

Figure 27

The charge $Q+$ has lines of force which flow outward. The $Q-$ charge shows force lines which flow inward, thus these charges are opposite.

The field produced by two equal and opposite charges is shown in Figure 28(a), and the field produced by equal charges with the same sign is shown in Figure 28(b). In Figure 28(a), the force lines complement each other, flowing out of one charge into the other. In Figure 28(b), the force lines oppose each other, causing the repulsion effect. Any charge particle, such as $q+$, which enters an electric field would experience a force according to Coulomb's Law and the direction of the force would be tangent to a given force line.

Electric Field Intensity, E, at any point in the field is the force per unit of positive charge at that point. Thus,

$E = F / q$,

where F is the force in newtons on charge q in coulombs. If a charge of $0.75 C$ in an electric field experiences a $0.5 N$ force, the field intensity would be

$E = F / q = 0.5/0.75$

$= 6.7 \ N/C.$

If an electric field acts on and moves a charge from one point in a field to another, then these points are said to differ in electrical potential. By moving the charge, the field does work on the charge. The potential difference, V, between two points in an electric field is the work done per unit charge as the charge is moved, and is measured in volts. One volt is that potential difference which does one joule of work when moving a one coulomb charge.

ELECTROSTATICS WITH CONDUCTORS

Conductors introduce some changes in any electric field which they inhabit. These are:

1. *The electric field E inside a conductor is zero.* If this is the case, a free electron *inside* the conductor will feel a force and will accelerate because of it. Since this goes against the assumption of electrostatic equilibrium, which requires no set force or any change, the electric field inside must be zero.

2. *The electric field at the surface of the conductor must be perpendicular to the surface.* If it is not perpendicular, i.e., the field has a component parallel to the surface, then any free electron at the surface will again experience a force and start accelerating.

3. *Any net change on a conductor resides on the surface.* If there is any *net* change *inside* the conductor, then there must be an electric field resulting from that change, inside the conductor, which is impossible since $E = 0$ inside.

ELECTRIC CIRCUITS

The existence of a potential difference is the energy which moves electric charges. When moving many charges through a conductor, the rate at which they flow is referred to as **electric current**, I. More specifically,

$I = Q/t$,

such that current is a measure of the amount of charge which passes a given point within a given time. As current flows, conductors may resist the movement. This opposition to current flow is called **resistance**. The resistance within a conductor depends on the nature and material of that conductor.

When conductors offer resistance, they convert some of the current's kinetic energy into heat. The actual amount of heat generated by a resistance can be determined by Joule's Law; the heat produced in a conductor is directly proportional to the resistance, the square of the current, and the time the current is maintained.

$\Delta H = I^2 Rt/J$,

where ΔH is the heat in calories, I is the current, R is resistance, t is the time, and J is the mechanical heat equivalent, 4.19 joules/calorie.

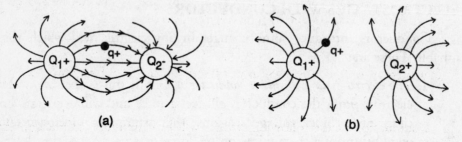

(a)   (b)

Figure 28

PROBLEM

What amount of heat is produced by a 10 ohm resistor which carries 0.3 amps of current for 3 minutes?

Solution

Since t must be expressed as seconds, $t = 3$ min $= 180$ sec. Therefore,

$H = I^2 Rt / J = (0.3)^2 (10) (180) / 4.19 = 38.7$ calories.

The relationship among potential differences, V, current, I, and resistance, R, is essential in the analysis of direct current electric circuits. This relationship is known as Ohm's Law,

$$V = IR.$$

Let's examine Figure 29.

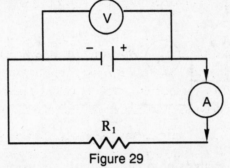

Figure 29

The potential difference in this circuit is provided by a one cell battery,

and would be measured with a voltmeter,

Assuming the resistance of the wire to be insignificant, the circuit resistance is equal to the resistance, R, which is 3 ohms. If our ammeter,

reads a current of 0.5 amps, what is our voltmeter reading? By Ohm's Law,

$$V = IR = (0.5) (3) = 1.5 \text{ volts.}$$

Examination of the following circuits will provide more insight into the laws for DC electric circuits.

Electrical circuits can be connected in series of parallel configurations. A series means that the electrical devices are connected such that the current *must* go from one device to the next. Parallel connections provide different paths for current flow.

Examination of Figure 30 shows the difference between a series and a parallel connection. Between A and B is a series of 3 cells. The set of resistors between C and D shows two paths for the current. Some current will pass through R_1 and R_2, and some will pass through R_3. R_1 and R_2 are in series since the current must go through both in that path. The resistor R_3 is parallel to the $R_1 - R_2$ series because any current through R_3 will *not* pass through the $R_1 - R_2$ series and vice versa.

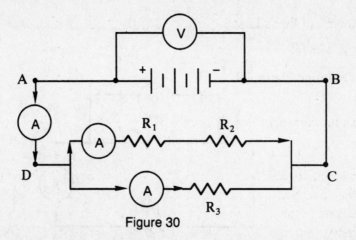

Figure 30

Mathematical analysis of circuits is more complex. When considering a series of voltages, they are added to a sum or total voltage as in Figure 31. Thus, for voltages in series,

$$V_t = V_1 + V_2 + V_3 \ldots + V_n.$$

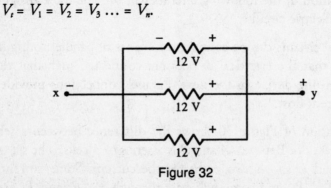

$$(-3\text{ V}) + (+4\text{ V}) + (+2\text{ V}) + (-6\text{ V}) = +3\text{ volts}$$

Figure 31

For parallel voltages, the connections are such that each device is essentially connected to the same two points as in Figure 32. This means that the voltage for each device is equal. Thus, for voltages in parallel,

$$V_t = V_1 = V_2 = V_3 \ldots = V_n.$$

Figure 32

When considering current through a series, we find that the same current passes through each device as in Figure 33.

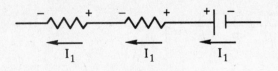

Figure 33

Thus, for currents through a series,

$$I_t = I_1 = I_2 = I_3 \ldots = I_n.$$

This seems logical since the current has no other path. For currents through parallel branches, we find that current which reaches a divided path *must* divide so as to send some current through all branches. The amount of current through a branch depends upon the resistances encountered in that branch. Thus, for parallel circuits,

$$I_t = I_1 + I_2 + I_3 \ldots + I_n$$

as shown in Figure 34.

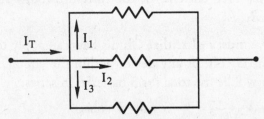

Figure 34

To examine resistances in series, they are added to a sum just as the voltages. Thus, for resistances in series,

$$R_t = R_1 + R_2 + R_3 \ldots + R_n$$

as shown by Figure 35.

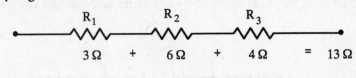

Figure 35

For resistances in parallel, we find a more complex situation. The resistance value equivalent to the parallel resistor set is the reciprocal sum of those resistors.

$$\frac{1}{R_{eq}} = \frac{1}{R_1} + \frac{1}{R_2} + \frac{1}{R_3} \cdots + \frac{1}{R_n}$$

as shown in Figure 36.

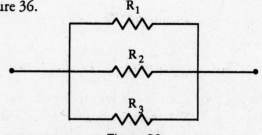

Figure 36

We can now apply these ideas to the circuit in Figure 37 both to analyze the circuit and better understand the relationships.

Given that the voltage for each cell is 3 V and $R_1 = 2\ \Omega$, $R_2 = 3\ \Omega$, and $R_3 = 7\ \Omega$, find the total current, I_t; the current through R_1– R_2, I_1; and the current through R_3, I_2.

To begin, we must realize that Ohm's Law can apply to the total circuit, any section of the circuit, or any device within the circuit. First, the reading on the voltmeter will be the total for 3 batteries in series;

$$V_t = V_1 + V_2 + V_3 = 3 + 3 + 3 = 9 \text{ volts.}$$

Since point *C* is connected to *A* and *D* is connected to *B*, then the voltage across the parallel resistor set must be 9 V. If we now calculate the total resistance of our set, we could calculate the total current by

$$I_t = \frac{V_t}{R_t}.$$

To calculate R_t, we must apply the rules series and parallel resistors. Since R_1

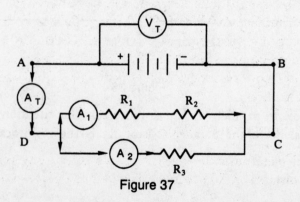

Figure 37

and R_2 are in series, they are added together. But, their series combination is parallel to R_3. Since there are no other resistances to consider, R_t will equal R_{eq} for our set. Thus,

$$\frac{1}{R_t} = \frac{1}{(R_1 + R_2)} + \frac{1}{R_3}$$

$$\frac{1}{R_t} = \frac{1}{5} + \frac{1}{7}$$

$$\frac{1}{R_t} = 0.2 + 0.143 = 0.343$$

$$R_t = \frac{1}{0.343} = 2.9\Omega$$

Now we may calculate the current I_t,

$$I_t = \frac{V_t}{R_t} = \frac{9}{2.9} = 3.1 \text{ amps.}$$

This means that 3.1 amps of current travel from the battery to point C. The current is then divided among the branches according to Ohm's Law. Since the voltage for both branches is 9 V, then

$$I_1 = \frac{V}{(R_1 + R_2)} = \frac{9}{5} = 1.8 \text{ amps}$$

$$I_2 = \frac{V}{R_3} = \frac{9}{7} = 1.3 \text{ amps}$$

Please note that $1.8 + 1.3 = 3.1$ amps. The sum of the divided currents must equal the total current.

Another device which may be used in a circuit is a capacitor. A capacitor is a combination of conducting plates which are separated by some insulating material. They are used to store electric charge within a system. The plates are given a potential difference which causes a charge buildup on each plate. The ratio of the charge on either plate to the potential difference is called **capacitance**. Capacitance is measured in farads. One farad is the capacitance when one coulomb of charge on a capacitor results in a potential difference of one volt between the plates.

PARALLEL PLATE CAPACITORS

A parallel plate capacitor consists of two conducting plates of area A separated by distance d. The volume between the plates is occupied by a vacuum, or air (or possibly a dielectric material). The capacitance is then given by the formula

$$C = \frac{\varepsilon_0 \cdot A}{d}$$

Note: ε_0 is the permitivity constant. You may also see this written as E_0.

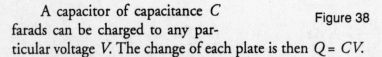

A

Figure 38

A capacitor of capacitance C farads can be charged to any particular voltage V. The change of each plate is then $Q = CV$.

The charge on a capacitor can be increased by using dielectric materials for insulators rather than air. The magnitude of the charge increase is different for different materials. If an air capacitor has a charge Q_1, and a second dielectric capacitor has a charge Q_2 under the same potential difference, then $Q_2 > Q_1$ by a factor of k, the dielectric constant for the given material. Thus, $Q_2 = kQ_1$.

As with other devices, the capacitance value for combinations of capacitors depends upon the connections within the circuit. Figure 39 shows capacitors in parallel which are added to a sum:

$$C_t = C_1 + C_2 + C_3 \ldots + C_n.$$

Also, capacitors in series add to a reciprocal sum:

$$\frac{1}{C_t} = \frac{1}{C_1} + \frac{1}{C_2} + \frac{1}{C_3} \ldots + \frac{1}{C_n}.$$

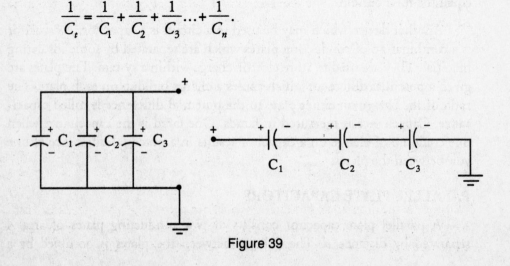

Figure 39

ELECTROMAGNETISM

Magnetism is a concept closely related to electricity, and shows many similarities to electrical phenomena. Magnetism is a property of charge in motion. In most situations, electrons within the structure of materials have two types of motion. First is the revolution of electrons about the nucleus of an atom. This gives the atom magnetic properties (Figure 40). The second is the motion of the electron spinning on its axis, causing magnetic effects. Most electrons are paired with opposite spins so as to neutralize their magnetism.

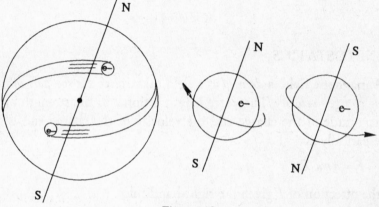

Figure 40

Although it is true that all atoms have these magnetic properties, we know that not all materials act as magnets. Iron is the most common magnetized substance. For the most part, atoms within the iron crystal are grouped in areas determined by their magnetic properties. These areas are called domains. The orientation of these domains is essentially random and crystallize in such a way so as to cancel the effects of each other. If the crystal is subjected to an intense magnetic field, the domains will all align themselves in the direction of the field and become a permanent magnet.

Just as electrical charges produce electric fields, magnets produce magnetic fields. Magnetic fields flow out of the north pole and into the south pole, as shown in Figure 41.

Once again we see that the opposite poles complement each other and have a force of attraction between them. Like poles would repel each other. The lines shown are magnetic lines of flux. A line of flux is drawn so that the tangent to the line at any point shows the direction of the magnetic field. Keep in mind that both magnetic and electric fields surround the source in three dimensions, not in a single plane as they are shown here.

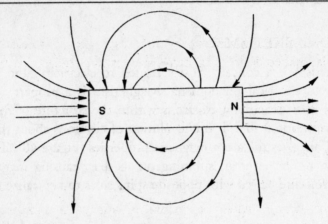

Figure 41

MAGNETOSTATICS

A **magnetic field** is *defined* as a field that exerts a force *perpendicular to a moving charge's velocity*. This force is proportional to the strength of the field, the magnitude of the charge and the velocity of the charge and is expressed mathematically as:

$$F = qv \times B$$

with the direction of *F* given the right-hand rule.

In the figure shown below, a uniform magnetic field points upwards. The force and velocity of the particle are drawn in various stages of its movement.

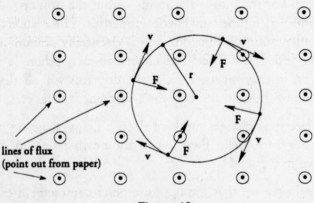

lines of flux
(point out from paper)

Figure 42

The particle follows a circular path of radius

$$r = \frac{mv}{qB}.$$

Note, however, that any component of particle velocity *parallel* to the magnetic field is unaffectd. So, in general, the actual particle trajectory is helical in nature.

The $q\mathbf{v} \times \mathbf{B}$ affects charges moving as currents in wires. The force on a length l of a current-carrying wire is

$$\mathbf{F} = i l \times \mathbf{B},$$

where l points in the direction of the current.

Current carrying wires are themselves sources of magnetic fields. The magnetic field surrounding a long current-carrying wire is $B = (\mu_0 i \,/\, 2\pi r)$ where i is the current and r is the distance from the wire.

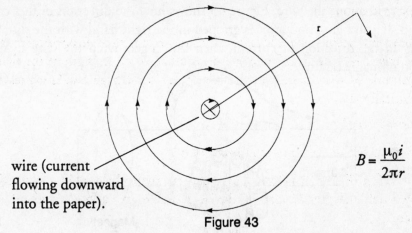

wire (current flowing downward into the paper).

$$B = \frac{\mu_0 i}{2\pi r}$$

Figure 43

The strength of a magnetic field is related to the flux density. **Flux density** is a measure of the number of flux lines per unit area perpendicular to the lines. This idea is shown in Figure 44.

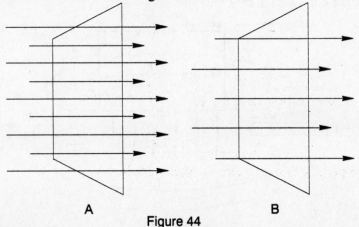

A   B

Figure 44

Given that the areas designated in *A* and *B* are equal, then the magnetic field in *A* is stronger than the field in *B* since more flux lines pass through the equal area. Thus, the field in *A* is more dense than the field in *B*.

Flux density can be calculated by

$$B = \phi \,/\, A,$$

where *B* is the flux density, ϕ is the number of flux lines, and *A* is the area of flux. Since flux lines are measured in webers, *B* is considered to be webers/m² which is called a tesla.

The flow of electric current will also produce a magnetic field. This is electromagnetic induction. As current flows through a wire, it induces a magnetic field about the wire. Figure 45 shows how the direction of flux can be found. If a straight conductor is grasped in the right hand with the thumb pointing in the direction of current, then the fingers wrap the wire in the direction of magnetic flux.

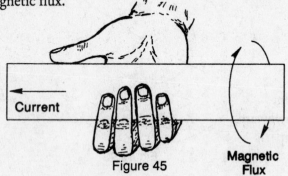

Figure 45

If conducting wire is looped into a coil, then a new situation occurs. Current traveling around a cylindrical core will generate a magnetic field through the core, shown by Figure 46.

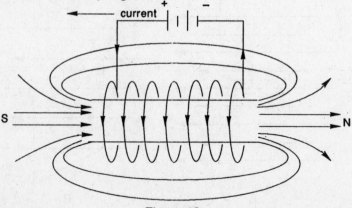

Figure 46

To find the direction of flux, Figure 47 shows that if the coil is grasped with the right hand so that the fingers wrap in the direction of the current, then the thumb will point in the direction of magnetic flux.

It is also possible to induce electricity with magnetism. As seen in Figure 48, a magnet, oriented with the north pole on the right side, moving to the right toward a loop of wire will induce a counterclockwise current in the wire loop. This is an illustration of Lenz's law which states that the induced current will be in a direction to oppose the change in magnetic flux that produced the current. The counterclockwise *induced* current produces a magnetic field (as found from the right-hand rule) with the north pole oriented on the left which opposes or repels the magnet moving toward the right. If the magnet were pulled away from the loop, the induced current would be clockwise and the induced magnetic field reversed to attract the magnet and thus oppose its motion moving away from the coil.

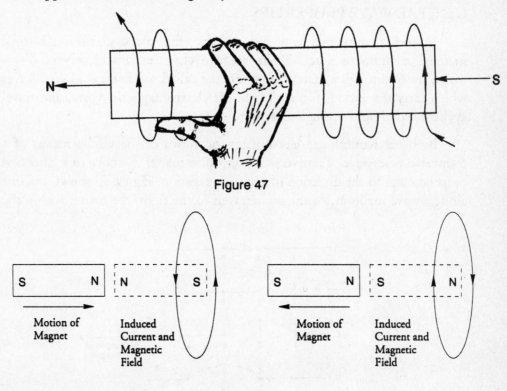

Figure 47

Figure 48

CHAPTER 4

WAVES AND OPTICS

GENERAL WAVE PROPERTIES

A **wave** is considered to be a disturbance that propagates through some material medium or space. There are two classifications of waves. Waves which travel through a material medium are called **mechanical waves**. Waves which carry the various forms of light are **electromagnetic waves**, and travel at the speed of light through a vacuum.

Both mechanical and electromagnetic waves can travel by means of a transverse type wave. **Transverse waves** cause matter to move in a direction perpendicular to the direction of wave propagation. Figure 49 shows 4 points along a wave medium. As the wave travels to the right, the matter within the

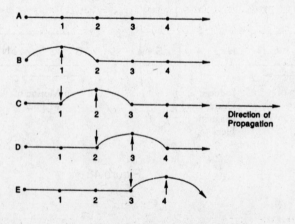

Figure 49

medium moves up, then down as the wave passes. Thus, the wave is transverse.

A second type of mechanical wave is the longitudinal or compression wave. **Longitudinal waves** cause material in the medium to move parallel to wave propagation. Figure 50 shows a compression wave pulse through a coil spring. When released, the compressed area attempts to spread out which will compress the coils to their right. This process continues throughout the length of the spring.

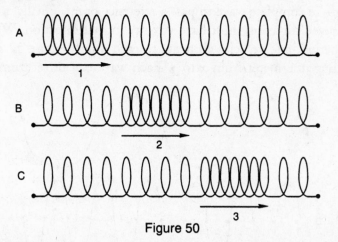

Figure 50

Sound waves are the best example of compression waves. The shock from a sound compresses the air near the source which sends a compression wave through the air in all directions. You hear the sound when the compression shock hits your eardrum.

If a source which creates a wave does so repeatedly at equal time intervals, then a periodic wave will result. Figure 51 shows a periodic transverse wave with equal disturbances over equal time periods.

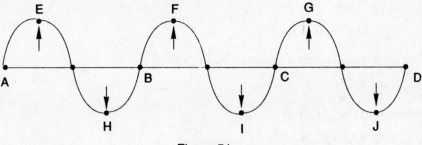

Figure 51

Shown are three complete waves, each having an upper displacement crest and a lower displacement trough. The distance from a point on a wave to the same point on the next is called one wavelength. For our wave, the wavelength, λ (lambda), could be measured from A to B, one crest and one trough; from E to F, crest to crest; or from H to I, trough to trough.

A wave which travels through one crest and one trough has completed one cycle. If we measure the number of waves which pass a given point in a specified time interval, then this is known as **wave frequency**. Frequency, f, is measured in cycles per second which is a hertz. The **period**, T, for a wave is the time for one complete wave to pass a reference point. Finally, a wave that moves in a given direction must have velocity in that direction. Wavelength, frequency, period, and velocity all relate to each other. Figure 52 shows two waves traveling one meter from x to y. Each wave can travel from x to y in one second.

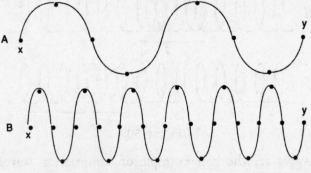

Figure 52

Looking at wave A, we find that in one second, two complete waves will pass point y which gives a frequency equal to 2 hz. For wave B, six waves pass y in one second which gives a frequency of 6 hz. Since the waves are traveling 2 per second in A, the period for wave A is $1/2$ second. In B, waves pass 6 per second and the period is $1/6$ second. Note that the frequency and period are reciprocals. Thus,

$$f = 1/T \quad \text{and} \quad T = 1/f.$$

Since each wave travels a distance, λ, in time T,

$$v = \lambda/T.$$

Substituting for $1/T$ gives

$$v = \lambda/T = (1/T)\,(\lambda) = f\lambda$$
$$v = f\lambda$$

This final equation is true for all periodic waves, transverse or longitudinal, regardless of medium material.

PROPERTIES OF STANDING WAVES

When two waves of the same wavelength and the same amplitude travel at the same speed but opposite directions, a standing wave emerges. At the same locations along the medium, the two waves always interfere destructively. These are called **nodes**. At other points, constructive interference continuously occurs and antinodes with large amplitudes result. Adjacent nodes are 1/2 apart, and so are adjacent antinodes. Standing waves can occur on a length L of a medium held "fixed" on both ends, so that each end is the site of a node. Then allowed wavelengths are given by

$$\lambda = \frac{2L}{n},$$

where $n = 1, 2, 3, \ldots$

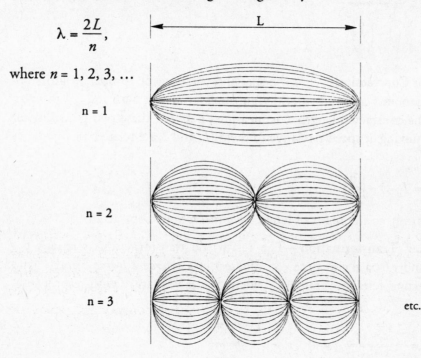

Figure 53

SPECIAL RELATIVITY

Postulates of Special Relativity

The most important postulates of the Theory of Relativity are:

1. All observers measure the speed of light through a vacuum to be the same as constant c.

2. The laws of physics are the same for all observers moving at constant velocity with respect to each other.

These two simple postulates produce a variety of effects.

Space-Time Effects

Time Dilation—If $T.$ is the same time between two events that occur at the same location and are measured on the clock of an observer at rest in this location, and T is the time between the very same two events but registered on the clock of an observer traveling at speed V relative to the location where the two events occur, then $T.$ and T are related by

$$T = \frac{T_0}{\sqrt{1 - \left(\dfrac{v}{c}\right)^2}}$$

Space Contraction—$L.$ is the spatial separation, or "proper length," between two points and measured by an observer at rest with respect to these points. The contracted length L is measured between these two points by an observer moving at speed v relative to them. $L.$ and L are related by

$$L = L_0 \sqrt{1 - \left(\frac{v}{c}\right)^2}$$

Note that only components of lengths *parallel to* v are contracted.

Lorenz Transformation—The relativistic transformation relations between x and t (space and time coordinates) in a *reference frame* S and x' and t' for a second reference frame S', where S' has velocity V with respect to S, are:

$$x' = \frac{x - vt}{\sqrt{1 - \left(\dfrac{v}{c}\right)^2}} \quad \text{and} \quad t' = \frac{t - \dfrac{v}{c^2} x}{\sqrt{1 - \left(\dfrac{v}{c}\right)^2}}$$

Velocity Transformation—Suppose frame S' has velocity V with respect to S. A particle has velocity V in S. Its velocity V' in frame S' is given by

$$V' = \frac{V - v}{1 - \dfrac{v^2}{c^2} V}$$

Mass and Energy Effects

At very high speeds, the mass of a particle appears to change. At rest, a particle has a "rest mass." Although it always "really" does have this mass, we speak of a "relative mass," m, whose

$$m = \frac{m_0}{\sqrt{1 - \dfrac{v^2}{c^2}}}.$$

The rest energy of a particle is $E_0 = m_0 c^2$. The relativistic energy of a particle, however, is related to the rest energy by

$$E^2 = E_0^2 + p^2 c^2 = m_0^2 c^4 + p^2 c^2 = mc^2 = \frac{m_0 c^2}{\sqrt{1 - \dfrac{v^2}{c^2}}},$$

where p, the relativistic momentum, is equal to

$$p = mv = \frac{m_0 v}{\sqrt{1 - \dfrac{v^2}{c^2}}}.$$

For massless particles with $m_0 = 0$, such as photons, $E_0 = m_0 c^2 = 0$ and we have $E^2 = p^2 c^2$ or merely $E = pc$.

One interesting idea regarding wave velocity is the **Doppler Effect**. This effect refers to a wave which originates from a source which is traveling with some velocity. In essence, the source velocity appears to be added to or subtracted from the wave velocity. The Doppler Effect is best explained by examining sound waves.

The frequency of a sound wave determines a characteristic known as pitch. Interpreting pitch is how the human ear distinguishes among frequen-

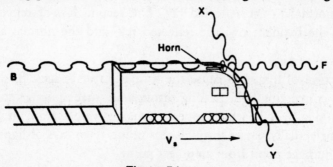

Figure 54

cies. The higher the frequency, the higher the pitch. If the source of sound is in motion relative to the listener, then the Doppler Effect occurs, and the pitch heard is not the true pitch of the wave. Figure 54 shows the Doppler Effect. Remember that sound travels by compression waves, but for this diagram they are shown as transverse.

The listeners at positions X and Y hear the wave perpendicular to the motion of the train. These waves are unaffected by the motion of the source, and the true pitch is heard. Listener F hears a wave which is traveling the same direction as the course. As the source approaches, the frequency heard increases and the pitch is higher. Listener B hears the opposite effect. Since the sound is moving opposite the source, the frequency heard decreases and the pitch is lower.

GEOMETRICAL PROPERTIES

Waves have many geometrical and optical properties. For the purposes of explanation, these descriptions will be made using light waves.

Waves can be reflected. This means that waves bounce off a surface, such as a mirror. The reflection of waves follow certain geometric principles. In

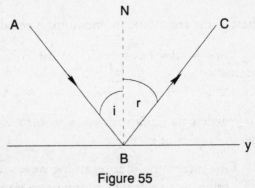

Figure 55

Figure 55, the line *xy* is the surface of a plane mirror. Line *AB* is an incident light ray which strikes the surface at *B*. The dotted line *NB* is the normal reference line perpendicular to the surface. Line *BC* is the reflected light ray. The first law of reflection states that the angle of incidence, measured from the normal to the incident ray, is equal to the angle of reflection, *r*, measured from the normal to the reflected ray. The second law of reflection simply states that the incident ray, the reflected ray, and the normal all lie in the same plane.

Reflection of light can cause the formation of images. **Real images** are formed by converging light passing through an image point, and **virtual images** are formed by light which appears to have diverged from an image point, but no light actually passes through this point. Two rays of light are needed to locate an image point from an object point.

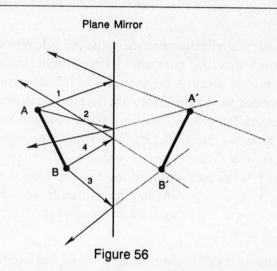

Figure 56

Figure 56 shows the location of the image of object line *AB*. Rays 1 and 2 begin at point *A* and are reflected according to the first law. *The point at which reflected rays intersect is the image point.* Since the reflected rays for 1 and 2 are diverging, they appear to have intersected behind the mirror. Tracing these reflected rays back, we find the intersection at *A'*. *B'* is found by tracing rays 3 and 4 in a similar manner. Line *A'B'* is the virtual image for line *AB* since there is no light behind the mirror. Note that for plane mirrors, the images are always virtual, erect, and equal in size to the object and appear to be the same distance behind the mirror as the object is in front.

Curved spherical mirrors present a greater challenge. Spherical mirrors are sections of a sphere used as a reflecting surface. The study of curved mirrors involves specific terminology. Figure 57 shows a concave converging

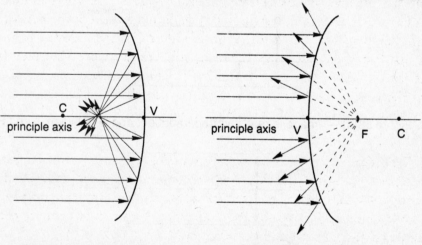

Concave-Converging Mirror   Figure 57   Convex-Diverging Mirror

mirror which has the reflecting surface inside the sphere, and a convex diverging mirror which has the reflecting surface ouside the sphere. The exact center of the mirror is called the vertex, *V.* An imaginary line which passes through the vertex perpendicular to the face of the mirror is the principle axis. Along the axis lies point *C,* which is the center point of curvature for the mirror and represents the center of the sphere from which the mirror was taken. Any line from *C* to the mirror is normal to the mirror and is a secondary axis. Point F is the focal point of the mirror. It is located exactly half the distance from *V* to *C.* Any light ray that is parallel to the principle axis will converge to or appear to diverge from the focal point. The distance from *V* to *F* is called focal length.

These mirrors will also form images whose characteristics can be determined graphically or mathematically.

When graphing images from spherical mirrors, the following rules simplify the process:

1. Light from an object parallel to the principle axis will be reflected back through or away from the focal point.

2. Light which passes through or is going towards the focal point will be reflected back parallel to the principle axis.

3. Light which passes through or is going towards the center of curvature will be reflected directly back to or away from the center of curvature.

Figures 58(a) – (f) show the six general curved mirror situations.

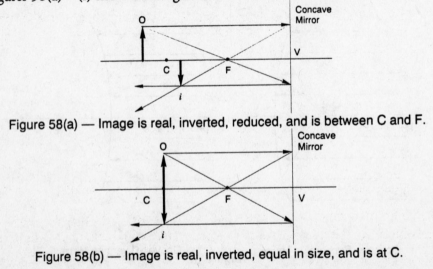

Figure 58(a) — Image is real, inverted, reduced, and is between C and F.

Figure 58(b) — Image is real, inverted, equal in size, and is at C.

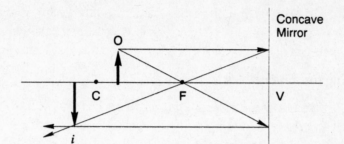

Figure 58(c) — Image is real, inverted, enlarged, and is beyond C.

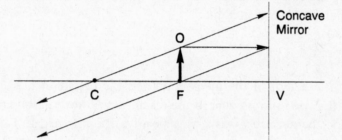

Figure 58(d) — The reflected rays are parallel; no image is formed.

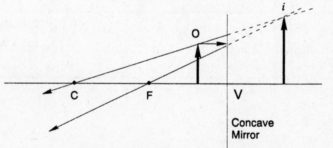

Figure 58(e) — Image is virtual, erect, enlarged, and is behind the mirror.

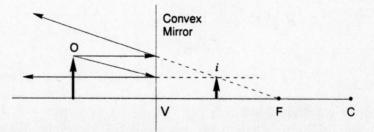

Figure 58(f) — Image is virtual, erect, reduced, and is between V and F.

The mathematical equation for mirrors relates the distance from V to the object, d_o, the distance from V to the image, d_i, and the focal length, f.

$$\frac{1}{f} = \frac{1}{d_o} + \frac{1}{d_i}$$

When solving for the variables, we find

$$f = \frac{d_o d_i}{(d_o + d_i)} : d_o = \frac{d_i f}{(d_i - f)} : d_i = \frac{d_o f}{(d_o - f)}.$$

The nature of diverging light is such that d_i is negative for virtual images, and f is negative for convex mirrors. All other quantities are considered positive. The size of an image is related by

$$\frac{h_i}{h_o} = \frac{d_i}{d_o},$$

where h_i is the height of the image and h_o is the height of the object. This shows that the size ratio is equal to the distance ratio for each situation. Since height cannot be negative, h_i is always positive and any negative sign on a d_i value is ignored.

PROBLEM

> A 4 cm high object is placed 12 cm from a concave mirror with a focal length of 8 cm. Where is the image? What is the height? What is its type?

Solution

Solve for d_i,

$$d_i = d_o f / (d_o - f) = (12)(8) / (12 - 8) = 96/4 = 24 \text{ cm},$$

and solve for h_i,

$$h_i = d_i h_o / d_o = (24)(4) / 12 = 8 \text{ cm}.$$

Since d_i was positive, the image is real.

PROBLEM

> A 10 cm high object is 6 cm from a convex mirror with a focal length of 5 cm. Where is the image? What is its height? What is its type?

Solution

Solve for d_i, remember d_i is negative for convex mirrors.

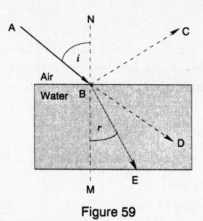

Figure 59

$$d_i = d_o f / (d_o - f) = (6) (-5) / [6 - (-5)] = -30/11 = -2.7 \text{ cm}$$

Solve for h_i, remember h_i is positive.

$$h_i = d_i h_o / d_o = (2.7) (10) / 6 = 4.5 \text{ cm}$$

Since d_i was negative, the image is virtual.

Another characteristic of waves is that they can be refracted. As light travels from one medium to a second medium with a different optical density, it will bend. Optical density is measured by how fast light will pass through the medium. The higher the optical density, the slower light will pass through. This change in velocity results in the bending of light we call refraction. Figure 59 shows how a ray is refracted.

Line *AB* is the incident ray. Line *NM* is the perpendicular normal at the point of refraction. Line *BC* represents a small amount of light reflected by the surface. Line *BD* is the original path of the incident ray, and *BE* is the refracted light ray. The incident ray and refracted ray are related by Snell's law:

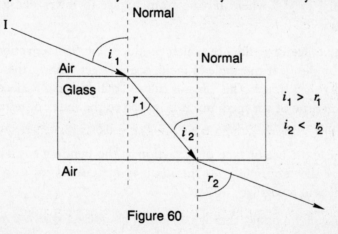

Figure 60

$n = \sin i / \sin r,$

where n is a property of an optical medium known as the **index of refraction**. It is the ratio of the sine of the incident angle to the sine of the refraction angle. The index of refraction can also be expressed in terms of the speed of light:

$n = c / v_m,$

where c is the velocity of light in a vacuum and v_m is the velocity of light in any medium.

The refraction of light can be summarized in three laws. First, the incident ray, the refracted ray, and the normal are in the same plane. Second, the index of refraction for any medium is constant for any incident angle. And third, light rays which pass from lower to higher optical densities are bent toward the normal. Rays from higher to lower densities are bent away from the normal. The third law is shown by Figure 60.

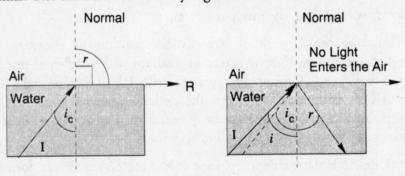

Figure 61

According to law three, it would be possible to reach an angle of refraction equal to 90° when moving from higher to lower densities, shown by Figure 61.

The angle of incidence which produces the 90° refraction is called the **critical angle**, i_c. If the angle of incidence is larger than i_c, then all light is reflected by the surface. This effect is called Total Internal Reflection. Since i_c is a characteristic of the medium, it is related to the index of refraction by $\sin i_c$ = $1/n$, thus $i_c = \arcsin 1/n$.

The most useful type of refraction is the bending of light with lenses. Much of the terminology is the same as for curved mirrors, but there are differences to recognize.

First, light passes through lenses. This means that a concave lens will diverge light and convex lenses will cause light to converge. These properties are opposite those for the corresponding mirrors. Another difference is that lenses have no reference to a center of curvature, although there are special situations regarding a distance twice the focal length, 2*f*. Finally, the rules for diagrams change slightly for lenses.

1. Light which enters the lens parallel to the principle axis will exit so as to pass through or appear to come from the focal point.

2. Light which passes through the focal point of a *convex lens* will exit the lens parallel to the principle axis.

3. Light which passes through the center of the lens, at *V,* is not bent and exits along the same path.

Figures 62 and 63 show the nature of these lenses and the general image formations.

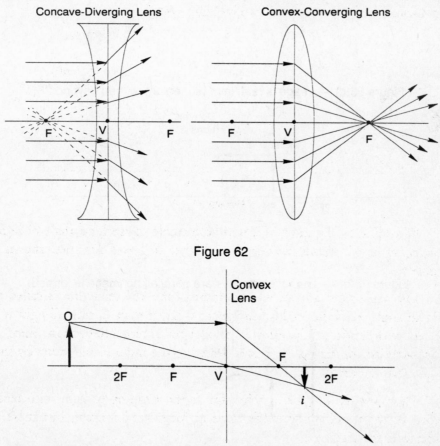

Concave-Diverging Lens   Convex-Converging Lens

Figure 62

Convex
Lens

Figure 63(a) — Image is real, inverted, reduced, and is between F and 2F.

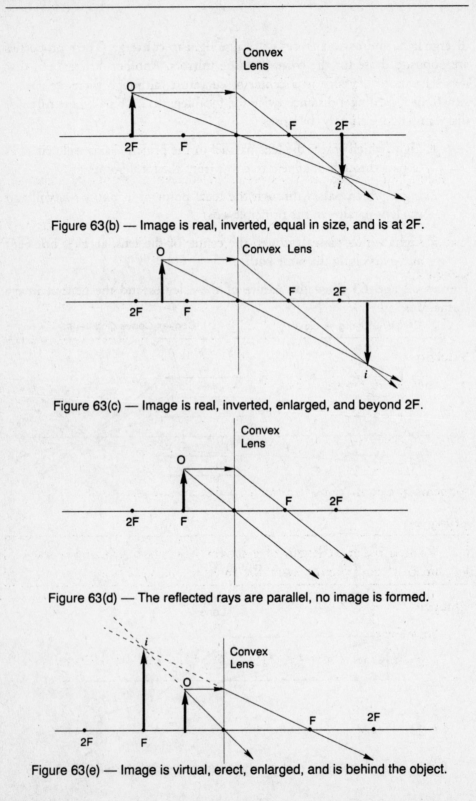

Figure 63(b) — Image is real, inverted, equal in size, and is at 2F.

Figure 63(c) — Image is real, inverted, enlarged, and beyond 2F.

Figure 63(d) — The reflected rays are parallel, no image is formed.

Figure 63(e) — Image is virtual, erect, enlarged, and is behind the object.

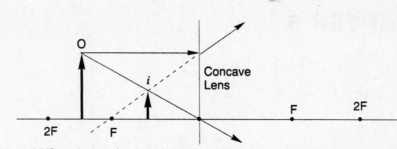

Figure 63(f) — Image is virtual, erect, reduced, and is between the object
and the lens.

The equations for lenses are the same as for curved mirrors. Remember
that d_i is negative for virtual images and f is negative for concave lenses.

PROBLEM

A 6 cm high object is 10 cm from a concave lens with a focal length
of 10 cm. Where is the image? What is its type? What is its height?

Solution

Solve for d_i, f is negative for concave lenses.

$$d_i = d_o f / (d_o - f) = (10)(-10) / [10 - (-10)] = -100/20 = -5 \text{ cm}$$

Since d_i is negative, the image is virtual. Solve for h_i,

$$h_i = d_i h_o / d_o = (5)(6) / 10 = 30/10 = 3 \text{ cm}.$$

Remember, h_i must be positive, so the − sign from d_i was dropped.

PROBLEM

What is the focal length of a convex lens which produces a real
image 15 cm from the lens if the object distance is 30 cm?

Solution

Solve for f,

$$f = d_o d_i / (d_o + d_i) = (30)(15) / (30 + 15) = 450 / 45 = 10 \text{ cm}.$$

CHAPTER 5

PHYSICAL OPTICS

PHYSICAL OPTICS

The behavior of waves can be affected by other waves or by instruments designed to produce a desired effect. When two or more waves come together, the resulting phenomenon is known as **interference**. Figure 64 shows two transverse waves. The maximum displacement of a crest or trough from the center is the amplitude of the wave. Here, amplitude a_1 is half that of a_2.

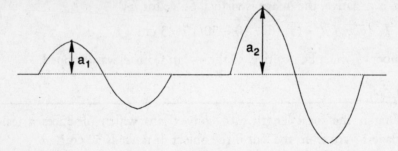

Figure 64

When waves interfere with each other, it is the amplitudes which are affected, which indirectly affects the energy of the wave. Figure 65 shows two identical waves, A and B, traveling from x to y.

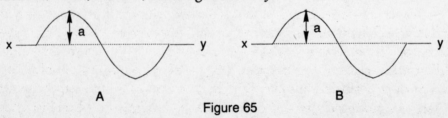

Figure 65

If these waves are added together, we have constructive interference. The crests of A and B will combine as well as their troughs. This would create a new wave, C, found in Figure 66.

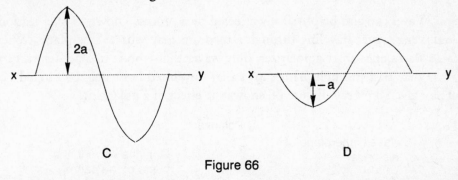

Figure 66

If wave A were to combine with wave D, then each crest would combine with a trough, effectively cancelling out both waves. This effect is destructive interference.

The examination of interference creates definite patterns within a wave system. Figure 67 shows a double point source interference pattern. Each solid line is a crest and the dotted lines are troughs. Considering these to be sources of light, dark regions appear at points of destructive interference and bright regions appear where constructive interference occurs.

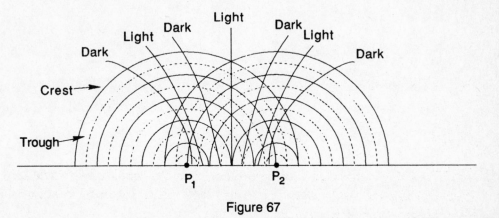

Figure 67

Waves can be bent by a process known as diffraction. **Diffraction** is the spreading of light into an area behind an obstruction. When light waves encounter an obstruction which is comparable in size to its wavelength, diffraction can occur. Items such as slit openings, pin holes, or sharp edges can produce a diffraction pattern. Diffraction separates light into its spectral colors and produces light and dark regions as in Figure 67. One instrument used to cause diffraction is called a diffraction grating. A grating is a transparent slide with etched lines which cause diffraction. Each grating could have hundreds or thousands of lines per centimeter of surface.

Waves can also be physically affected by a process known as polarization. Transverse waves traveling through a medium may vibrate in a plane. When these waves encounter a polarizer, only waves that vibrate in a predetermined plane may pass through. This shows that unwanted light may be filtered out of any given light ray. Figure 68 shows the effect of a polarizer.

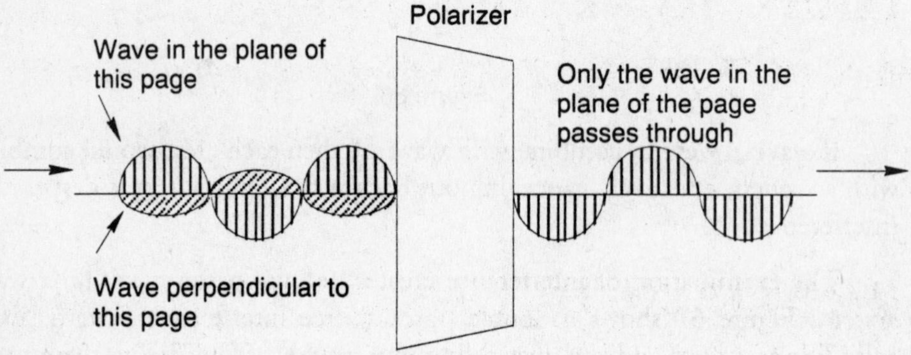

Figure 68

CHAPTER 6

HEAT, KINETIC THEORY, AND THERMODYNAMICS

THERMAL PROPERTIES

Much of the energy we deal with day to day is heat energy. Hot objects cool off over time and some substances burn and release heat. When a substance is hot, it has more thermal energy than when it is cold. The thermal energy of matter is the total potential and kinetic energy associated with the internal motion of the constituent particles. The term *heat* is actually a reference to the amount of thermal energy which is released, absorbed, or transferred from one body to the next.

Although heat and temperature are related, they are different quantities. A temperature is a quantity proportional to the *average* kinetic energy of the internal particles. For scientific purposes, temperature measurements must be made on the Celsius or Kelvin scales. The Kelvin scale is an absolute scale containing no negative temperatures. 0K is called the absolute zero of temperature. At this point, molecular motion is at a minimum, thus it is the lowest possible temperature. In the lab, temperatures can be made on the Celsius scale and then converted to Kelvin. The magnitude of 1C° is equal to that of 1K. The difference is that 0° Celsius is assigned to the freezing point of water. 0K is 273° below this point. Therefore,

$$K = °C + 273.$$

When a body absorbs heat, its temperature will increase. The amount of heat needed to change the temperature of a body 1° is the **heat capacity**.

heat capacity $= \Delta Q / \Delta T$,

where ΔQ is the heat needed to cause the temperature change ΔT. Since heat capacity is affected by the mass of material, it is not considered a descriptive property of matter. If, however, we consider different substances with equal mass, we have a property unique to each substance known as specific heat. **Specific heat** is the heat capacity per unit mass of substance. Specific heat, c, is given by

$c = \Delta Q / m\Delta T$.

From this we can see that $\Delta Q = mc\Delta T$, which allows the change in heat to be calculated since m and T are measurable, and c can be found on a prepared table of specific heat values. Examine the following problems:

PROBLEM

What is the specific heat of copper if a 150g sample absorbs 6930 calories which increases the temperature from 20°C to 520°C?

Solution

Solve for c,

$c = \Delta Q / m\Delta T = 6930 / (150)(500) = 6930 / 75000 = 0.0924$ cal/g°C.

PROBLEM

How many calories of heat are required to raise the temperature of 875g of copper 200°C?

Solution

Solve for ΔQ,

$\Delta Q = mc\Delta T = (875)(0.0924)(200) = 16,170$ cal.

Another specific property of substances is **thermal expansion**. Except in a few instances, materials expand when heated and contract when cooled. If we consider the expansion of solids in one dimension, then we are referring to linear expansion. The change in length per unit length of a solid for a 1° change is called the **coefficient of linear expansion**. From this we conclude that the longer an object is, the greater the expansion will be per degree. This is shown in Figure 69.

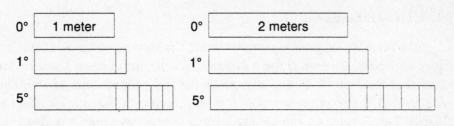

Figure 69

First note that the expansion shown here is greatly exaggerated for the purposes of the diagram. The rods begin at 0°. At 1°, the rods will expand according to their coefficients. Since the 2 meter rod is twice as long, its expansion is twice as much per degree. This is also illustrated at 5°. This means that the change in length, Δl, is equal to the product of the original length, l, its temperature change, ΔT, and the coefficient of linear expansion, α, such that

$$\Delta l = \alpha l \Delta T.$$

The coefficient for aluminum is 2.3×10^{-5} / °C. If a 12 meter aluminum rod is heated from 20° to 100°, what is the length of the rod at 100°?

$$\Delta l = \alpha l \Delta T = (2.3 \times 10^{-5})\,(12)\,(80) = 0.022 \text{ m}$$

The new length of the rod is

$$12 \text{ m} + 0.022 \text{ m} = 12.022 \text{ m}.$$

We must remember that solids expand in three dimensions. If two dimensions are examined, then the coefficient of area expansion is twice the linear coefficient. For three dimensions, the coefficient of volume expansion is 3 times the linear coefficient.

Liquids also expand when heated. Since liquids have no definite shape, we consider the volume expansion, ΔV, such that $\Delta V = \beta V \Delta T$. β is the coefficient of volume expansion.

Water is an exception to the expansion rules. When water is in the solid form of ice, it has an open hexagonal crystal structure which is necessary because of the bond angles of water molecules. This structure requires more space than if the molecules were free to move within the bond angle of another water molecule. Because of this, water has its maximum density at 40°C at which point heating or cooling will cause expansion.

KINETIC THEORY

The behavior of gases is complex since the volume of a gas is not fixed. There are several laws which help explain the behavior of gases. **Charles' Law** states that the volume of any dry gas is directly proportional to its Kelvin temperature, if the pressure upon the gas is constant. Figure 70 illustrates Charles' Law. Under P_1, the gas has a larger volume at a higher temperature. The Charles' Law equation is

$$V' = VT' / T,$$

where V' is the new volume, T is the original temperature, V is the original volume, and T' is the new temperature. To make a calculation, the temperatures must be in Kelvin. Charles' Law can be applied to the following problem:

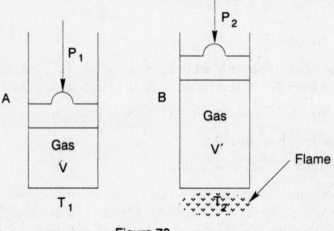

Figure 70

PROBLEM

What is the new volume of 3 liters of oxygen which is heated from 20°C to 50°C under constant pressure?

Solution

Convert °C to K,

$$K = °C + 273°$$

$$20 + 273 = 293 \text{ and } 50 + 273 = 323.$$

Solving for V',

$$V' = VT' / T = (3)(323) / 293 = 3.3 \text{ liters.}$$

Boyle's Law states that the volume of any dry gas is inversely proportional to the pressure exerted on it, if the temperature is constant. Figure 71 illustrates Boyle's Law. The increase in the pressure from P_1 to P_2 decreases the volume of the gas.

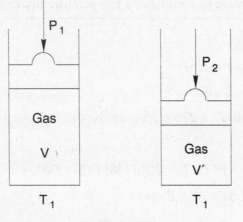

Figure 71

Since the pressure and volume are inversely proportional, their product is a constant. This means that

$$PV = k \text{ and } P'V' = k.$$

The Boyle's Law equation is

$$V' = VP/P'.$$

Pressure is measured in atmospheres, atm. One atmosphere is the pressure of the earth's atmosphere at sea level, and is called standard pressure. Standard temperature is 0°C or 273K. These values are often referred to as STP (standard temperature and pressure). Boyle's Law can be applied to the following problem:

PROBLEM

What pressure is needed to reduce 10 liters of a gas at STP to a volume of 2 liters?

Solution

Solve for P',

$$P' = VP/V' = (10)\,(1)\,/\,2 = 5 \text{ atm.}$$

The combination of these two laws gives the Combined Gas Law Equation:

$$PV \, / \, T = P' V' \, / \, T'$$

PROBLEM

What is the new volume of 20 liters of gas at STP which experience a pressure increase of 2 atm and a temperature increase of 75°?

Solution

A 2 atm increase means

$P' = 1 + 2 = 3$ atm

$T = 273$ and $T' = 273 + 75 = 348$K

Solving for V',

$V' = PVT' \, / \, P'T = (1) \, (20) \, (348) \, / \, (3) \, (273)$

$= 6960 \, / \, 819 = 8.5$ liters.

Amedeo Avogadro found that at the same temperature and pressure, different gases had densities proportional to the molecular weight. The **molecular weight** is the sum of all the atomic masses for all atoms that form the molecule. He also found that if you have a mass in grams of a substance equal to the molecular weight of the molecule, then the number of particles present in that mass would be equal for all substances. This is known as the **gram equivalent weight**. For example, helium has an atomic mass of 2. Avogadro said that 2 grams of helium contains 6.02×10^{23} atoms of helium. Further, if you had 44 grams of carbon dioxide with a molecular weight of 44, then you would have 6.02×10^{23} particles of $CO_2 \cdot 6.02 \times 10^{23}$ which is called Avogadro's Number.

One gram-molecular weight is commonly called a **mole**. One mole of a substance is that mass which contains Avogadro's Number of particles. Under these conditions, any $PV \, / \, T$ ratio is the same for one mole of any gas, and can be expressed as a constant, R. R is the Universal Gas Constant.

$$R = PV \, / \, T$$

Since this is true for any number of moles present, $nR = PV \, / \, T$. This equation is most commonly written as

$$PV = nRT$$

which is known as the **Ideal Gas Law**.

PROBLEM

To apply the ideal gas law, 15g of carbon dioxide, CO_2, occupy a volume of 13 liters under 1.5 atm of pressure. What is the temperature of the CO_2?

Solution

Determine the number of moles of CO_2.

$CO_2 = C + O + O = 12 + 16 + 16 = 44$ g/mol

15 grams × 1 mol/44 g = 0.34 mol CO_2

Solving for T,

$T = PV / nR = (1.5) (13) / (0.34) (0.082) = 699K.$

For one mole of a gas at STP, the volume is 22.4 liters. The value of R is

$R = PV / nT = (1$ atm$) (22.4$ L$)/(1$ mol$) (273) = 0.082$ L atm/mol K.

THERMODYNAMICS

Heat energy can be changed into other types of energy. This is the concept of **thermodynamics**. The following information deals with converting heat into mechanical energy. The energy which is transferred is the internal energy a substance possesses. **Internal energy** is the total potential and kinetic energy of the particles within the substance. These particles include the molecules, atoms, ions, and subatomic particles.

Heat is one form of internal energy. Mechanical energy is considered work and is measured in joules. An equivalent amount is measured in calories. One calorie is equal to 4.19 joules of work. This factor is the mechanical heat equivalent.

The transformation of heat into mechanical energy is governed by the First and Second Laws of Thermodynamics. The first law states that the energy supplied to a system in the form of heat is equal to the work done by the system plus the change in internal energy of the system. Thus, there is no loss of energy. To state the law mathematically, ΔQ is the quantity of heat added to a substance with internal energy equal E_i. This addition causes an increase in internal energy to E_f and also does a quantity of work, W. Thus,

$\Delta Q = (E_f - E_i) + W.$

First Law of Thermodynamics

A system's *internal energy* is a characteristic property of the system. We can map the states of a system on what is known as a *PV* diagram. On a *PV* diagram, every point represents a gas being on a certain pressure *P*, and volume *V*, and its final state is state *f*, with pressure P_f and volume V_f. It can go from states *i* to *f* by a number of possible processes:

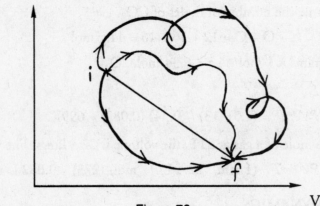

Figure 72

Suppose the gas expands isothermally. Then *T* = constant. Thus, since

$$PV = NRT,$$

PV does not change during the expansion.

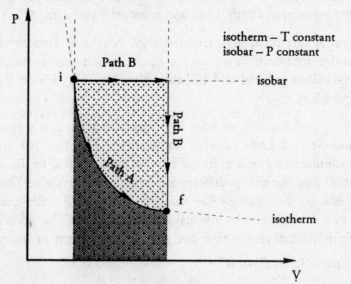

isotherm – T constant
isobar – P constant

Figure 73

In the *PV* diagram above, Path A represents an isothermal expansion from state *i* to state *f.* Path B represents another process, an isobaric expansion followed by an isovolumetric compression.

The expanding gas does work whose magnitude is equal to the area under the curve that represents the process on a *PV* diagram. If the gas is not expanding but *contracting,* (*V* goes *down*) during a process, then it *absorbs* work whose magnitude is equal to the area under the curve (meaning the work is done on the gas).

The First Law of Thermodynamics can be written as

$$\Delta Q = \Delta E + W,$$

where ΔQ is the total heat and W is the work done *by* (not *on*) the system. For the isothermal process described by Path A, $\Delta E = 0$, so $\Delta Q_a = W_a$. Energy *leaves* the system as *work* and *enters* as *heat.* No heat applied to the gas is retained; it is all converted into work.

Now for Path B: Here again, $\Delta E = 0$ so $Q_b = W_b$. But the areas under the curves are clearly different. Thus, W_a cannot $= W_b$. In fact, W_b is bigger. So ΔQ_a cannot $= \Delta Q_b$.

We can now envision a *closed cycle* where the gas follows Path B, then follows Path A backwards, i.e., goes down from *f* to *i* along the isotherm. On Path B, ΔH_b is put into the system and W_b comes out. *On the reversed path A, an amount of work W_a is put into the system and Q_a is released by it.* So on the cycle, $\Delta Q_b - Q_a$ is put into the system and $W_a - W_b$ joules of work come out.

Second Law of Thermodynamics

The second law states that it is impossible to construct an engine whose only effect is to extract heat from a source at a single temperature and convert all the heat into work. The examination of a basic heat engine can help clarify the second law.

In an engine, the working substance goes through a given cycle. The heat taken by the cycle is converted into work. However, any heat which is not converted must be delivered to a low temperature heat reservoir or "heat sink." The heat sink absorbs the exhaust from the cycle. Figure 74 illustrates the basic process for heat engines.

In essence, the second law says that heat flows from objects with high temperatures to objects with low temperatures. In a single temperature system, no heat flows.

The efficiency of a heat engine, e, is equal to the work done during one cycle divided by the heat added during the cycle.

$$e = W / \Delta Q$$

From the first law, we find that the work is the difference between the heat taken in and the heat exhaust,

$$W = \Delta Q_i - \Delta Q_e$$

Therefore,

$$e = (\Delta Q_i - \Delta Q_e) / Q_i$$
$$e = 1 - \Delta Q_e / \Delta Q_i$$

Since the ratio of the heats is equal to the ratio of the temperatures,

$$e = 1 - T_e / T_i \times 100\%.$$

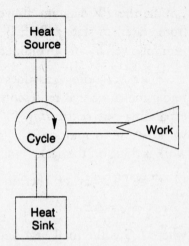

Figure 74

From this we conclude that the efficiency can be increased by raising the temperature of the source, lowering the temperature of the sink, or both. Maximum efficiency is achieved by keeping the source temperature as high as possible while keeping the sink temperature as low as possible. Examine the following problems:

PROBLEM

> What is the efficiency of a heat engine which has an input temperature of 300°C and a sink temperature of 150°C?

Solution

Solving for e,

$$e = 1 - T_e / T_i = 1 - (150 / 300) = 1 - 0.5 = 0.5$$
$$e = 0.5 \times 100\% = 50\%$$

PROBLEM

> What input temperature is necessary to increase the efficiency of the engine in the above problem by 30% if the sink temperature remains the same?

Solution

Solving for T_i, for $e = 80\%$,

$$T_i = T_e / (1 - e) = 150 / (1 - 0.8) = 150 / 0.2 = 750°C.$$

CHAPTER 7

MODERN PHYSICS

NUCLEAR STRUCTURE AND TRANSFORMATION

Early atomic scientists believed that atoms were composed of an equal number of positive and negative electrical charges even though the actual internal structure of these charges was undetermined. Ernest Rutherford performed an experiment which led to a new theory of atomic structure.

Rutherford shot a beam of positively charged alpha particles through a thin layer of gold foil. The alpha particle had a velocity of 1.6×10^7 m/s and the thickness of the foil was 1×10^{-7} m. He found that most of the particles passed through the foil as if it had not been there. But unexpectedly, he found that one of 8,000 alphas was deflected backward by the foil. From this and other data, Rutherford concluded that the positive charge in an atom must be concentrated at a single point. This is the only possible structure which could repel an alpha as was observed. Therefore, Rutherford's atom contained a nucleus in which 99.95% of the mass is concentrated, holds all the positive charge within the atom, and is surrounded by the negative charge. The positive nuclear particles are now known as **protons**. Protons have a mass of 1.007276470 amu which is equivalent to $1.6726485 \times 10^{-27}$ kg. This mass is 1836/1837 of the mass of hydrogen which contains one proton as the nucleus and one electron. Thus, the electron's mass is only 1/1837 of the mass of hydrogen, 9.1×10^{-31} kg or 0.00054858026 amu.

The number of protons in the atom nucleus is called the **atomic number**. If the nucleus is composed entirely of protons, then the mass of atom would be the sum of all the proton masses. This is not the case, however, since atomic masses are considerably larger than this sum. James Chadwick isolated a neutral particle he called a **neutron**. From his experiments it was evident that neutrons were regular components of atomic nuclei with a size comparable to a proton and a slightly higher mass of 1.008665012 amu or 1.6749543 × 10^{-27} kg. Thus, the atom nucleus is composed of positive protons and neutral neutrons. Once again, these nucleons provide for 99.95% of the atomic mass.

It may seem strange that many protons may be compacted into the nucleus of an atom without repelling each other electrically. Protons and neutrons in a nucleus are held together by the **nuclear binding force**. Nuclear binding is a unique attraction force which acts between nucleons which are closer than 2.0 × 10^{-15} m. The magnitude of the binding energy can be found by considering the nuclear mass defect. Measurements show that the mass of a nucleus is always less than the sum of the masses of its individual particles. This is true because of mass to energy conversion according to

$$E = mc^2.$$

Thus, when particles combine to form a nucleus, a small amount of mass is converted to energy. The energy released is the nuclear binding energy. To find the binding energy of a helium nucleus, examine the following information:

> helium nucleus = 2 protons + 2 neutrons
>
> 2 protons = 2 × 1.007276 = 2.014552 amu
>
> 2 neutrons = 2 × 1.008665 = 2.017330 amu
>
> total of 4 nucleons = 4.031882 amu
>
> mass of helium nucleus = 4.001509 amu
>
> nuclear mass defect = 0.030373 amu

Nuclear energies are measured in electron volts. One electron volt is the energy needed to move an electron through a potential difference of 1 volt. Since electron volts are small, energies are more commonly measured in Megaelectron volts, 1 × 10^6 electron volts. The conversion of one amu to energy yields 931 MeV. To find the binding energy of helium,

> 0.030373 amu × 931 MeV/amu = 28.3 MeV or 7.1 MeV/nucleon.

One important characteristic of many nuclei is **radioactivity**. This is the spontaneous breakdown of unstable nuclei with the emission of particles and/ or rays. This process is most commonly referred to as **radioactive decay**. A heavy nucleus can decay by emitting two kinds of particles, alpha or beta, or by the emission of gamma rays. The alpha particle is a helium nucleus. Alphas travel at one-tenth the speed of light, are positively charged, and can be stopped by a sheet of paper. Betas are electrons which travel near the speed of light, have a negative charge, and have more penetrating power than alphas. Gamma rays are waves which carry no mass and no charge, travel at the speed of light, and have high energies.

The emission of these radiation particles cause conversion to a new isotope of the same element, or cause a transformation to a new element. Uranium 238 is radioactive and decays by a series of reactions. We can examine nuclear transformations by looking at some of these uranium decay reactions. Uranium 238 decays by the emission of an alpha particle. The reaction is

$$^{238}_{92}U \rightarrow {}^{234}_{90}Th + {}^{4}_{2}He$$

The letters shown are the element symbols. The number written as the superscript is the atomic mass of the isotope, and the number written as the subscript is the number of protons in the nucleus, which is the atomic number. Uranium 238 emits an alpha which carries away 2 protons and 2 neutrons. Thus the mass is reduced by 4 nucleons, $238 - 4 = 234$. Losing 2 protons gives the atomic number of $92 - 2 = 90$. This means that the element now present is element 90, Thorium. This thorium isotope has a mass of 234 amu. In nuclear equations, the sum of the masses and the proton numbers must be equal on either side. Reactions which emit gamma rays do not change the atom, since gammas carry no mass and no protons. Thorium 234 is also radioactive and will decay by the emission of a beta particle. By looking at the following equation, we can predict the resulting element and its mass.

$$^{234}_{90}Th \rightarrow {}^{0}_{-1}e + {}^{?}_{?}?$$

The symbol for beta shows that it carries no mass and a −1 proton number. These numbers are significant in that betas must come from a transformation which results in the loss of a neutron and the gain of a proton. Thus, the mass is the same but the element will change. Since,

$$234 = 0 + ? \text{ and } 90 = -1 + ?$$

then

$$^{234}_{90}Th \rightarrow {}^{0}_{-1}e + {}^{234}_{91}Pa.$$

Thus, the element produced is Protactinium 234. After 14 such reactions which produce radioactive products, Uranium 238 will be reduced to a very stable Lead 206 atom.

As a particular number of radioactive atoms decay, it is logical that the amount of decay activity will decrease over time since there are fewer atoms of the original element left. The time period associated with a decay rate is called **half-life**. Simply, the half-life is the time necessary for exactly half of the radioactive atom to decay. The following chart and graph show an example half-life analysis for Iodine 131. Given that the half-life for Iodine 131 is 8 days:

Time in days	Number of I – 131 atoms	Number of half lives
0	100%	0
8	50%	1
16	25%	2
24	12.5%	3
32	6.25%	4
40	3.125%	5

Shown graphically, we see how the decay activity decreases over time.

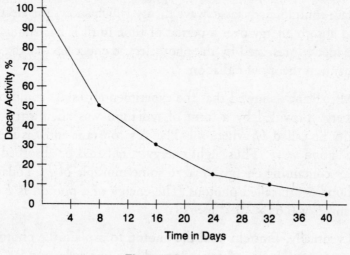

Figure 75

Radioactive decay is not the only nuclear process. Other reactions may occur by the bombardment of one nucleus with another. One example is the bombardment of Beryllium with alpha particles,

$$^{9}_{4}\text{Be} + ^{4}_{2}\text{He} \rightarrow ^{12}_{6}\text{C} + ^{1}_{0}\text{n} + \text{energy}$$

which produces carbon 12 and a free neutron as well as the release of the binding energy.

Nuclear fission is another reaction that releases a great amount of energy. Fission occurs in some isotopes of atoms with large nuclei. Fission is the splitting of the nucleus into smaller nuclei. Uranium 235 is a common fission fuel for power plants. When a Uranium 235 nucleus absorbs a neutron, the Uranium nucleus will divide to produce any number of different element combinations. In any case, the energy released is very large and can be used for the production of electricity. The products produced most often by Uranium 235 fission are Barium, Krypton, and free neutrons.

$$^{235}_{92}\text{U} + ^{1}_{0}\text{n} \rightarrow ^{138}_{56}\text{Ba} + ^{95}_{36}\text{Kr} + 3^{1}_{0}\text{n} + \text{energy}$$

QUANTUM THEORY AND ATOMIC STRUCTURE

Around 1900, physicists were examining a phenomenon they called the Photoelectric Effect. The **photoelectric effect** is the emission of electrons by a substance when illuminated by electromagnetic radiation. If an electron on the surface of the substance could absorb enough energy, it would escape the crystal with a given velocity. Experiments showed that the photoelectrons are ejected only when they can instantly absorb the energy required to do so. This fact contradicted classic wave theory which shows the electron should be able to absorb energy over a period of time until it has enough for ejection. The evidence presented by the photoelectric effect lead to the conception of the quantum theory of radiation.

Max Planck showed that the experimental results could be explained if the energy provided by a form of radiation was an integral multiple of a quantity he called hf, where h is Planck's constant and f is the frequency of the radiation wave. Thus, light energy is radiated or absorbed in indivisible bundles containing energy equal to some multiple of hf. Today, these quantum bundles are called photons. The energy of a photon is $E = hf$. Planck's constant, h, is 6.63×10^{-34} J·s.

Eventually, Einstein used the photon to explain the photoelectric effect. The maximum kinetic energy possessed by a photoelectron is

$$^{1}/_{2}\, mv^2 = hf - w,$$

where *m* and *v* are the mass and velocity of the photoelectron, *h* is Planck's constant, *f* is the frequency, and *w* is the energy needed or the work done for the electron to escape the surface. If the photon's energy was just enough to free it with a zero velocity, that is *hf* = *w*, then *f* is called the **cut off frequency**. This means that any photons with a frequency below cut off cannot cause photoemission regardless of exposure time. Thus, the earlier problems faced by wave theory are solved by the quantized photon theory.

The concept of quantized energy led to new theories regarding atomic structure. Neils Bohr theorized that the electron around the nucleus of an atom must exist in distinct or quantized orbitals since they do not radiate energy. Also, the closer the orbital is to the nucleus, the lower the energy is for that orbital.

If an electron in an atomic orbital can absorb a photon with the exact amount of energy so as to land in a higher level, it will do so. Similarly, if an excited electron emits a photon, it will fall to a lower orbital and the energy of the photon will be equal to the energy difference between the orbitals. This is shown by Figure 76.

Before absorption, we have an electron in level 1 which absorbs a 5eV photon. Since the difference between level 1 and level 3 is 5eV, the electron will jump to level 3. Once in level 3, there are two possible results. The first is that the electron could emit a 5eV photon and return to level 1. The second possibility is that the electron would emit a 3eV photon and fall to level 2, then emit a second photon with 2eV energy as it falls to level 1.

Bohr's idea has since been modified to incorporate such ideas as electron spin, magnetic effects, and angular momentum factors which he did not include in his atomic explanations.

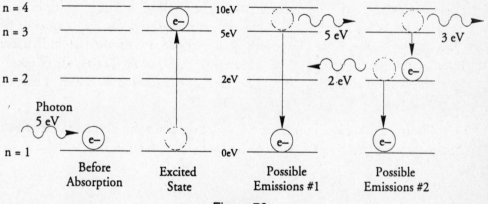

Figure 76

Dimension	Units
Length	Meter
Time	Second
Mass	Kilogram

	Dimension	Units
Derived Dimensions	Acceleration	m/s^2
	Velocity	m/s
	Force	$kg \cdot m/s^2$
	Momentum	$kg \cdot m/s$
	Torque	$kg \cdot m^2/s^2$
	Angular Momentum	$kg \cdot m^2/s^2$
	Electrostatic Charge	Coulomb (C)
	Energy/Work	Joule ($kg \cdot m^2/s^2$)
	Power	Watt ($kg \cdot m^2/s^3$)
	Potential Difference	Volt ($kg \cdot m^2/C \cdot s^2$)
	Current	Ampere (C/s)

ADVANCED PLACEMENT EXAMINATION IN
PHYSICS

C Course Review

CHAPTER 8

CLASSICAL MECHANICS

VECTORS

A vector is a measure of both direction and magnitude. Vector variables are usually indicated in **boldface**, or with an arrow, such as $\bar{v}$.

THE COMPONENTS OF A VECTOR

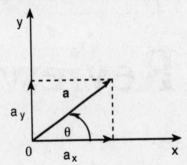

a_x and a_y are the components of a vector a. The angle θ is measured counter-clockwise from the positive x-axis. The components are formed when we draw perpendicular lines to the chosen axes.

Figure 1 — The Formation of Vector Components on the Positive $x - y$ axis

The components of a vector are given by:

$$A_x = A \cos \theta$$

$$A_y = A \sin \theta$$

A component is equal to the product of the magnitude of vector **A** and cosine of the angle between the positive axis and the vector.

The magnitude can be expressed in terms of the components:

$$A = \sqrt{A_x^2 + A_y^2}$$

Finally, the angle θ is given by:

$$\theta = \tan^{-1} \frac{A_y}{A_x}$$

Like scalars, which are measures of magnitude, vectors can be added, subtracted, and multiplied.

To add or subtract vectors, simply add or subtract the prospective x and y coordinates. For example,

$$\mathbf{A} - \mathbf{B} \Rightarrow A_x - B_x = C_x$$
$$A_y - B_y = C_y$$

Therefore, **C** is the sum vector.

There are two forms of multiplication: the dot product and the vector, or cross product. The dot product yields a scalar value:

$$\mathbf{a} \cdot \mathbf{b} = ab \cos \theta$$

The cross product of two vectors yields a vector:

$$\mathbf{a} \times \mathbf{b} = \mathbf{c}$$
$$\text{and}$$
$$|\mathbf{c}| = ab \sin \theta$$

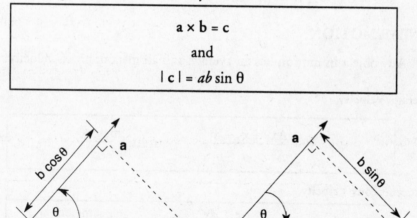

(a) Dot Product   (b) Cross Product

Figure 2 — Vector Multiplication

The direction of the vector product $\mathbf{a} \times \mathbf{b} = \mathbf{c}$ is given by the "Right-Hand Rule":

1) With **a** and **b** tail-to-tail, draw the angle θ from **a** to **b**.

2) With your right hand, curl your fingers in the direction of the angle drawn. The extended thumb points in the direction of **c**.

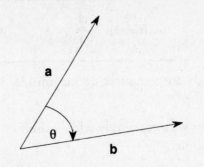

Figure 3 — The direction of the vector product,

$\mathbf{c} = \mathbf{a} \times \mathbf{b}$ ($|\mathbf{c}| = ab\sin\theta$), is into the page.

Properties of the cross product:

$$\mathbf{A} \times \mathbf{B} = -\mathbf{B} \times \mathbf{A}$$

$$\mathbf{A} \times (\mathbf{B} + \mathbf{C}) = (\mathbf{A} \times \mathbf{B}) + (\mathbf{A} \times \mathbf{C})$$

$$c(\mathbf{A} \times \mathbf{B}) = (c\mathbf{A}) \times \mathbf{B} = \mathbf{A} \times (c\,\mathbf{B}), \text{ where } c \text{ is a scalar.}$$

$$|\mathbf{A} \times \mathbf{B}|^2 = A^2 B^2 - (\mathbf{A} \cdot \mathbf{B})^2$$

LINEAR MOTION

Any object in motion has an average and an instantaneous velocity:

Average Velocity

$$V = \frac{\Delta x}{\Delta t} = \frac{x_2 - x_1}{t_2 - t_1} \qquad \text{units: } \frac{\text{meters}}{\text{sec}}$$

Instantaneous Velocity

$$V = \lim_{\Delta t \to 0} \frac{\Delta x}{\Delta t} = \frac{dx}{dt} = v(t) \qquad \text{units: } \frac{\text{meters}}{\text{sec}}$$

Just as the average and instantaneous velocities are the rate of change of position with respect to time, acceleration is the rate of change of velocity with respect to time.

$$\frac{dx}{dt} = v; \quad \frac{dv}{dt} = a$$

From this, the following basic kinematic equations of motion can be derived:

1. $$v = v_0 + at$$

2. $$v^2 = v_0^2 + 2a(x - x_0)$$

3. $$x = x_0 + v_0 t + {}^1\!/_2 \, at^2$$

4. $$x = x_0 + {}^1\!/_2 \, (v_0 + v)t$$

where v_0 and x_0 are initial values.

TWO-DIMENSIONAL MOTION

For two-dimensional, or planar, motion, simply break the velocity and acceleration vectors down into their x and y components. Once this is done, the preceding one-dimensional equations can apply.

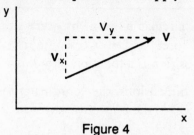

Figure 4

A special case of two-dimensional motion is *Uniform Circular Motion.* For a particle to be held on a circular path, a radial acceleration must be applied. This acceleration is called *centripetal acceleration.*

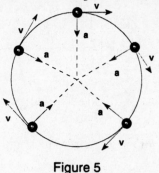

Figure 5

Centripetal Acceleration

$$a = \frac{v^2}{r}$$

where a = acceleration

            v = tangential component of velocity

r = radius of the path

For uniform circular motion, a can also be written as:

$$a = \frac{4\pi^2 r}{T^2}$$

where T, the period or time for one revolution, is given by:

$$T = \frac{2\pi r}{v}$$

The tangential component of the acceleration is the rate at which the particle speed changes:

$$a_T = \lim_{\Delta t \to 0} \frac{\Delta v}{\Delta t} = \frac{dv}{dt}$$

When dealing with circular motion, or other situations involving motion relative to a central force field, it is often appropriate to use cylindrical coordinates, where the position is a function of radius and angle (r, θ).

In the case of three dimensions, the coordinates become (r, θ, z), where the z-coordinate is identical to the respective cartesian z-coordinate.

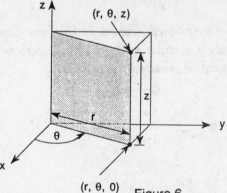

Figure 6

In describing such motion, α represents angular acceleration

$$\left(\frac{d\omega}{dt} \right)$$

and ω represents angular velocity.

$$\left(\frac{d\theta}{dt} \right)$$

If angular acceleration, α, is constant, then equations correlating to those previously stated for linear motion can be shown to apply.

Similarity Table

Rotational Motion	Linear Motion Equivalent
α = constant	a = constant
$\omega = \omega_0 + \alpha t$	$v = v_0 + at$
$\theta = \dfrac{\omega_0 + \omega}{2} t$	$x = \dfrac{v_0 + v}{2} t$
$\theta = \omega_0 t + \frac{1}{2} \alpha t^2$	$x = v_0 t + \frac{1}{2} a t^2$
$\omega^2 = \omega_0^2 + 2\alpha\theta$	$v^2 = v_0^2 + 2ax$
θ_0, θ = initial and final angular displacements	
ω_0, ω = initial and final angular velocities	

Another type of coordinate system used is the spherical coordinate system, with components (ρ, ϕ, θ).

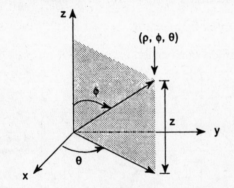

Figure 7

$r = \rho \sin \phi$	$x = r \cos \theta$	$x = \rho \sin \phi \cos \theta$
$z = \rho \cos \phi$	$y = r \sin \theta$	$y = \rho \sin \phi \sin \theta$
$\theta = \theta$	$z = z$	$z = \rho \cos \phi$

NEWTON'S LAWS

First Law

Every body remains in its state of rest or uniform linear motion, unless a force is applied to change that state.

Second Law

If the vector sum of the forces **F** acting on a particle of mass m is different from zero, then the particle will have an acceleration, **a**, directly proportional to, and in the same direction as, **F**, but inversely proportional to mass *m*. Symbolically,

$$F = m\mathbf{a}$$

(if mass is constant).

Third Law

For every action, there exists a corresponding equal and opposing reaction, or the mutual actions of two bodies are always equal and opposing.

Newton's Laws all refer to the effects of forces on particles or bodies. These forces can be represented in vector form.

Force

A) is a push or pull that a body exerts on another.

B) can be represented by a vector.

C) adds and subtracts vectorially.

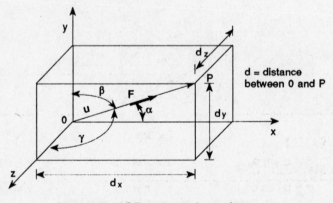

Figure 8 — $\mathbf{OP} = d_x\mathbf{x} + d_y\mathbf{y} + d_z\mathbf{z}$

Unit Vector

$$\mathbf{u} = \frac{\mathbf{OP}}{OP} = \frac{1}{d}\left(d_x\mathbf{x} + d_y\mathbf{y} + d_z\mathbf{z}\right)$$

Force F

$$\mathbf{F} = F\mathbf{u} = \frac{F}{d}\left(d_x\mathbf{x} + d_y\mathbf{y} + d_z\mathbf{z}\right)$$

Components

$$F_x = \frac{Fd_x}{d}, \quad F_y = \frac{Fd_y}{d}, \quad F_z = \frac{Fd_z}{d}$$

Distance

$$d = \sqrt{d_x^2 + d_y^2 + d_z^2}$$

Directional Cosines of F

$$\alpha = \cos^{-1} \frac{d_x}{d}$$

$$\beta = \cos^{-1} \frac{d_y}{d}$$

$$\gamma = \cos^{-1} \frac{d_z}{d}$$

Unit Vector Expressed in Terms of Angles

$$\mathbf{u} = \cos\alpha\,\mathbf{x} + \cos\beta\,\mathbf{y} + \cos\gamma\,\mathbf{z}$$

Relationship Between Angles

$$\cos^2\alpha + \cos^2\beta + \cos^2\gamma = 1$$

MOMENTUM

LINEAR MOMENTUM

$$\mathbf{p} = m\mathbf{v} \quad \rightarrow \quad \text{units: } \frac{\text{kg} \cdot \text{m}}{\text{sec}}$$

where p = linear momentum of particle
m = mass of particle
v = velocity of particle

NEWTON'S SECOND LAW

$$\mathbf{F} = \frac{d\mathbf{p}}{dt} = \frac{d(m\mathbf{v})}{dt}$$

where F = the net force on the particle.

LINEAR MOMENTUM OF A SYSTEM OF PARTICLES

Total Linear Momentum

$$P = \sum_{i=1}^{n} p_i = p_1 + p_2 + \ldots + p_n$$
$$= m_1 v_1 + m_2 v_2 + \ldots + m_n v_n$$

where P = total linear momentum of system

p_i, m_i, v_i = linear momentum, mass, and velocity of ith particle, respectively

Newton's Second Law for a System of Particles (Momentum Form)

$$F_{ext} = \frac{dP}{dt}$$

where F_{ext} = sum of all external forces.

Momentum is conserved. The total linear momentum of the system remains unchanged if the *sum* of all forces acting on the system is zero.

According to Newton's Second Law:

$$\frac{dP}{dt} = \sum F_{ext} = 0$$

ANGULAR MOMENTUM

Angular Momentum = l

Vector Equation

$$l = r \times P$$

Scalar Equation

$$l = rP \sin\theta$$

where l = angular momentum

r = radius

P = linear momentum

θ = angle formed by **r** and **P**

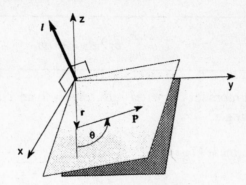

Figure 9 — Angular Momentum

The rotational correlation to force is torque, which relates to angular momentum by the equation:

$$\tau = \frac{\partial l}{\partial t}$$

Torque is simply:

$$(\mathbf{F}_{tangential}) \times (\mathbf{r}) = \tau$$

Another way of defining angular momentum is the moment of inertia times the angular velocity:

$$l = I\omega,$$

where I corresponds to mass (ω being angular velocity).

Determination of I:

Integration Method

Area — General Formula

$$I = \int_A s^2 \, dA$$

where s = perpendicular distance from the axis to the area element.

EXAMPLE

For a Rectangular Area

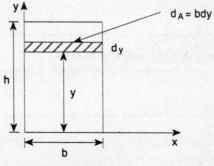

Figure 10

$$I_x = \int_0^b by^2 \, dy = \frac{1}{3} bh^3$$

This is the moment of inertia with respect to an axis passing through the base of the rectangle.

Moments of Inertia of Masses

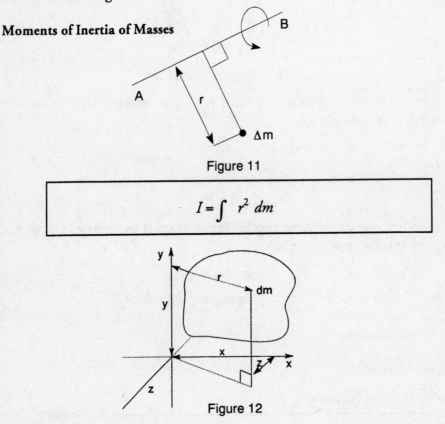

Figure 11

$$I = \int r^2 \, dm$$

Figure 12

In polar coordinates, the polar moment of inertia is noted as *J*.

Polar Moment of Inertia

$$J_0 = \int r^2 \, dA$$

Rectangular Moments of Inertia

$$J_0 = I_x + I_y$$

The radius of gyration can be determined once the moment of inertia and the area are known.

$$I_x = k_x^2 A; \quad I_y = k_y^2 A$$

Rectangular Component Form

$$k_x = \sqrt{\frac{I_x}{A}}$$

$$k_y = \sqrt{\frac{I_y}{A}}$$

Polar Form

$$k_0 = \sqrt{\frac{J_0}{A}}$$

Relation Between Rectangular Component Form and Polar Form

$$k_0^2 = k_x^2 + k_y^2$$

Masses

$$I = k^2 m$$

$$k = \sqrt{\frac{I}{m}}$$

Impulse and Momentum

Impulse-Momentum Method — An alternate method to solving problems in which forces are expressed as a function of time. It is applicable to situations wherein forces act over a small interval of time.

Linear Impulse-Momentum Equation

$$\int_1^2 \mathbf{F} \, dt = \text{impulse} = m\mathbf{v}_2 - m\mathbf{v}_1$$

Ideal impulse produces an instantaneous change in momentum and velocity of the particle without producing any displacement.

$$M\mathbf{v}_1 + \Sigma \, \mathbf{F} \, \Delta t = M\mathbf{v}_2$$

Any force which is non-impulsive may be neglected, e.g., weight, or small forces.

ENERGY AND WORK

The work done by a force **F** through a displacement $d\mathbf{r}$ is defined:

$$dw \equiv \mathbf{F} \cdot d\mathbf{r} \text{ in Joules. (SI units)}$$

Over a finite distance from point 1 to point 2:

$$W_{1-2} = \int_1^2 \mathbf{F} \cdot d\mathbf{r}$$

Work-Energy Principle

Kinetic energy for a particle of mass M and velocity v is defined as

$$\text{K.E.} = \frac{1}{2} m v^2$$

Kinetic energy is the energy possessed by a particle by virtue of its motion.

Principle of Work and Energy — Given that a particle undergoes a displacement under the influence of a force **F**, the work done by **F** equals the change in kinetic energy of the particle.

$$W_{1-2} = (KE)_2 - (KE)_1$$

Results of the Principle of Work and Energy:

A) Acceleration is not necessary and may not be obtained directly by this principle.

B) The principle may be applied to a system of particles if each particle is considered separately.

C) Those forces that do not contribute work are eliminated.

Kinetic energy and Newton's Law:

$$F = mv \frac{dv}{dx} = \frac{d}{dx}(KE),$$

where KE = a function of x.

(This applies only in an inertial reference frame.)

Power and Efficiency

Power is defined as the time-rate of change of work and is denoted by dw/dt,

$$\text{Power} = \frac{dw}{dt} = \mathbf{F} \cdot \mathbf{v}$$

Mechanical Efficiency

$$\eta = \frac{\text{Power out}}{\text{Power in}}$$

NOTE: η is *always* < 1.

Potential Energy

Potential Energy ≡ The stored energy of a body or particle in a force field associated with its position from a reference frame.

If *PE* represents potential energy,

$$PE = mgh$$

$$U_{1-2} = (PE)_1 - (PE)_2$$

A negative value would indicate an increase in potential energy.

Types of potential energy include:

1) Gravitational Potential Energy:

$$PE_g = -G\frac{M_1 M_2}{r}$$

2) Spring Potential Energy:

$$PE = \frac{1}{2}ky^2$$

Conservation of Energy

Conservative Case

For a particle under the action of conservative forces:

$$(KE)_1 + (PE)_1 = (KE)_2 + (PE)_2 = E \qquad (1)$$

The sum of kinetic and potential energy at a given point is constant.

Equation (1) can be written as:

$$E = \frac{1}{2}mv^2 + (PE)$$

The potential energy must be less than or equal to the total energy.

In a conservative system, if $PE = E$, then $V = 0$.

In a nonconservative system, relating potential and kinetic energy with the nonconservative force $\mathbf{F}'$:

$$d(PE + KE) = \int \mathbf{F}' \cdot d\mathbf{r}$$

1) The direction of $\mathbf{F}'$ is opposite to that of $d\mathbf{r}$.

2) Total energy E decreases with motion.

3) Friction forces are nonconservative.

HARMONIC MOTION

Simple Harmonic Motion — Linear motion of a body where the acceleration is proportional to the displacement from a fixed origin and is always directed towards the origin. The direction of acceleration is always opposite to that of the displacement.

Equation of motion:

or

$$mx'' + kx = 0$$

$$x'' + p^2 x = 0 \tag{2}$$

where $p^2 = k/m$.

General solution of Equation (2):

$$x = c_1 \sin pt + c_2 \cos pt$$

where c_1 and c_2 may be obtained from initial conditions.

An alternate form of Equation (2):

$$x = x_m \sin (pt + \phi)$$

where x_m = the amplitude
ϕ = the phase angle

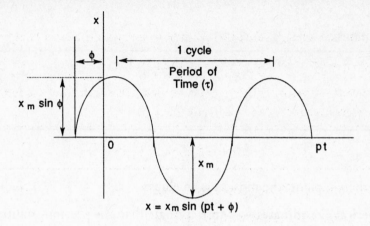

$$x = x_m \sin (pt + \phi)$$

Figure 13 — Period — $\tau = 2\pi / P$

Frequency — $f = 1 / \tau = P / 2\pi$

For small angles of vibration, the motion of a simple pendulum can be approximated by simple harmonic motion.

For small angles of vibration,

$$\phi = s / l$$

Equation of Motion:

$$\phi'' + \frac{g}{l}\phi = 0$$

The solution is:

$$\phi = \phi_0 \cos (\omega_0 t + \alpha_0),$$

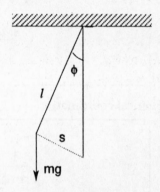

Figure 14

where $\omega_0 = \sqrt{g/l}$

ϕ_0 = max amplitude of oscillation
α_0 = phase factor

The period of oscillation is:

$$T_0 = \frac{2\pi}{\omega_0} = 2\pi\sqrt{\frac{l}{g}}$$

The spherical pendulum refers to the simple pendulum-like arrangement, but with motion in three dimensions.

The equations of motion become:

$$x'' + (g/l)x = 0$$

$$y'' + (g/l)y = 0$$

with solutions:

$$x = A \cos (\omega t + r)$$

$$y = B \cos (\omega t + \delta)$$

where $\omega = \sqrt{g/l}$.

On the x–y plane, the motion is an ellipse.

Spherical Coordinates — More accurate than the previous solution.

Equations of Motion:

$$ma_r = F_r = Mg \cos \theta - T$$

$$ma_\phi = F_\phi = - Mg \sin \phi$$

$$ma_{\phi\theta} = F_{\phi\theta} = 0$$

In spherical coordinates:

$$\phi'' - \psi'^2 \sin \phi \cos \phi + g \sin \phi = 0$$

$$\frac{1}{\sin \phi} \frac{d}{dt} (\alpha' \sin^2 \phi) = 0$$

Forced (Driven) Harmonic Oscillator

For periodic driving force:

Equation of Motion:

$$\frac{d^2 x}{dt^2} = -\omega^2 x + \frac{F_0}{m} \cos \omega_f t$$

where ω_f = driving frequency
F_0 = max. magnitude of the driving force

The solution will be equal to the sum of the complementary solution and the particular solution.

$$X = \underbrace{A \cos \omega t + B \sin \omega t}_{X_c} + \underbrace{\frac{F_0 / m}{\omega^2 - \omega_f^2} \cos \omega_f t}_{X_p}$$

Resonance occurs when $\omega_f \approx \omega$.

Damped Oscillator

A common damping force is:

$$F = c\frac{dx}{df}$$

If an object's motion is damped in this manner, then the equation of motion is:

$$m\frac{d^2x}{dt^2} + c\frac{dx}{dt} + kx = 0$$

$$a_1 = \frac{-c}{2m} - \sqrt{\left(\frac{c}{2m}\right)^2 - \frac{k}{m}}$$

$$a_2 = \frac{-c}{2m} + \sqrt{\left(\frac{c}{2m}\right)^2 - \frac{k}{m}}$$

The critical damping coefficient is defined as:

$$C_{\text{critical}} = 2m\sqrt{\frac{k}{m}}$$

Now, three cases must be considered with respect to C_{critical}:

A) If $c > C_{\text{critical}}$, a_1 and a_2 are both real, the motion is nonoscillating, and the system is overdamped. The general solution is given by:

$$x = Ae^{a_1 t} + Be^{a_2 t}$$

B) If $c = C_{\text{critical}}$, $a_1 = a_2$ and the system is critically damped with general solution:

$$x = (A + Bt)e^{-\left(\frac{C_{\text{critical}}}{2m}\right)t}$$

C) If $c < C_{\text{critical}}$ a_1 and a_2 are complex and imaginary and the system is underdamped with the solution given by:

$$X = E\left[e^{-(c/2m)t}\sin\left(\sqrt{\frac{k}{m} - \left(\frac{C}{2m}\right)^2}\,t + \psi\right)\right]$$

where constants A, B, E, and ψ are determined from initial conditions. The graph representing the above equation is shown in the following figure:

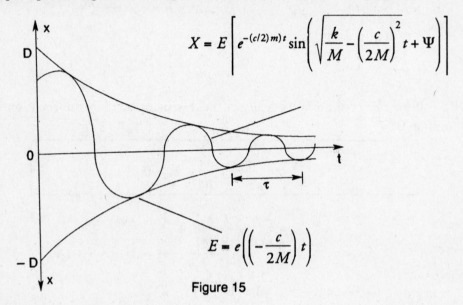

$$X = E\left[e^{-(c/2)m)t}\sin\left(\sqrt{\frac{k}{M} - \left(\frac{c}{2M}\right)^2}\,t + \Psi\right)\right]$$

$$E = e\left(\left(-\frac{c}{2M}\right)t\right)$$

Figure 15

Damped Force (Driven) Vibration

The equation of motion becomes:

$$m\frac{d^2x}{dt^2} + c\frac{dx}{dt} + kx = F\sin\omega t$$

Assuming $X_p = A\sin(\omega t - \psi)$

$$A = \frac{F/k}{\sqrt{\left[1 - \frac{4m^2\omega^2}{C_{\text{critical}}^2}\right]^2 + \left[\frac{4m\omega C}{C_{\text{critical}}^2}\right]^2}}$$

$$\psi = \tan^{-1}\left[\frac{c\omega/k}{\left(1 - \frac{m\omega^2}{k}\right)}\right]$$

NOTE: Angle ψ is the phase difference between the resulting steady-state vibration and the applied force.

The magnification factor is defined as:

$$\text{Magnification factor} = \frac{A}{F/k} = \frac{1}{\sqrt{\left[1 - \frac{4m^2\omega^2}{C_{\text{critical}}^2}\right]^2 + \left[\frac{4m\omega c}{C_{\text{critical}}^2}\right]^2}}$$

The graph is shown in the following figure. Resonance occurs only when the damping is zero and the frequency ratio is one.

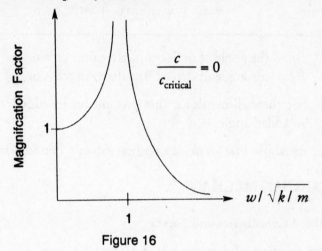

Figure 16

COLLISIONS

When kinetic energy is conserved the collision is Elastic. Otherwise, the collision is said to be Inelastic.

A)   For an elastic collision,

$$\frac{1}{2}\,m_1 v_{1_i}^2 + \frac{1}{2}\,m_2 v_{2_i}^2 = \frac{1}{2}\,m_1 v_{1_f}^2 + \frac{1}{2}\,m_2 v_{2_f}^2$$

B)   For an inelastic collision, some kinetic energy is transformed into internal energy. However, linear momentum is still conserved. If the two bodies stick and travel together with a common final velocity after collision, it is said to be completely inelastic. From conservation of momentum, we have

$$m_1 v_{1_i} + m_2 v_{2_i} = (m_1 + m_2)v_f$$

Collisions in Two and Three Dimensions

Since momentum is linearly conserved, the resultant components must be found and then the conservation laws applied in each direction.

A)   The x–component

$$m_1 v_{1_i} = m_1 v_{1_f} \cos\theta_1 + m_2 v_{2_f} \cos\theta_2 \qquad \text{(i)}$$

B) The y-component

$$m_2 v_{2_i} = m_1 v_{1_f} \sin \theta_1 + m_2 v_{2_f} \sin \theta_2 \qquad \text{(i)}$$

where θ_1 = the angle of deflection, after the collision, of mass m_1.
θ_2 = the angle of deflection, after the collision, of mass m_2.

C) For three dimensions, there would be an added z-component and an added angle, θ_3.

For the above cases, i denotes initial value; f denotes final value.

LAGRANGIAN MECHANICS

Generalized Coordinates and Forces

The position of a particle is described by employing the concept of a coordinate system. Given, for example, a coordinate system such as the spherical or the oblate spherical coordinates, etc., a particle in space may be characterized as an ordered triple of numbers called coordinates.

A constrained particle in motion on a surface requires two coordinates, and a constrained particle on a curve requires one coordinate to characterize its location.

Given a system of m particles, 3M coordinates are required to describe the location of each particle. This is the configuration of the system. (If constraints are imposed on the system, fewer coordinates are required.)

A rigid body requires six coordinates, three for orientation and three for the reference point, to completely locate its position.

Generalized coordinates — A set of coordinates, $q_1, q_2, \ldots, q_m$, equal to the number of degrees of freedom of the system.

If each q_i is independent of the others, then it is known as holonomic.

The rectangular coordinates for a particle expressed in generalized coordinates:

$x = x(q)$ Motion on a curve (one degree of freedom)

$x = x(q_1, q_2)$ Motion on a surface (two degrees of freedom)
$y = y(q_1, q_2)$

$x = x(q_1, q_2, q_3)$ Spatial motion (three degrees of freedom)
$y = y(q_1, q_2, q_3)$
$z = z(q_1, q_2, q_3)$

Small changes in coordinates:

$$\delta x = \frac{\partial x}{\partial q_1}\delta q_1 + \frac{\partial x}{\partial q_2}\delta q_2 + \frac{\partial x}{\partial q_3}\delta q_3$$

$$\delta y = \frac{\partial y}{\partial q_1}\delta q_1 + \frac{\partial y}{\partial q_2}\delta q_2 + \frac{\partial y}{\partial q_3}\delta q_3$$

$$\delta z = \frac{\partial z}{\partial q_1}\delta q_1 + \frac{\partial z}{\partial q_2}\delta q_2 + \frac{\partial z}{\partial q_3}\delta q_3$$

For a system of m particles in generalized coordinates:

$$\delta x_i = \frac{\partial x_i}{\partial q_k}\delta q_k \qquad \begin{array}{l} k = 1, 2, \ldots, m \\ 1 < i < m \end{array}$$

$$\delta y_i = \frac{\partial y_i}{\partial q_k}\delta q_k \qquad \begin{array}{l} k = 1, 2, \ldots, m \\ 1 < i < m \end{array}$$

$$\delta z_i = \frac{\partial z_i}{\partial q_k}\delta q_k \qquad \begin{array}{l} k = 1, 2, \ldots, m \\ 1 < i < m \end{array}$$

expressed in tensor notation.

Generalized forces:

Work done $\qquad \delta w = \mathbf{F} \cdot \delta \mathbf{r} = F_i \cdot \delta x_i$

For one particle, $\qquad 1 < i < 3$

and for m particles, $\qquad 1 < i < 3m$

In terms of generalized coordinates:

$$\delta w = F_i \frac{\partial x_i}{\partial q_k}\delta q_k$$

or $\qquad \delta w = Q_k \delta q_k$, where $\quad Q_k = F_i \frac{\partial x_i}{\partial q_k}$

and is known as the generalized force.

Conservative Systems

Forces expressed in terms of the potential energy function:

$$\boxed{F_i = \frac{-\partial v}{\partial x_i}}$$

where v is the potential energy.

In terms of the generalized force,

$$Q_k = -\frac{\partial v}{\partial x_i}\frac{\partial x_i}{\partial q_k} = -\frac{\partial v}{\partial q_k}$$

LAGRANGE'S EQUATION

For a system, kinetic energy, KE, is:

$$T = KE = \frac{1}{2}m_i x'^2_i \quad i = 1, 2, ..., 3M$$

where

$$x'_1 = \frac{\partial x_i}{\partial q_k}q'_k + \frac{\partial x_i}{\partial t} \quad k = 1, 2, ..., M$$

The Lagrange equation of motion using the equations above is:

$$\frac{d}{dt}\frac{\partial T}{\partial q'_k} = Q_k + \frac{\partial T}{\partial q_k} \quad k = 1, 2, ..., M$$

or if the motion is conservative and if the potential energy is a function of generalized coordinates, then the equation becomes:

$$\frac{d}{dt}\left(\frac{\partial T}{\partial q'_k}\right) = \frac{\partial T}{\partial q_k} - \frac{\partial v}{\partial q_k} \quad k = 1, 2, ..., M$$

Lagrange's Function (L)

$L = T - V$, where T and V are in terms of generalized coordinates.

Lagrange's equation in terms of L:

$$\frac{d}{dt}\left(\frac{\partial L}{\partial q'_k}\right) = \frac{\partial L}{\partial q_k} \quad k = 1, 2, ..., M$$

Lagrange's equation for nonconservative generalized forces:

If

$$Q_k = Q' - \frac{\partial v}{\partial q_k}$$

where Q' is nonconservative, then Lagrange's equation becomes

$$\frac{d}{dt}\frac{\partial L}{\partial q'_k} = Q'_k + \frac{\partial L}{\partial q_k}$$

and is useful, for example, when frictional forces are present.

General procedure for obtaining the equation of motion:

A) Choose a coordinate system.

B) Write the kinetic energy equation as a function of these coordinates.

C) Find the potential energy, if the system is conservative.

D) Combining these terms in Lagrange's equation results in the equation of motion.

Lagrange's Equations with Constraints

Holonomic Constraint — Constraints of the form:

$$\frac{\partial q}{\partial q_k}\, \delta q = 0$$

Non-Holonomic Constraint — Constraints of the form:

$$h_k\, \delta q_k = 0$$

Differential equations of motion by the method of undetermined multipliers (The Non-Holonomic Case):

Multiply the equation by a constant λ and add the result to the integrand of:

$$\int_{t_a}^{t_b} \left[\frac{\partial L}{\partial q_k} - \frac{d}{dt}\frac{\partial L}{\partial q'_k} \right] \delta q_k\, dt = 0$$

Select λ such that the terms in brackets equals zero,

$$\frac{\partial L}{\partial q_k} - \frac{d}{dt}\frac{\partial L}{\partial q'_k} + \lambda h_k = 0 \quad (k = 1, 2, \ldots, m)$$
$$h_k q'_k = 0$$

There now exist $m + 1$ equations to obtain $m + 1$ unknowns, i.e.,

$$(q_1, q_2, \ldots, q_n, \lambda.)$$

This technique may be employed with moving constraints or with several constraints by having corresponding undetermined coefficients with corresponding h's in the Lagrangian equations.

CHAPTER 9

ELECTRICITY AND MAGNETISM

ELECTRIC FIELDS

Definition of an Electric Field

$$E = \frac{F}{q_0}$$

where E = electric field
            F = electric force
          q_0 = positive test charge

COULOMB'S LAW

By definition, the force between two point charges of arbitrary positive or negative strengths is given by the Coulomb's law as follows:

$$F = k \frac{Q_1 Q_2}{4\pi\varepsilon_0 d^2}$$

where
  Q_1 and Q_2 = positive or negative charges on either object in coulombs
           d = distance separating the two point charges
           k = the constant of proportionality
             = $(4\pi\varepsilon_0)^{-1} = 9 \times 10^9$ newton-meter^2 / coul.
          ε_0 = permittivity in free space
             = 8.854×10^{-12} F/m

NOTE: $\varepsilon = \varepsilon_0 \, \varepsilon_r$ for media other than free space, where ε_r is the relative permittivity of the media.

The force F can be expressed in vector form to indicate its direction as follows:

$$F = \frac{Q_1 Q_2}{4\pi\varepsilon_0 d^2} \, \mathbf{a}_d$$

The unit vector $\mathbf{a}_d$ is in the direction of d

$$\mathbf{a}_d = \frac{\mathbf{d}}{\left|\mathbf{d}\right|} = \frac{\mathbf{d}}{d}$$

Naturally, Q_1 and Q_2 can each be either positive or negative. As a consequence of this, the resultant force can be either positive (repulsive) or negative (attractive).

Flux

By definition, the electric flux, ψ (from Faraday's experiment), is given by:

$$\psi = Q,$$

where Q is the charge in coulombs.

The electric flux density $\mathbf{D}$ is a vector quantity. In general, at a point M of any surface S (see figure), $\mathbf{D} ds \cos\theta = d\psi$ (where $d\psi$ is the differential flux through the differential surface ds of M, and θ is the angle of $\mathbf{D}$ with respect to the normal vector from ds). (**NOTE:**

$$\mathbf{D} = \frac{d\psi}{ds}$$

is the case where $\mathbf{D}$ is normal to ds and the direction and magnitude of the electric flux density varies along the surface.)

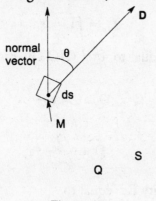

Figure 17

GAUSS'S LAW

Gauss's law states that the net electric flux passing out of a closed surface is equal to the total charge within that surface.

Hence, since

$$d\psi = \mathbf{D} \cdot d\mathbf{s}$$

$$\psi = \int \mathbf{D} \cdot d\mathbf{s}$$

and by Gauss's law,

$$\psi_{net} = \oint_s \mathbf{D} \cdot d\mathbf{s} = Q_s$$

where Q_s is the total number of charges enclosed by the surface.

Application of Gauss's Law

The following spherical surface is **chosen** to enclose a given charge to be determined: Q_s

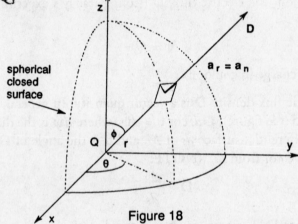

Figure 18

Applying Gauss's law, the charge Q_s enclosed by the spherical surface is

$$Q_s = \oint_s \mathbf{D} \cdot d\mathbf{s},$$

where ds in this case is equal to $4\pi r^2$ (**NOTE:** r is the radius of the sphere). Hence,

$$Q_s = D4\pi r^2$$

and

$$D = \frac{Q_s}{4\pi r^2} \cdot \mathbf{a}_r$$

Since electric field intensity **E** is equal to

$$\frac{Q}{4\pi\varepsilon_0 d^2} a_d$$

and d is equal to r in this case, then $\mathbf{D} = \varepsilon_0\mathbf{E}$.

Some hints for choosing a special Gaussian surface:

A)   The surface must be closed.

B) D remains constant through the surface and normal to the surface.

C) D is either tangential or normal to the surface at any point on the surface.

It is easier to solve a problem if we can choose a special Gaussian surface. In other words, this surface should be chosen to conform to the flux at any given point on the closed surface about the charge.

ELECTRIC POTENTIAL, ENERGY, AND WORK

Electric Potential Difference:

$$V_B - V_A = \frac{W_{AB}}{q_0} \text{ units: volts}$$

where V_B = electric potential at Point B
V_A = electric potential at Point A
W_{AB} = work done by external force
q_0 = electrical test charge

More generally:

The potential difference between two points p and p', symbolized as $V_{p'p}$ (or $\phi p'p$), is defined as the work done in moving a unit positive charge by an external force from the initial point p to the final point p'.

$$V_{p'p} = -\int_p^{p'} \mathbf{E} \cdot d\mathbf{L} = V_{p'} - V_p$$

The unit for potential difference is the Volt (V) which is Joules/coulomb.

CAPACITORS

The capacitance of two oppositely charged conductors in a uniform dielectric medium is

$$C = \frac{Q}{V_0}$$

The unit for capacitance is the Farad (F)

$$F = \frac{C}{V}$$

where Q = the total charge in *either* conductor
V_0 = the potential difference between the two conductors

EXAMPLE

Capacitance of the parallel-plate capacitor:

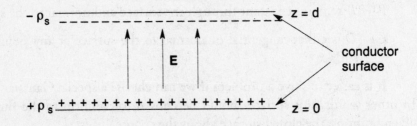

Figure 19

$$E = \frac{\rho_s}{\varepsilon} a_z$$

ε is the permittivity of the homogeneous dielectric.

$$D = \rho_s \cdot a_z$$

On lower plate:

$$D_n = D_z = \rho_s$$

D_n is the normal value of **D**.

On upper plate:

$$D_n = -D_z$$

V_0 = The potential difference

$$= -\int_{upper}^{lower} E \cdot dL$$

$$= -\int_d^0 \frac{\rho_s}{\varepsilon} d_z = \frac{\rho_s d}{\varepsilon}$$

$$\boxed{C = \frac{Q}{V_0} = \frac{\varepsilon S}{d}}$$

$Q = \rho_s S$ and $V_0 = \frac{\rho_s d}{\varepsilon}$

considering conductor planes of area S are of linear dimensions much greater than d.

Total energy stored in the capacitor:

$$\boxed{\begin{array}{c} W_E = \frac{1}{2}\int_{vol} \varepsilon E^2 \, dv = \frac{1}{2}\int_0^S \int_0^d \frac{\varepsilon \rho_s}{\varepsilon^2} \, dz \, ds \\[2mm] W_E = \frac{1}{2} C V_0^2 = \frac{1}{2} Q V_0 = \frac{1}{2} \frac{Q^2}{C} \end{array}}$$

Multiple Dielectric Capacitors

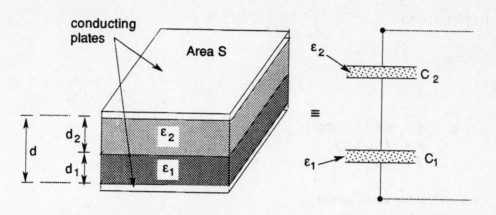

Figure 20 — A parallel-plate capacitor containing two dielectrics with the dielectric interface parallel to the conducting plates;

$$C = 1/\{ (d_1 / \varepsilon_1 S) + (d_2 / \varepsilon_2 S) \}.$$

$$C = \cfrac{1}{\left(\dfrac{1}{C_1}\right) + \left(\dfrac{1}{C_2}\right)},$$

where

$$C_1 = \frac{\varepsilon_1 S}{d_1}$$

$$C_2 = \frac{\varepsilon_2 S}{d_2}$$

V_0 = A potential difference between the plates

$\quad\ = E_1 d_1 + E_2 d_2$

$$E_1 = \frac{V_0}{d_1} + \left(\frac{\varepsilon_1}{\varepsilon_2}\right) d_2$$

ρ_{s_1} = The surface charge density $= D_1 = \varepsilon_1 E_1$

$$= \cfrac{V_0}{\left(\dfrac{d_1}{\varepsilon_1}\right) + \left(\dfrac{d_2}{\varepsilon_2}\right)} = D_2$$

$$C = \frac{Q}{V_0} = \frac{\rho_s \cdot S}{V_0} = \cfrac{1}{\left(\dfrac{d_1}{\varepsilon_1 s}\right) + \left(\dfrac{d_2}{\varepsilon_2 s}\right)} = \cfrac{1}{\left(\dfrac{1}{C_1}\right) + \left(\dfrac{1}{C_2}\right)}$$

CURRENT AND RESISTANCE

DEFINITIONS

Current

$$i = \frac{dq}{dt} \text{ amperes,}$$

where i = electric current
q = net charge
t = time

Current Density and Current

$$j = \frac{i}{A} \text{ amperes} / m^2,$$

where j = current density
i = current
A = cross-sectional area

Mean Drift Speed

$$v_D = \frac{j}{ne},$$

where v_D = mean drift speed
j = current density
n = number of atoms per unit volume

Resistance

$$R = \frac{V}{i} \text{ ohms } (\Omega),$$

where R = resistance
V = potential difference
i = current

Resistivity

$$\rho = \frac{E}{j} \text{ ohm} - \text{meters } (\Omega\, m),$$

where ρ = resistivity
E = electric field
j = current density

Power

$$P = VI = I^2R = \frac{V^2}{R} \text{ watts (W)},$$

where P = power
            I = current
            V = potential difference
            R = resistance

CIRCUITS

Electromotive Force, *EMF*(ε)

$$\varepsilon = \frac{dw}{dq}$$

where ε = electromotive force
            w = work done on charge
            q = electric charge

Current in a Simple Circuit

$$i = \frac{\varepsilon}{R}$$

where i = current
            ε = electromotive force
            R = resistance

Resistances

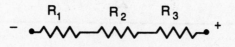

Figure 21

$$R_{\text{Total}} = (R_1 + R_2 + R_3)\ \Omega \text{ (in series)}$$

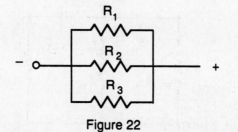

Figure 22

$$\frac{1}{R_{\text{Total}}} = \left(\frac{1}{R_1} + \frac{1}{R_2} + \frac{1}{R_3} \right) \text{ (in parallel)}$$

The Loop Theorem

$$\Delta V_1 + \Delta V_2 + \Delta V_3 \ldots = 0$$

For a complete circuit loop

EXAMPLE

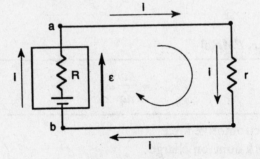

Figure 23 — Simple Circuit with Resistor

$$V_{ab} = \varepsilon - iR = + ir$$

Then

$$\varepsilon - iR - ir = 0$$

NOTE: If a resistor is traversed in the direction of the current, the voltage change is represented as a voltage drop, $- iR$. A change in voltage while traversing the *EMF* (or battery) in the direction of the *EMF* is a voltage rise $+\varepsilon$.

Circuit with Several Loops

$$\sum_n i_n = 0$$

EXAMPLE

$$i_1 + i_2 + i_3 = 0$$

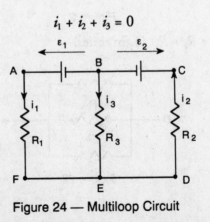

Figure 24 — Multiloop Circuit

RC CIRCUITS (RESISTORS AND CAPACITORS)

RC charging and discharging

Differential Equations

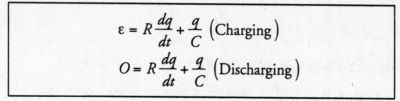

$$\varepsilon = R\frac{dq}{dt} + \frac{q}{C} \quad \left(\text{Charging}\right)$$

$$0 = R\frac{dq}{dt} + \frac{q}{C} \quad \left(\text{Discharging}\right)$$

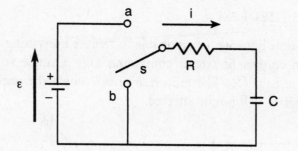

Figure 25 — An RC Circuit

Charge in the Capacitor

$$q = (C\varepsilon)\left(1 - e^{\frac{-t}{RC}}\right) \quad \text{(Charging)}$$

$$q = (C\varepsilon)\, e^{\frac{-t}{RC}} \qquad \text{(Discharging)}$$

Current in the Resistor

$$i = \left(\frac{\varepsilon}{R}\right) e^{\frac{-t}{RC}} \quad \text{(Charging)}$$

$$i = -\left(\frac{\varepsilon}{R}\right) e^{\frac{-t}{RC}} \quad \text{(Discharging)}$$

where $e = 2.71828$ (Exponential Constant).

KIRCHOFF'S CURRENT LAW

The algebraic sum of all currents entering a node equals the algebraic sum of all currents leaving it.

$$\sum_{n=1}^{N} i_n = 0$$

KIRCHOFF'S VOLTAGE LAW (SAME AS LOOP THEOREM)

The algebraic sum of all voltages around a closed loop is zero.

THEVENIN'S THEOREM

In any linear network, it is possible to replace everything except the load resistor by an equivalent circuit containing only a single voltage source in series with a resistor (R_{th} Thevenin resistance), where the response measured at the load resistor will not be affected.

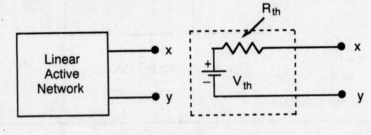

Figure 26

Procedures to Find Thevenin Equivalent

1) Solve for the open circuit voltage V_{oc} across the output terminals.

$$V_{oc} = V_{th}$$

2) Place this voltage V_{oc} in series with the Thevenin resistance which is the resistance across the terminals found by setting all independent voltage and current sources to zero (i.e., short circuits and open circuits, respectively).

RLC CIRCUITS AND OSCILLATIONS

These oscillations are analogous to, and mathematically identical to, the case of mechanical harmonic motion in its various forms. (AC current is sinusoidal.)

SIMPLE RL AND RC CIRCUITS

Source Free RL Circuit

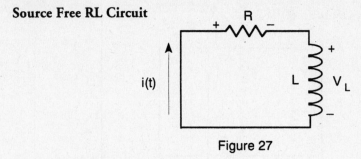

Figure 27

Properties: Assume initially $i(0) = I_0$

A) $v_R + v_L = Ri + L\dfrac{di}{dt} = 0$

B) $i(t) = I_0 e^{-Rt/L} = I_0 e^{-t/\tau}$, τ = time constant = $\dfrac{L}{R}$

C) Power dissipated in the resistor =

$P_R = i^2 R = I_0^2 Re^{-2Rt/L}$

D) Total energy in terms of heat in the resistor =

$W_R = \frac{1}{2} LI_0^2$

Source Free RC Circuit

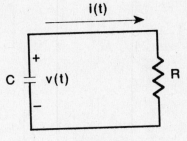

Figure 28

Properties: Assume initially $v(0) = V_0$

A) $C\dfrac{dv}{dt} + \dfrac{v}{R} = 0$

B) $v(t) = v(0)e^{-t/RC} = V_0 e^{-t/RC}$

C) $\dfrac{1}{C}\displaystyle\int_{-\infty}^{t} i(\tau)\, d\tau + i(t)R = 0$

$i(t) = i(0)e^{\frac{-t}{RC}}$

THE RLC CIRCUITS

Parallel RLC Circuit (source free)

Circuit diagram:

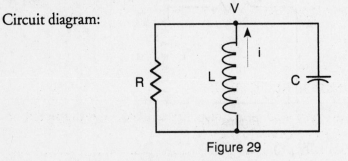

Figure 29

KCL equation for parallel RLC circuit:

$$\frac{v}{R} + \frac{1}{L}\int_{t_0}^{t} v\, dt - i(t_0) + C\frac{dv}{dt} = 0;$$

and the corresponding linear, second-order homogeneous differential equation is:

$$C\frac{d^2v}{dt^2} + \frac{1}{T}\frac{dv}{dt} + \frac{v}{L} = 0.$$

General solution:

$$V = A_1 e^{S_1 t} + A_2 e^{S_2 t},$$

where $\quad S_{1,2} = \dfrac{-1}{2RC} \pm \sqrt{\left(\dfrac{1}{2RC}\right)^2 - \dfrac{1}{LC}}$

or $\qquad S_{1,2} = -\alpha \pm \sqrt{\alpha^2 - \omega_0^2},$

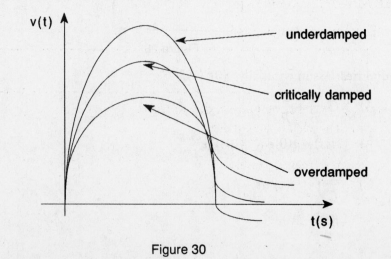

Figure 30

where α = exponential damping coefficient neper frequency

$$= \frac{1}{2RC}$$

and ω_0 = resonant frequency

$$= \frac{1}{\sqrt{LC}}$$

COMPLETE RESPONSE OF RLC CIRCUIT

The general equation of a complete response of a second order system in terms of voltage for an RLC circuit is given by:

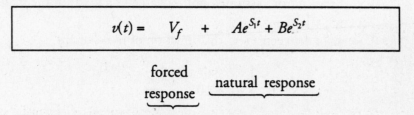

(i.e., constant for DC excitation).

NOTE: *A* and *B* can be obtained by

1)   Substituting v at $t = 0^+$

2)   Taking the derivative of the response, i.e.,

$$\frac{dv}{dt} = 0 + S_1 A\, e^{S_1 t} + S_2 B\, e^{S_2 t},$$

where $\dfrac{dv}{dt}$ at $t = 0^+$ is known .

THE MAGNETIC FIELD

Force in a magnetic field

$$\mathbf{F}_b = q\mathbf{v} \times \mathbf{B}$$

where $\mathbf{F}_b$ = force on particle due to field
q = charge on particle
$\mathbf{v}$ = velocity of particle
$\mathbf{B}$ = magnetic field

MAGNETIC FIELDS AND CURRENTS

THE BIOT-SAVART LAW

$$dB = \frac{\mu_0 i}{4\pi} \frac{\sin\theta\, dl}{r^2}$$

where B = magnetic field
  μ_0 = permeability constant
  i = current through a wire
  l = length of wire
  r = distance from assumed point charge to a point in the magnetic field
  θ = angle between r and the direction of the element

NOTE:

$$\mu_0 = 4\pi \times 10^{-7} \frac{T \cdot m}{A}$$

Integral form:

$$B = \frac{\mu_0 i}{4\pi} \oint_c \frac{d\mathbf{l}' \times \mathbf{a}_R}{r^2},$$

where primed terms refer to points along the source of the field.

AMPERE'S LAW

The line integral of the tangential component of **B** is exactly equal to the current enclosed by that path.

$$\oint B \cdot d\mathbf{L} = I$$

Curl of a Vector Field

The curl of any vector is defined as a vector where the direction is given by the right-hand rule, and the magnitude is given by the limit of the quotient of the closed line integral and the area of the enclosed path as the area approaches 0.

$$(\text{curl } H)_n = \lim_{\Delta s_n \to 0} \frac{\oint H \cdot d\mathbf{L}}{\Delta s_n}$$

Δs_n is the area enclosed by the closed line integral, and n is any component; this is normal to the surface enclosed by the closed path.

STOKE'S THEOREM

$$\oint_l \mathbf{F} \cdot d\mathbf{l} = \int_S (\nabla \times \mathbf{F}) \cdot ds$$

F is any vector field, s is a surface bounded by l. It gives the relation between a closed line integral and surface integral.

By using the Divergence Theorem and Stoke's theorem we can derive a very important identity:

$$\nabla \cdot \nabla \times \mathbf{A} \equiv 0$$

where $\mathbf{A}$ = is any vector field.

MAGNETIC FLUX AND MAGNETIC FLUX DENSITY

$B = \mu_0 H$, B is the magnetic flux density in free space.

Unit of B is webers per square meter (Wb / m^2) or Tesla (T), a new unit.

$\mu_0 = 4\pi \times 10^{-7}$ H/m (permeability of free space)

H is in amperes per meter (A/m).

$$\oint_S \mathbf{B} \cdot ds = 0$$

This is Gauss's law for the magnetic field

$$\nabla \cdot \mathbf{B} = 0$$

after application of the divergence theorem. This is the fourth and last equation of Maxwell.

FARADAY'S LAW

Faraday's Law can be stated as follows:

$$\text{emf} = \oint \mathbf{E} \cdot d\mathbf{L} = -\frac{d\phi}{dt} (v)$$

The minus sign is by Lenz's Law which indicates that the induced e.m.f. is always acting against the changing magnetic fields which produce that e.m.f.

Faraday's Law describes the relationship between electric and magnetic fields.

INDUCTANCE (*L*)

$$L = \frac{N\phi}{I} = \frac{\text{Total flux linkage}}{\text{current linked}}$$

Unit of inductance is *H* which is equivalent to *Wb / A.*

Applications

Inductance per meter length of a coaxial cable of inner radius *a* and outer radius *b*.

$$L = \frac{\mu_0}{2\pi} \ln \frac{b}{a} \text{ H/m.}$$

A toroidal coil of *N* turns and *IA*,

$$L = \frac{\mu_0 N^2 s}{2\pi R},$$

where   *R* = mean radius of the toroid.

Different expressions for inductance:

$$L = \frac{2 W_H}{I^2}$$

$$L = \frac{\int_{vol} \mathbf{B} \cdot \mathbf{H} \, dv}{I^2}$$

$$= \frac{1}{I^2} \int_{vol} \mathbf{H} \cdot (\nabla \times \mathbf{A}) \, dv$$

$$L = \frac{1}{I^2} \left[\int_{vol} \nabla \cdot (\mathbf{A} \times \mathbf{H}) \, dv + \int_{vol} \mathbf{A} \cdot (\nabla \times \mathbf{H}) \, dv \right]$$

$$L = \frac{1}{I^2} \int_{vol} \mathbf{A} \cdot \mathbf{J} \, dv$$

$$L = \frac{1}{I^2} \int_{vol} \left(\int_{vol} \frac{\mu \mathbf{J}}{4\pi R} \, dv \right) \cdot \mathbf{J} \, dv$$

Mutual inductance between circuits 1 and 2,

$$L_{12} = \frac{N_2 \cdot \phi_{12}}{I_1}$$

where   *N* = the number of turns

$$L_{12} = \frac{1}{I_1 I_2} \int_{\text{vol}} (\mu H_1 \cdot H_2) \, dv$$

$$L_{12} = L_{21}$$

MAXWELL'S EQUATIONS

Maxwell's equation in differential form:

$$\nabla \times E = -\frac{\partial B}{\partial t}$$

$$\nabla \times H = J + \frac{\partial D}{\partial t}$$

$$\nabla \cdot D = \rho$$

$$\nabla \cdot B = 0$$

Auxiliary equations relating **D** and **E**:

$$D = \varepsilon E \qquad D = \varepsilon_0 E + P$$
$$B = \mu H \qquad B = \mu_0 (H + M)$$
$$J = \sigma E \qquad J = \rho U$$

Lorentz force equation:

$$F = \rho(E + U \times B)$$

Maxwell's equations in integral form:

$$\oint E \cdot dL = -\int_s \frac{\partial B}{\partial t} \cdot ds$$

$$\oint H \cdot dL = I + \int_s \frac{\partial D}{\partial t} \cdot ds$$

$$\oint_s D \cdot ds = \int_{\text{vol}} \rho \, dv$$

$$\oint B \cdot ds = 0$$

These four integral equations enable us to find the boundary conditions on **B**, **D**, **H**, and **E** which are necessary to evaluate the constants obtained in solving Maxwell's equations in partial differential form.

ELECTROMAGNETIC WAVES

Maxwell's equations in phasor form:

$$\nabla \times \mathbf{H}_s = j\omega\,\varepsilon_0\mathbf{E}_s$$
$$\nabla \times \mathbf{E}_s = -j\omega\,\mu_0\mathbf{H}_s$$
$$\nabla \cdot \mathbf{E}_s = 0$$
$$\nabla \cdot \mathbf{H}_s = 0$$

Wave equations:

$$\nabla \times \nabla \times \mathbf{E}_s = \nabla(\nabla \cdot \mathbf{E}_s) - \nabla^2\mathbf{E}_s = -j\omega\mu_0\nabla \times \mathbf{H}_s$$
$$= \omega^2\mu_0\varepsilon_0\mathbf{E}_s = -\nabla^2\mathbf{E}_s$$

$$\nabla^2\mathbf{E}_s = -\omega^2\mu_0\varepsilon_0\mathbf{E}_s$$

$$\nabla^2 E_{xs} = \frac{\partial^2 E_{xs}}{\partial x^2} + \frac{\partial^2 E_{xs}}{\partial y^2} + \frac{\partial^2 E_{xs}}{\partial z^2}$$
$$= -\omega^2\mu_0\varepsilon_0\, E_{xs}$$

For

$$\frac{\partial^2 E_{xs}}{\partial y^2} = \frac{\partial^2 E_{xs}}{\partial z^2} = 0$$

i.e., E_{xs} independent of x and y.

This can be simplified to

$$\frac{\partial^2 E_{xs}}{\partial z^2} = -\omega^2\mu_0\varepsilon_0\, E_{xs}$$

$$E_x = E_{x_0}\cos\left[\omega(t - z\sqrt{\mu_0\varepsilon_0})\right]$$

and
$$E_{x'} = E_{x'_0}\cos\left[\omega(t + z\sqrt{\mu_0\varepsilon_0})\right]$$

E_{x0} = value of E_x at $z = 0$, $t = 0$.

Velocity of the travelling wave:

To find the velocity U, let us keep the value of E_x to be constant, therefore,

$$t - z\sqrt{\mu_0\varepsilon_0} = \text{constant}$$

Take differentials; we have

$$dt - \frac{1}{U} dz = 0$$

$$\frac{dz}{dt} = U$$

in free space.

Velocity of light $= U = \dfrac{1}{\sqrt{\mu_0 \varepsilon_0}} = 3 \times 10^8$ m/s

Wave length $= \lambda = \dfrac{U}{f} = \dfrac{2\pi U}{\omega}$

The field is moving in the Z direction with velocity U. It is called a travelling wave.

Form of the H field:

If $\mathbf{E}_s$ is given, $\mathbf{H}_s$ can be obtained from

$$\nabla \times \mathbf{E}_s = -j\omega \mu_0 \varepsilon_0 \mathbf{H}_s$$

$$\frac{\partial E_{xs}}{\partial z} = -j\omega \mu_0 \mathbf{H}_{ys}$$

$$= E_{x_0}(-j\omega \sqrt{\mu_0 \varepsilon_0})e^{-j\omega \sqrt{\mu_0 \varepsilon_0} z}$$

$$\boxed{H_y = E_{x_0} \sqrt{\frac{\varepsilon_0}{\mu_0}} \cos\left[\omega\left(t - z\sqrt{\mu_0 \varepsilon_0}\right)\right]}$$

$$\boxed{\frac{E_x}{H_y} = \frac{\mu_0}{\varepsilon_0}}$$

is a constant where

$$\boxed{\eta = \sqrt{\frac{\mu}{\varepsilon}}}$$

where η = The intrinsic impedance: It is the square root of the ratio of permeability to permittivity and is measured in Ω.

$$\eta_0 = \sqrt{\frac{\mu_0}{\varepsilon_0}} = 377\Omega$$

$\eta_0 = \eta$ of free space

The term uniform plane wave is used because the H and E fields are uniform throughout any plane, Z = constant, and it is also called a transverse electromagnetic (TEM) wave since both the *E* and *H* fields are perpendicular to the direction of propagation.

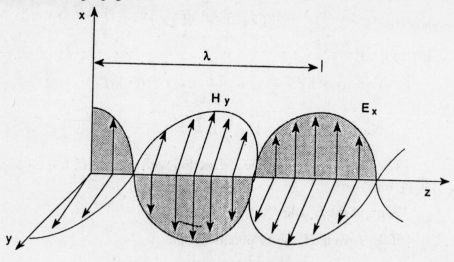

Figure 31 — A Uniform TEM Wave

ADVANCED PLACEMENT EXAMINATION IN
PHYSICS

AP Physics B
Test 1

AP PHYSICS B
TEST 1

Section I

(Answer sheets appear in the back of this book.)

TIME: 90 Minutes
70 Questions

DIRECTIONS: Each of the questions or incomplete statements below is followed by five answer choices or completions. Choose the best answer to each question.

---

1. According to the following equation,

$$^{27}_{13}\text{Al} + {}^4_2\text{He} \rightarrow {}^{30}_{15}\text{P} + X + \text{energy},$$

particle X is which atomic particle?

(A) Neutrons

(B) Positrons

(C) Alpha particles

(D) Protons

(E) Helium atoms

2. Two charges are separated by 2.0 m. The force of attraction between them is 4 N. If the distance between them is doubled, the new force between them is

(A) .5 N.

(B) 1 N.

(C) 2 N.

(D) 4 N.

(E) 8 N.

3. The relationship between the pressure and volume of an ideal gas when temperature is held constant is

(A) logarithmic.

(B) geometric.

(C) inverse.

(D) direct.

(E) ratio.

4. The time it takes for a plane to change its speed from 100 m/s to 500 m/s with a uniform acceleration in a distance of 1200 m is

(A) 1 s.

(B) 2 s.

(C) 3 s.

(D) 4 s.

(E) 5 s.

5. The graph shows the speed of an object as a function of time. The average speed of the object during the time interval shown is

(A) 3 m/s.

(B) 5 m/s.

(C) 7 m/s.

(D) 8 m/s.

(E) 10 m/s.

6. A graph of displacement vs. time for an object moving in a straight line is shown below. The acceleration of the object must be

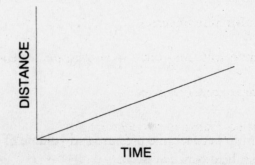

(A) zero.

(B) increasing.

(C) decreasing.

(D) constant and greater than zero.

(E) equal to *g*.

7. Why does a marble table feel cooler to the touch than a wooden table top?

(A) Because the marble table never asbsorbs enough heat to reach room temperature.

(B) Because the heat conductivity of marble is higher than wood, heat flows more readily from your fingers.

(C) Because the heat conductivity of marble is higher than wood, heat flows more readily into your fingers.

(D) Because the heat conductivity of wood is higher than marble, heat flows more readily from your fingers.

(E) Because the heat conductivity of wood is higher than marble, heat flows more readily into your fingers.

8. A gas at atmospheric pressure and room temperature is contained in a cylinder which is sealed on one end, and contains a frictionless movable cylinder at the other end. If the gas expands adiabatically, the piston is pushed out. Increasing the volume,

(A) the pressure remains the same.

(B) the temperature increases.

(C) the temperature may increase or decrease, depending on the gas.

(D) the temperature decreases.

(E) there is no change in temperature.

QUESTION 9 refers to the following figure.

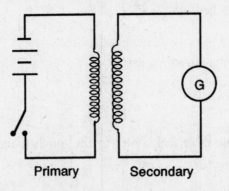

Primary   Secondary

9. The primary coil of an induction coil has a battery and switch in series with it. The secondary coil has a galvanometer in series with it as shown. Consider the following situations:

I.   The switch is closing.

II. The switch is held closed.

III. The switch is opening.

IV. The switch is held opened.

During which situation(s) will the galvanometer read?

(A) II only   (B) III only

(C) II and IV only   (D) I only

(E) I and III only

10. Which of the following comments regarding the addition of heat to a system is false?

(A) The conduction of heat always involves a transfer of heat.

(B) The addition of heat always causes a rise in temperature.

(C) In a perfectly isolated system, any heat lost by one part of the system always equals the heat gained by another part of the same system.

(D)   Heat and temperature are not the same thing.

(E)   Temperature can change even though no heat is lost or gained.

11.   According to the laws of resistance, doubling the thickness of a given wire and making it ten times longer will cause its resistance to be

(A)   40 times greater.   (B)   20 times greater.

(C)   5 times greater.   (D)   2.5 times greater.

(E)   0.05 as much as before.

QUESTIONS 12 and 13 refer to the following graphs.

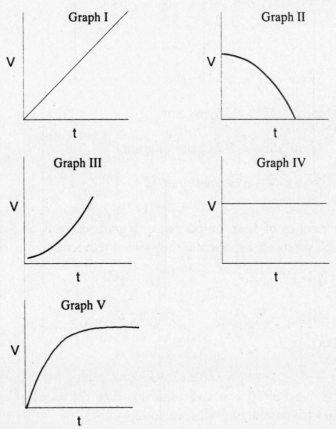

12.   A graph that best describes the motion of a mass at rest and pulled by a constant force is

(A) Graph I.   (B) Graph II.

(C) Graph III.   (D) Graph IV.

(E) Graph V.

13. The graph that best describes the motion of a mass pulled by a force that is equal to the frictional force acting on it is

(A) Graph I.   (B) Graph II.

(C) Graph III.   (D) Graph IV.

(E) Graph V.

QUESTION 14 refers to the following specific heats of some common substances.

    I.   Lead — 0.03 calories/gram C

   II.   Silver — 0.06 calories/gram C

  III.   Iron — 0.11 calories/gram C

  IV.   Aluminum — 0.21 calories/gram C

   V.   Water — 1.0 calories/gram C

14. Ten calories of heat are added to 1 gram of each of the substances. Which substance experiences the greatest temperature increase?

(A) I   (B) II

(C) III   (D) IV

(E) V

15. If the speed of light in a vacuum is c, then the speed of light in a medium with an index of refraction of 2 will be

(A) $c/2$.   (B) $2c$.

(C) *c*/4.   (D) 4*c*.

(E) 8*c*.

QUESTION 16 refers to the following diagram.

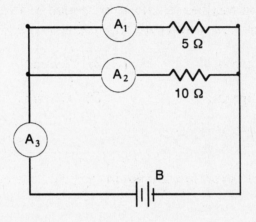

16. If ammeter A_3 reads 6 amps, ammeter A_1 will read how many amps?

(A) 2 amps   (B) 3 amps

(C) 4 amps   (D) 5 amps

(E) 6 amps

17. A block of weight W is pulled along a horizontal surface at a constant speed V by a force F, which acts at an angle θ with the horizontal, as shown below. The normal force exerted on the block by the surface is equal to

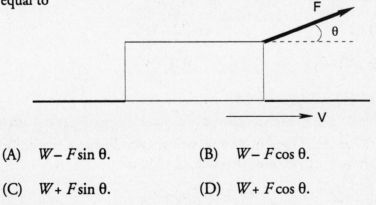

(A) $W - F \sin \theta$.   (B) $W - F \cos \theta$.

(C) $W + F \sin \theta$.   (D) $W + F \cos \theta$.

(E) W.

QUESTIONS **18 and 19** refer to the following graphs.

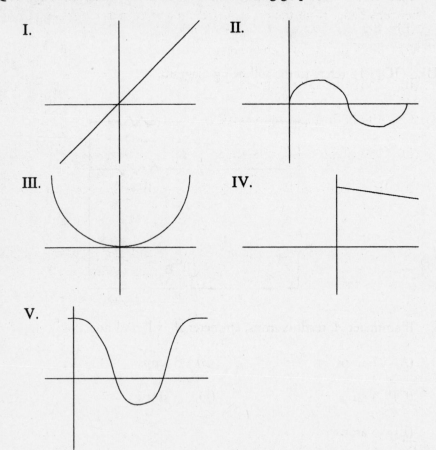

18. Which graph best represents the potential energy in a spring (vertical scale) as a function of displacement from equilibrium (horizontal scale) considering the up and down motion of a small mass on that spring?

    (A) I   (B) II

    (C) III   (D) IV

    (E) V

19. Which graph best represents the total energy (vertical) versus time (horizontal) of a small mass on a spring oscillating up and down?

    (A) I   (B) II

    (C) III   (D) IV

    (E) V

20. A uniform rope of weight 100 newtons hangs from a hook. A box of 50 newtons hangs from the rope. What is the tension in the rope?

   (A)   50 N throughout the rope

   (B)   75 N throughout the rope

   (C)   100 N throughout the rope

   (D)   150 N throughout the rope

   (E)   It varies from 100 N at the bottom of the rope to 150 N at the top.

21. Which velocity vs. time graph best represents the speed of a falling styrofoam ball as a function of time, taking air resistance into account?

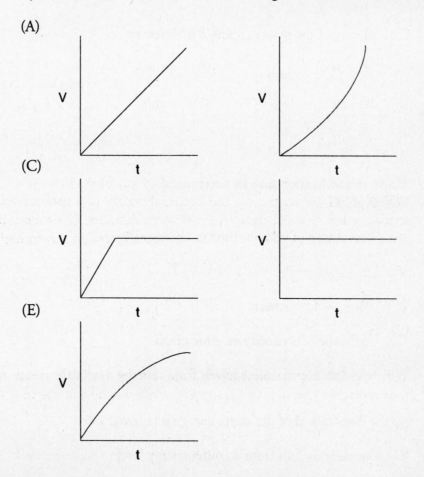

QUESTION 22 refers to the following diagram.

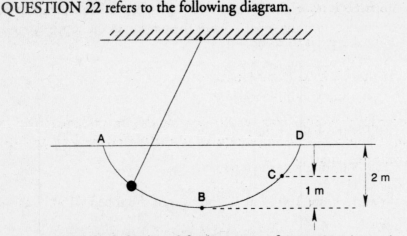

A mass swings freely back and forth in an arc from point *A* to point *D*, as shown above. Point *B* is the lowest point, *C* is located 1.0 meters above *B*, and *D* is 2.0 meters above *B*. Air resistance is negligible. $g = 10$ m/s².

22. The velocity of the mass at point *B* is closest to

    (A)   10 m/s.   (B)   40 m/s.

    (C)   20 m/s.   (D)   6 m/s.

    (E)   15 m/s.

23. Uniform acceleration may be determined by any of the following methods EXCEPT

    (A)   the change of velocity/time to change velocity.

    (B)   speed/time.

    (C)   constant force/mass.

    (D)   the slope of a velocity vs. time graph.

    (E)   the distance an object travels from rest/the time it travels squared.

24. In the Bohr model of the atom, energy is radiated when

    (A)   an electron falls from an outer energy level to an inner level.

    (B)   an electron is stripped from an atom.

(C)   an ion is formed.

(D)   light shines on an atom.

(E)   an atom is in its ground state.

25.   In order for the torque on a current-carrying loop in a magnetic field to be at a minimum, the angle between the plane of the loop and the magnetic field must be

(A)   0°.   (B)   30°.

(C)   45°.   (D)   60°.

(E)   90°.

QUESTION 26 refers to the following before and after diagram. Mass *m* at rest splits into two parts — one with a mass 2/3 *m* and one with a mass 1/3 *m*. After the split, the part with mass 1/3 *m* moves to the right with a velocity *v*.

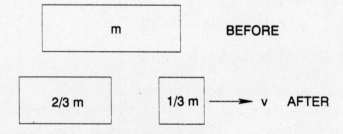

26.   The velocity of the 2/3 *m* part after the split is

(A)   1/3 *v.*   (B)   1/2 *v.*

(C)   2/3 *v.*   (D)   2 *v.*

(E)   3 *v.*

27.   Two unequal masses falling freely from the same point above the earth's surface would experience the same

(A)   acceleration.

(B)   decrease in potential energy.

(C)   increase in kinetic energy.

(D)   increase in momentum.

(E)   change in mass.

QUESTION 28 refers to the following diagram.

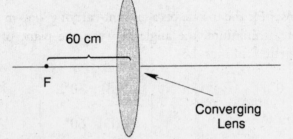

28.   An object is placed 30 centimeters to the left of the lens shown. Where will the image of the object be located?

(A)   60 cm to the left of the lens

(B)   20 cm to the left of the lens

(C)   20 cm to the right of the lens

(D)   30 cm to the right of the lens

(E)   60 cm to the right of the lens

29.   In a circuit with a current flow of I, which of the following expressions for the power dissipated by a resistance R is incorrect?

(A) $W = R/E$ (B) $W = EI$

(C) $W = E^2/R$ (D) $W = I^2R$

(E)   None of the above.

30.   According to the following equation,

$$^{27}_{13}\text{Al} + {}^4_2\text{He} \rightarrow {}^{30}_{15}\text{P} + X + \text{energy},$$

phosphorus is produced by bombarding aluminum atoms with what type of atomic particle?

(A)   Neutrons   (B)   Positrons

(C)   Alpha particles   (D)   Protons

(E)   Helium atoms

31.   When the sun is low on the horizon in the evening, it appears "redder." The best explanation for this is that

(A)   the sun is further away from the earth.

(B)   the sun is cooler in the evening.

(C)   the earth's atmosphere scatters the shorter wavelength, blue light.

(D)   the earth's atmosphere absorbs blue and green wavelengths.

(E)   the earth's atmosphere diffracts the light from the sun.

QUESTION 32 refers to the following diagram.

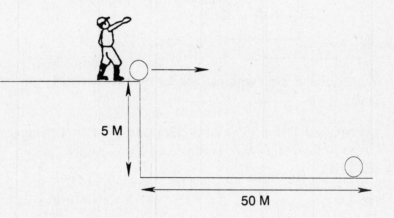

32.   Given that the ball lands in one second, how fast did the child throw the ball horizontally?

(A)   5 meters/sec   (B)   50 meters/sec

(C)   100 meters/sec   (D)   500 meters/sec

(E)   1000 meters/sec

For **QUESTIONS 33 and 34** choose from the five circuit diagrams of 4 resistors of 10 ohms each wired in five of the possible combinations.

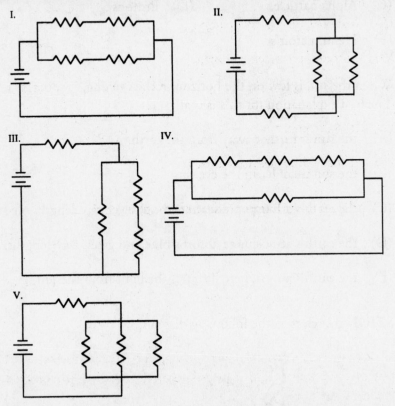

33. Which of the five combinations shown produces the least total resistance?

    (A) I   (B) II

    (C) III   (D) IV

    (E) V

34. Which of the five possible combinations produces the largest total resistance?

    (A) I   (B) II

    (C) III   (D) IV

    (E) V

35. If a negatively charged rod is held near an uncharged metal ball, the metal ball

   (A) becomes negatively charged.

   (B) becomes positively charged.

   (C) becomes polar.

   (D) is unaffected.

   (E) Affect cannot be determined.

QUESTIONS 36 and 37 refer to the following diagram.

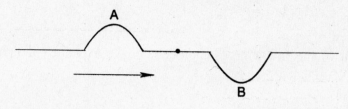

36. Two pulses are shown traveling in opposite directions on a rope. After one second, crest *A* and trough *B* are at point *P*. What is the shape of the rope at this instant?

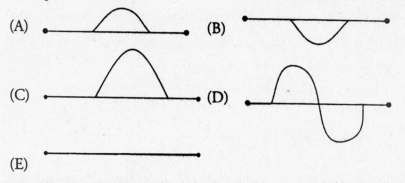

37. What is the shape of the rope at the end of two seconds?

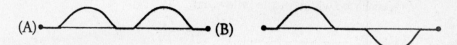

(C) 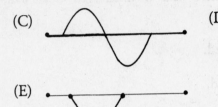 (D)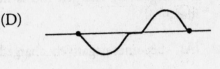

(E)

38. If a particular metal in a photo cell releases a current when blue light shines on it, it must also release a current when it is struck with

   (A)   ultraviolet light.   (B)   infrared light.

   (C)   microwaves.   (D)   radio waves.

   (E)   red light.

39. All of the following phenomena can be explained if light is a wave EXCEPT

   (A)   reflection.   (B)   refraction.

   (C)   photoelectric effect.   (D)   diffraction.

   (E)   interference.

QUESTION 40 refers to the following diagram.

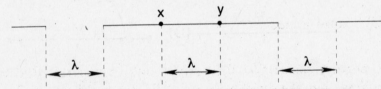

40. Two wave pulses, each of wavelength λ are traveling toward each other along a rope as shown above. When both pulses are in the region between points *x* and *y* and which are a distance λ apart, the shape of the rope will be which of the following?

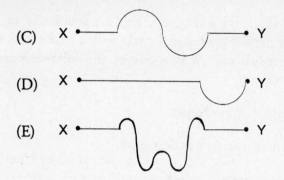

(C) X •————⌒⌣————• Y

(D) X •————————⌣——• Y

(E) X •——⌒—⌒—• Y

QUESTION 41 refers to the following figure.

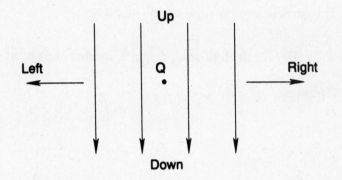

41. If the charge on *Q* is doubled, the electrical force acting on it

(A) remains constant.   (B) is twice as large.

(C) is 1/2 as much.   (D) is 4 times larger.

(E) is 1/4 as much.

42. A negative charge *Q* is fired into a uniform magnetic field *B* shown pointing into the page (by the *x*'s). Which answer best describes its motion in the field?

(A) Straight

(B) Parabolic

(C) Circular

(D) Vibrates

(E) Stops

43. A charged particle is shot into a magnetic field perpendicular to the particle's motion. The particle moves in a circle with a radius of 5 cm. The radius increases to 10 cm. Which one of the following could explain this change in radius?

    (A) The particle lost half of its charge.

    (B) The particle's kinetic energy was decreased.

    (C) The particle slowed down.

    (D) The magnetic field was increased.

    (E) The particle lost a neutral chunk of mass.

QUESTION 44 refers to the following diagram and list of possible changes.

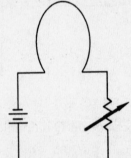

    I.   Decreases

    II. Increases

    III. Remains the same

    IV. Equals zero

    V.   None of the above

44. If the coil is rotated in an external magnetic field and the voltage across the coil is decreased, the external force required to rotate the coil at a constant velocity

    (A) I   (B) II

    (C) III   (D) IV

    (E) V

45. A 70 kg person runs with a horizontal velocity of v and jumps into a 10 kg raft floating just off shore. Assuming no water resistance, what will be the velocity of the raft and person?

    (A) 1/7 v (B) 7 v

(C) 8/7 *v*   (D) 1/8 *v*

(E) 7/8 *v*

46. The baseball bat pictured is balanced at point *x*. This implies that

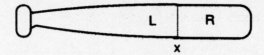

(A) side *L* weighs the same as side *R*.

(B) side *L* has a mass which is the same as the mass of side *R*.

(C) the torque of side *L* equals the torque of side *R*.

(D) the density of the wood on side *L* is less than the density of side *R*.

(E) None of the above.

47. A skier starts from rest at the top of a hill and follows the path shown in the diagram on the following page. Assuming no friction, what will be his speed at point *X*?

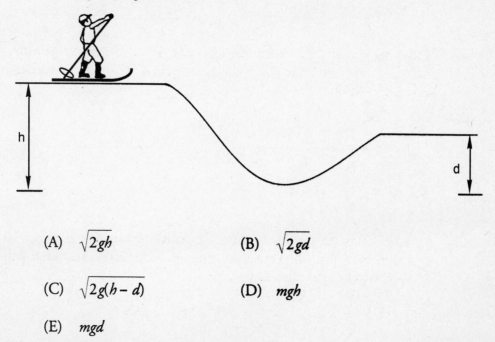

(A) $\sqrt{2gh}$ (B) $\sqrt{2gd}$

(C) $\sqrt{2g(h-d)}$ (D) *mgh*

(E) *mgd*

48. When a positively charged conductor touches a neutral conductor, the neutral conductor will

    (A)   gain protons.   (B)   gain electrons.

    (C)   lose protons.   (D)   lose electrons.

    (E)   stay neutral.

49. In the diagram, a mass on a spring is pulled down a distance, – x, from its equilibrium position, P, and released. As the object moves back to P and up an additional distance, + x, its acceleration graph looks as follows (assume upward acceleration is positive):

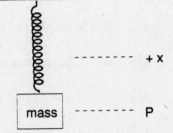

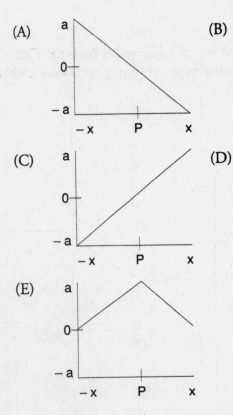

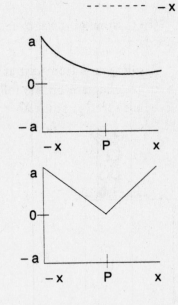

50. A stream of radioactive particles is traveling 0.90 *c* relative to a scientist in the laboratory. Compared to the half-life of the same particles at rest in the scientist's frame of reference, the scientist will measure the half-life of the moving particles as

    (A) 5.3 times longer.   (B) 0.19 times longer.

    (C) 2.3 times longer.   (D) 0.44 times longer.

    (E) The same as if the particles were standing still relative to the scientist.

QUESTION 51 refers to the following figure.

The figure here shows an object at 12 cm from a convex lens with a focal length of 4 cm. Draw an appropriate ray diagram, and answer the following questions concerning the image.

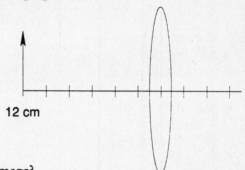

12 cm

51. What is the location of the image?

    (A) 6 cm to the left of the lens

    (B) 6 cm to the right of the lens

    (C) 10 cm to the right of the lens

    (D) 12 cm to the left of the lens

    (E) 8 cm to the right of the lens

52. What is the ideal efficiency of a steam engine that takes steam from the boiler at 200 degrees C and exhausts it at 100 degrees C?

    (A) 50%   (B) 25%

    (C) 21%   (D) 11%

    (E) 2%

QUESTIONS 53 and 54 are based on the below heating curve for 10 grams of a substance.

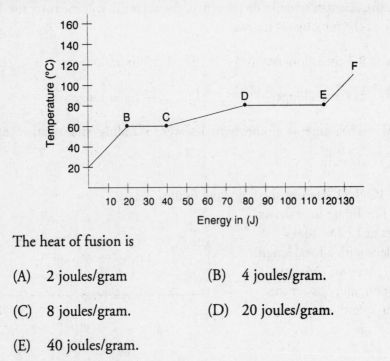

53. The heat of fusion is

(A) 2 joules/gram

(B) 4 joules/gram.

(C) 8 joules/gram.

(D) 20 joules/gram.

(E) 40 joules/gram.

54. Entropy is increasing between

(A) A and B.

(B) B and C.

(C) C and D.

(D) All of the above.

(E) None of the above.

55. Two objects of equal mass are a fixed distance apart. If the mass of each object could be tripled, the gravitational force between the objects would

(A) decrease by 1/3.

(B) decrease by 1/9.

(C) triple.

(D) increase by nine times.

(E) decrease by nine times.

56. Light falls on a photoelectric material and no electrons are emitted. Electrons may be emitted if which of the following is increased?

    I.   Intensity of the light

    II.   Frequency of the light

    III. Wavelength of the light

    (A)   I only   (B)   II only

    (C)   III only   (D)   I and II only

    (E)   I and III only

57. Compared to the force exerted on *B* at a separation of 12 meters, the force exerted on sphere *B* at a separation of 6 meters would be

    (A)   1/2 as great.   (B)   2 times as great.

    (C)   1/4 as great.   (D)   4 times as great.

    (E)   9 times as great.

QUESTION 58 refers to the following diagram.

58. A wire in the plane of the page carries a current *I* directed toward the top of the page, as shown above. If the wire is located in a uniform magnetic field *B* directed out of the page, the force on the wire resulting from the magnetic field is

    (A)   directed into the page.   (B)   directed out of the page.

(C)   directed to the right.   (D)   directed to the left.

(E)   zero.

QUESTIONS 59 and 60 refer to the following figure and information.

I. Y_0

II. Y_1

III. Y_2

IV. Y_1 and Y_2

V. Y_0 and Y_1

59.   Where is the net force on mass M a minimum?

(A)   I   (B)   II

(C)   III   (D)   IV

(E)   V

60.   Where is the acceleration of mass M a maximum?

(A)   I   (B)   II

(C)   III   (D)   IV

(E)   V

61.   A rotating object which suddenly contracts to a smaller radius rotates with a higher angular velocity because

(A)   smaller objects turn more quickly than larger ones.

(B)   the object's density must increase.

(C)   the rotational inertia of smaller objects is greater.

(D)   the angular velocity of rotating objects must remain the same.

(E)   angular momentum must be conserved.

Use the following table of refractive indices to answer question 62.

1.   Air   ($N = 1.00$)
2.   Water   ($N = 1.22$)
3.   Glass   ($N = 1.50$)
4.   Oil   ($N = 2.00$)
5.   Diamond   ($N = 2.40$)

62.   A ray of light passes through air, glass, and then water. Select the answer that best describes what happens to the velocity of the ray of light shown as it passes from air into glass and then out of glass into water.

(A)   Decreases, then increases

(B)   Decreases, then decreases again

(C)   Increases, then decreases

(D)   Increases, then decreases again

(E)   No change

63.   A nuclide with a half-life of 2 days is tested after 6 days. What fraction of the sample has decayed?

(A)   1/2   (B)   1/4

(C)   3/8   (D)   3/4

(E)   7/8

64.   X-rays striking a piece of gold foil may cause

(A)   electrons to be emitted.

(B)   isotopes of gold to form.

(C)   addition of protons to gold atoms.

(D) addition of neutrons to gold atoms.

(E) nuclear transmutation of gold into another element.

65. If the distance between the plates of a parallel plate capacitor are doubled, what must you do to the area of the plates to return to the original capacitance?

(A) Cut the plate area in half.

(B) Cut the plate area by one-fourth.

(C) Double the plate area.

(D) Make no change because the change in distance between the plates does not change the capacitance.

(E) Increase the area by four times.

66. The electric field at a point near a charged object, P, is

(A) the force on a unit negative charge at that point.

(B) the force on a unit positive charge at that point.

(C) the direction of the electric potential at that point.

(D) the acceleration of an electron at that point.

(E) the energy contained in the field at that point.

67. As an object is continuously, uniformly accelerated its velocity levels off, never exceeding the speed of light. Which of these is true?

(A) The kinetic energy and momentum also level off.

(B) The kinetic energy continues to increase but the momentum levels off.

(C) Both the kinetic energy and the momentum continue to increase.

(D) The momentum increases but the kinetic energy levels off.

(E) There is no connection between velocity, kinetic energy, and momentum.

QUESTION 68 refers to the following diagram.

The diagram below shows a 10 newton force pulling an object up a hill at a constant rate of 4 meters per second.

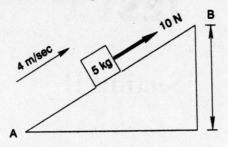

68. How much work is done in moving the object from Point A to Point *B*?

(A) 100 J (B) 120 J

(C) 200 J (D) 300 J

(E) 1000 J

69. Copper has a work function of 4.8 eV. What wavelength of the electro-magnetic spectrum will produce photoelectrons with the lowest kinetic energy?

(A) 4.1×10^{-26} m (B) 9.5×10^{-25} m

(C) 2.6×10^{-7} m (D) 1.3×10^{-6} m

(E) 5.8×10^{-7} m

70. Compared to a 10 eV photon, a 2 eV photon has

(A) higher frequency. (B) lower frequency.

(C) higher speed. (D) lower speed.

(E) lower wavelength.

AP PHYSICS B
TEST 1

Section II

TIME: 90 Minutes
6 Free Response Questions

DIRECTIONS: Carefully read each question and then make sure to answer *each part* of the question. You must show your work.

---

1. Radiation with a wavelength of 300 nm shines on a metal and produces photoelectrons with a velocity of 3.00×10^5 m/s.

   (a) Determine the energy carried by one photon of this radiation.

   (b) Determine the work function for this metal.

   (c) Determine the maximum wavelength of radiation that will produce photoelectrons for this metal.

2. A 10 kg, solid wooden cylinder with a 0.2 m radius has a 3 m length of string wrapped around its circumference. If you hold the end of the string and drop the cylinder,

   (a) what will be its acceleration?

   (b) how long will it take the cylinder to unwrap from the string?

3. $_{92}U^{238}$ (238.0508 amu) decays to $_{90}Th^{234}$ (234.0436 amu) giving off an alpha particle (4.0026 amu) and a 2.5×10^{-11} m gamma ray. (1 amu = 1.7×10^{-27} kg)

   (a) How much energy is released after the reaction?

   (b) What is the energy of the gamma ray?

4. An astronaut and his gear have a total mass of 90 kg, including a backpack with propellants. If he is motionless in space relative to his space ship and fires 3 kg of propellant from his pack at 15 m/sec in 5 sec,

    (a) what will be his final speed?

    (b) how long will it take him to travel the 50 m back to his ship?

5. You are given three 8Ω resistors and a 12 V battery. Design a circuit that will have 1 amp of current flowing from the battery.

6. A golf club strikes a 0.045 kg golf ball with an average force of 210 N for 0.006 sec. If the ball leaves the tee at a 30° angle,

    (a) what will be the velocity of the ball?

    (b) if we disregard air friction, how high will the ball go?

    (c) how far will the ball travel horizontally?

TEST 1
Section I

1.	(A)	19.	(D)	37.	(D)	55.	(D)
2.	(B)	20.	(E)	38.	(A)	56.	(B)
3.	(C)	21.	(E)	39.	(C)	57.	(D)
4.	(D)	22.	(D)	40.	(B)	58.	(C)
5.	(C)	23.	(B)	41.	(B)	59.	(A)
6.	(A)	24.	(A)	42.	(C)	60.	(D)
7.	(B)	25.	(E)	43.	(A)	61.	(E)
8.	(D)	26.	(B)	44.	(E)	62.	(A)
9.	(E)	27.	(A)	45.	(E)	63.	(E)
10.	(B)	28.	(A)	46.	(C)	64.	(A)
11.	(D)	29.	(A)	47.	(C)	65.	(C)
12.	(A)	30.	(C)	48.	(D)	66.	(B)
13.	(D)	31.	(C)	49.	(A)	67.	(C)
14.	(A)	32.	(B)	50.	(C)	68.	(A)
15.	(A)	33.	(D)	51.	(A)	69.	(C)
16.	(C)	34.	(B)	52.	(C)	70.	(B)
17.	(A)	35.	(C)	53	(A)		
18.	(C)	36.	(E)	54.	(D)		

DETAILED EXPLANATIONS OF ANSWERS

TEST 1

Section I

1. **(A)**
    In Question 1, the rules for the conservation of charge and mass in nuclear reactions must be utilized. On the left-hand side of the equation, there are represented a total of 15 protons (2 + 13), and there are also 15 represented on the right side. On the left side, a total mass number of 31 (neutrons and protons) is represented, while on the right only 30 are represented. Since protons are conserved from right to left, and the mass number of P is 30, X must be a neutron.

2. **(B)**
    Force varies inversely with the square of the distance. By doubling the distance, the force becomes one-fourth as large ($1/2^2$), 1 N.

3. **(C)**
    The ideal gas law states as P increases, V decreases and vice versa, to the first power of each variable. Thus V is proportional to $1/P$.

    $$PV = nRT$$

where n is amount in moles and R is the universal gas constant.

4. **(D)**
    Time equals distance divided by average velocity if the acceleration is uniform. The average velocity is

    (100 m/s + 500 m/s) / 2 or 300 m/s.

1200 m / 300 m/s = 4 s and the correct choice is (D).

5. **(C)**
    The average speed for each second during which the speed is either constant or changes uniformly may be calculated.

$$0 - 1s, \qquad V_{av} = 2.5 \text{ m/s};$$
$$1 - 2 \text{ s}, \qquad V_{av} = 7.5 \text{ m/s};$$
$$2 - 3 \text{ s}, \qquad V_{av} = 10 \text{ m/s};$$
$$3 - 4 \text{ s}, \qquad V_{av} = 10 \text{ m/s};$$
$$4 - 5 \text{ s}, \qquad V_{av} = 5/\text{ms}.$$

These average speeds may in turn be averaged:

$$(2.5 + 7.5 + 10 + 10 + 5) / 5 = 35/5 = 7 \text{ m/s}.$$

Thus, the average speed is 7 m/s and the correct choice is (C).

6.   **(A)**
The slope of the line is constant, indicating that the distance covered per time is constant. An object traveling in a straight line must be traveling at a constant velocity to cover the same distance in the same time. Acceleration is a measure of the change in velocity per time. No change in velocity results in zero acceleration.

7.   **(B)**
Because marble is a good conductor of heat it has a high conductivity and heat will be able to flow easily from your finger into the rock making it feel cool.

8.   **(D)**
Because work is done by the gas on the piston (it exerts a force in the direction the piston moves), and no heat is allowed to enter or leave, the internal energy of the gas decreases, and therefore the temperature must decrease. In an adiabatic process, a system does not exchange heat with the surroundings, and the change in internal energy is the negative of the work done. Mathematically,

$$\Delta U = Q - W;$$

for adiabatic processes $Q = 0$; thus,

$$\Delta U = - W.$$

9.   **(E)**
Induction occurs only when the electromagnetic field is changing (I and III) not while it is constant (II and IV).

10. **(B)**
    Heat added that causes a state change does not result in a temperature change (i.e., the melting of a solid).

11. **(D)**
    According to the laws of resistance,

$$R = \frac{\rho L}{A} = \frac{\rho L}{\pi r^2}.$$

Resistance is directly proportional to the length but inversely proportional to the cross-sectional area. Doubling the thickness of the wire increases the area by a factor of 4, since area depends on the square of the radius. This by itself would decrease the resistance by a factor of 4, making answers (A) and (B) incorrect. Increasing the length by a factor of 10 makes the resistance 10 times greater; thus, answer (C) is incorrect. The net effect then is 10/4 greater, or 2.5 times as great. Thus answer (E) is incorrect.

12. **(A)**
    A mass at rest being acted on by a constant force will accelerate constantly, or its change in velocity per unit time will be a constant (with a beginning velocity of zero). Thus, a plot of velocity versus time for this mass would be a straight diagonal line passing through the origin.

13. **(D)**
    If the force pulling on a mass equals the force of friction between the mass and the surface it is sitting on, then the net force on the mass is zero. According to Newton's First Law, if the net force is zero, an object will move at a constant velocity, or remains motionless. Graph IV describes a mass moving with a constant velocity.

14. **(A)**
    A specific heat value, if read like a sentence, explains the number of calories required to raise one gram of a substance one degree centigrade. Therefore, the substance in the table with the lowest specific heat will experience the greatest temperature increase, when equal numbers of calories are added to an equal mass of each substance.

15. **(A)**
    The index of refraction of a medium defined as the ratio of the speed of light in a vacuum to the speed of light in the medium. Thus,

$I.R. = c/$speed in medium;

2 = *c*/speed in medium;

speed in medium = *c*/2.

16. **(C)**
Since the current through the 5 ohm resistor must flow through A_1, and since 5 ohms is 1/2 as large as the 10 ohm resistor, then twice as much current will flow through it. Therefore, 4 of the 6 amps flow through the 5 ohm resistor, and 2 amps flow through the 10 ohm resistor.

17. **(A)**
The normal force is the net force pushing the block against the horizontal surface. The force pulling the block downward is its weight. The vertical component of F tends to lift the block away from the surface and is equal to $F\sin\theta$. Therefore, the net force pushing the two surfaces together is

$W - F\sin\theta.$

18. **(C)**
Hook's Law refers to the energy in a spring as

$PE = 1/2\ kx^2,$

where k is the spring constant and x is the displacement. This function has a parabolic shape.

19. **(D)**
Total energy remains constant but slowly some escapes the mass-spring system in the form of thermal energy to the environment.

20. **(E)**
Newton's Third Law states that forces occur in pairs. The tension in the rope is the force which the hook has to "pull back with," or the total force "transmitted" to the hook by the rope in order to keep the rope and whatever is connected to it from accelerating downward. If the 100 newton rope did not have a mass attached to it, the hook would have to exert a force upward of 100 newtons, and if only half the rope was attached it would exert 50 N, etc. Therefore, the hook must support the weight of a certain length of the rope plus the 50 newton mass.

21. **(E)**
A falling object has increasing air resistance as it speeds up, eventually reaching terminal speed as the air resistance equals the force of gravity. (A) would be true without air resistance. (B) would imply an increasing (non-

uniform) acceleration. (C) would imply an abrupt appearance of air resistance and (D) would imply no acceleration.

22. **(D)**
Question 22 can be answered easily if you realize that the potential energy at Point *A* equals the kinetic energy at Point *B*. Knowing the mass is not necessary since it is constant and cancels out when PE is set to equal KE, the velocity is then easily calculated.

$$PE = KE$$
$$mgh = \frac{1}{2}mv^2$$
$$\sqrt{2gh} = v$$
$$\sqrt{2(10 \text{ m/s}^2)2\text{m}} = v$$
$$6.3 \text{ m/s} = v$$

23. **(B)**
The exception is (B), which determines distance. (A), (C), or (E) can be used to determine acceleration with the appropriate information. (D) is a graphical method of determining acceleration.

24. **(A)**
In the Bohr model, an atom radiates energy when an electron moves from the outer energy level to an inner energy level.

25. **(E)**
As a current-carrying loop rotates in a magnetic field, the torque changes from a maximum when the plane of the loop is parallel to a minimum when it is perpendicular to the direction of the *B* field. Thus, an angle of 0 degrees, answer (A), between the plane of the loop and the magnetic field would produce a maximum torque that would decrease as the angle increases to 90 degrees, answer (E), to produce the minimum torque.

26. **(B)**
Since momentum is conserved,

$$1/3 \ v = 2/3 X;$$
$$X = 1/2 \ v.$$

27. **(A)**
      Two unequal masses will have different kinetic energies, potential energies, and momentums since these parameters are a function of mass. This fact eliminates choices (B), (C), and (D). Choice (E) is nonsensical since mass is conserved. Choice (A) is the obvious choice, since all objects, regardless of their masses, experience the same acceleration g near the earth's surface.

28. **(A)**
      This problem is easily solved if you are familiar with the thin lens equation

$$\frac{1}{F} = \frac{1}{o} + \frac{1}{i};$$

where F is the focal length, o is the distance of the object from the lens, and i is the distance of the image from the lens. Therefore,

$$\frac{1}{60} = \frac{1}{30} + \frac{1}{i};$$

and $i = -60$. Therefore, the image is 60 cm to the left of the lens.
      Note: It must also be remembered that the sign of F for a converging lens is positive, and the signs of o and i are negative if the image is virtual.

29. **(A)**
      All of the expressions except this one give an answer of joules/time or watts.

30. **(C)**
      This question requires you to be able to recognize the symbol for an alpha particle:
      He.

31. **(C)**
      The dust, water particles, etc., in the earth's atmosphere scatter the shorter wavelengths, blue and green light waves. When the sun is on the horizon, the light from the sun must travel a longer distance through the earth's atmosphere, decreasing the amount of blue and green wavelengths reaching the earth's surface.

32. **(B)**
      The time it takes for the ball to travel 50 meters horizontally is exactly equal to the time it takes for the ball to travel 5 meters to the ground. For an

object to travel 50 meters in one second, it must be traveling at a velocity of 50 meters per second.

33. **(D)**
   In choice (I) two resistors in series (20) plus the other two in series (20), are in parallel for a total of 10 ohms. In answer (II) one in series (10), plus two in parallel (5), plus one in series (10), would give the largest of the combinations described, a total of 25 ohms. In answer (III) two in series (20), with one in parallel (10), would be equivalent to 20/3 or 6 and 2/3 plus one more in series (10) would produce a total of 16 2/3. For answer (IV) three in series (30), plus one (10) in parallel, would add up to produce 30/4 or 7.5 ohms. Finally, answer (V) with one in series (10), with three in parallel 10/3 or 3.33 would produce an equivalent resistance of 13.33 ohms.

34. **(B)**
   See explanation 33.

35. **(C)**
   The electrons in the ball are repelled away from the rod and move to the far side of the ball, leaving the side nearest the rod positive. Even though the net charge on the ball is zero, the separation of the charges cause the ball to become polar.

36. **(E)**
   When crest *A* is directly over trough *B*, the two pulses add together destructively, and cancel each other at that instant.

37. **(D)**
   After two seconds the pulses move past each other and continue moving in their respective directions.

38. **(A)**
   The photo effect states that electrons will not be ejected from an atom unless incident electromagnetic radiation has at least a minimum frequency value. The only EM radiation having a greater frequency than blue light is ultraviolet.

39. **(C)**
   Waves and particles have both been shown to undergo reflection and refraction, which eliminates answers (A) and (B). Only waves exhibit the capability of being refracted and interfere with each other, which eliminates answers (D) and (E). Albert Einstein won the Nobel Prize for proving that

for the photoelectric effect to occur, light must have the properties of particles.

40. **(B)**
    Both pulses have a wavelength equal to the distance between x and y, but are 180 degrees out of phase. Therefore, when both pulses are between x and y simultaneously, they will destructively interfere to give no displacement from the horizontal.

41. **(B)**
    The force experienced by a charged particle in an electrical field is found by multiplying the charge on the particle by the magnitude of the electrical field;

$$F = EQ.$$

Therefore, if Q is doubled, the force it experiences is doubled.

42. **(C)**
    A negative charge moving to the right will be deflected downward due to a force perpendicular to its velocity. Since the direction of motion is now changed, and since the force always acts perpendicular to the particle's velocity, the particle moves in a clockwise circular path. A positive charge would travel in a counterclockwise direction.

43. **(A)**
    The radius of the path of a charged particle traveling in a magnetic field is given by

$$r = mv/qB.$$

Of the five choices, the only one that will make a larger radius is a decrease in charge.

44. **(E)**
    Lentz's law states that the direction of an induced current is such that its own magnetic field opposes the original change in the flux that induced the current. In the situation described above, the coil rotates through a magnetic field at a constant velocity, and the magnetic lines "cut" buy the coil continuously vary from zero to a maximum. The current induced in the coil therefore varies from zero to a maximum causing a magnetic field around the coil. This induced magnetic field will therefore vary from zero to a maximum and thus the external force required to rotate it against the external magnetic field at a constant velocity will have to vary from zero to a maximum.

45. **(E)**

From the conservation of momentum we know that the total momentum before the collision of the raft and person must equal the total momentum after the collision, so

$$m_{person}\ v_{person} = (m_{person} + m_{raft})\ v_{raft\ and\ person}$$

or

$$(70\ kg)\ v_{person} = (70\ kg + 10\ kg)\ v_{raft\ and\ person}$$

$$v_{raft\ and\ person} = 7/8\ v_{person}$$

46. **(C)**

If the object were unbalanced, the object would rotate. Rotation involves torque which is calculated by the product of force perpendicular to rotation and distance from rotation that the force is applied. Because side L is longer than R, yet it supplies equal torque, side L must weigh less than side R, thus eliminating (A) and (B). While (D) could be true, the situation does not imply it.

47. **(C)**

At the top of the hill the skier has a potential energy of mgh. As he drops he will lose potential energy and it will be changed to kinetic energy ($1/2\ mv^2$). The amount of kinetic energy that is gained will equal the difference between the potential energy at the top and the potential at X. This means

$$mgh - mgd = 1/2\ mv^2$$

or

$$mg(h - d) = 1/2\ mv^2.$$

If we cancel mass and rearrange the equation we have

$$v = \sqrt{2g(h - d)}.$$

48. **(D)**

All protons are contained in the nucleus of atoms and are quite immobile. Therefore answers (A) and (C) are unreasonable. Electrons, on the other hand, tend to distribute themselves uniformly on the surface of conductors. A positively charged conductor has lost some electrons, and will attract some of the electrons away from the neutral conductor, causing it to lose electrons, leaving it positively charged.

49. **(A)**

(A) varies with the restoring force of the spring which varies linearly and directly with x according to Hooke's Law. Since it accelerates upwards at first the answer must start with positive a, eliminating (C) and (E). Since it decelerates after the equilibrium point, we can eliminate (B) and (D).

50. **(C)**

Say that t_0 is a time interval measured by an observer that is at rest relative to the radioactive particles and t is a time interval measured by the scientist at rest relative to the laboratory. As the particles pass the scientist at 0.9 c, the theory of special relativity says that

$$t = t_0 / \sqrt{1 - (v/c)^2}.$$

If you substitute 0.9 c for v, you have

$$t = t_0 / \sqrt{1 - (9.0c/c)^2} = t_0 / \sqrt{1 - 0.81}$$

or

$$t = t_0 / 0.44.$$

This tells us that if the half-life of the particle is t_0 when it is standing still relative to the scientist, it will be $t_0 / 0.44$ when the particle is moving with a speed of 0.90 c with respect to the scientist. This is the same as $t_0(1/0.44)$ or $2.3 t_0$.

51. **(A)**

A properly constructed ray diagram places the image 6 cm to the right of the lens.

Also by using the thin lens equation,

$$\frac{1}{f} = \frac{1}{i} + \frac{1}{o}.$$

Remember the focal length is positive for a convex lens and negative for a concave lens.

$$\frac{1}{4} - \frac{1}{12} = \frac{1}{o}$$
$$6 \text{ cm} = o$$

The positive 6 means the image is real and thus to the right of the lens.

52. **(C)**

First you must change the temperatures to Kelvin, which becomes 473 and 373. Then you use

$\{T_1 - T_2\} / T_1$

to get .21, or 21%. Answer (A) is often incorrectly attained when you forget to change the temperatures to Kelvin.

53. **(A)**

The heat of fusion is the heat required to melt 1 gram of the substance. Twenty joules are used between *B* and *C* to melt the 10 grams. Thus,

20 J / grams = 2 joules / gram.

54. **(D)**

Disorder increases during each of the segments.

55. **(D)**

Question 55 can be solved if you are familiar with the relationship which states that the gravitational force between two objects is directly proportional to the product of their masses, and inversely proportional to the square of the distance between them.

$$F = \frac{GM_1 m_2}{r^2}$$

G = gravitational constant

M_1 = mass of object 1

m_a = mass of object 2

r = distance between objects

If the distance between two objects is held constant, then the force is directly proportional to any change in the mass of the objects or

$F \propto M_1 m_2$.

This means that if the mass of one of the objects is tripled, then the force triples and if the mass of both of them is tripled the force will increase by nine times.

56. **(B)**

Not all frequencies of light cause photoelectric emission from a given material. Instead each photoelectric material exhibits a threshold frequency necessary to dislodge electrons.

Increasing this threshold frequency increases the number of electrons. Increasing the wavelength decreases the frequency and no electrons will be emitted. Increasing the intensity will increase the number of light particles, photons, hitting the material, but if these photons are not emitted at the threshold frequency then they will not dislodge any electrons. Thus, choice II is the only parameter that, when increased, will cause emission of an electron.

57. **(D)**
   If Coulomb's equation is considered it can be reasoned that if the changes on A and B remain the same, and the distance between them is halved and then squared, then the denominator is reduced by four times. Since the denominator, r^2, is four times smaller, the quotient

$$kqA/r^2$$

will be four times greater.

58. **(C)**
   The direction of the magnetic force on a current-carrying wire is perpendicular for both the current flow and the magnetic field strength B. When a right hand is held so that the fingers an be curled from the direction of I into the direction of B, the thumb points in the direction of the force.

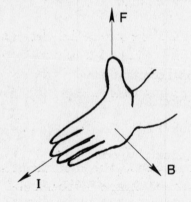

59. **(A)**
   If the mass is allowed to hang freely, it will position itself at Y_0. The net force at this point is zero. (Force up equals force down.)

60. **(D)**
   The acceleration reaches a maximum when the force acting on the mass is maximum. This occurs at Y_1 and Y_2.

61. **(E)**
   Angular momentum is a product of factors which include mass, velocity, and radius and is conserved. As one is reduced, another must increase to

compensate. Therefore, as radius is reduced, velocity must increase (assuming the mass of the object does not change).

An object's speed is not inherently determined by its size, eliminating (A). When a rotating object withdraws its mass into a smaller radius about the axis of rotation, it does not mean that its density necessarily changes (e.g., a figure skater rotating with extended arms can pull her arms in but her density would not change). This eliminates (B). The rotational inertia of smaller objects is generally less, due to their smaller radius, thus eliminating (C). An object cannot both increase its angular velocity and keep its angular velocity the same, so (D) must be eliminated.

62. **(A)**

As light passes from a less dense medium to a more dense medium it slows down (air to glass), and speeds up as it goes from more dense to less dense (glass to water). Since the refractive index is the ratio of the speed of light in a medium to the speed of light in a vacuum, the higher the value, the more dense the medium.

63. **(E)**

After only 2 days, 1/2 the sample has decayed and 1/2 remains, so answer (A) is incorrect. After 4 days, 1/2 of the 1/2, or 1/4, remains, so 3/4 has decayed. Thus, answers (B), (C), and (D) are not possible. After 6 days, 1/2 of the 1/4, or 1/8, remains, which means 7/8 of the original amount has decayed.

64. **(A)**

X-rays are not energetic enough to affect the nucleus of atoms. Choices (B), (C), (D), and (E) involved changes in the nucleus.

65. **(C)**

The capacitance of a parallel plate capacitor is proportional to the area of the plates and inversely proportional to the distance between the plates.

$C \propto A/d.$

If we double the distance, the area will have to be doubled to compensate.

66. **(B)**

The electric field, E, is the force on a unit positive charge to a point.

67. **(C)**

As the particle is accelerated, the mass of the particle, from our point of view, would increase. Because both momentum and kinetic energy rely on mass and velocity, both of these quantities will continue to increase.

68. **(A)**

The work done is equal to the increase in potential energy of the mass from Point *A* to Point *B*; or

$$PE = mgh = 5 \text{ kg } (10 \text{ m/sec}^2) \, 2 \text{ m} = 100 \text{ J}.$$

69. **(C)**

First change the energy of the work function to joules,

$$4.8 \text{ eV } (1.6 \times 10^{-19} \text{ J/eV}) = 7.7 \times 10^{-19} \text{ J}.$$

We know that the work function represents the energy needed just to remove an electron from the metal and thus the lowest kinetic energy, because

$$E = hc / \lambda$$

h is planks constant and *c* is the speed of light. If we rearrange we have

$$\lambda = 6.6 \times 10^{-34} \text{ J sec } (3.0 \times 10^8 \text{ m/sec})/7.7 \times 10^{-19} \text{ J}$$

$$\lambda = 2.6 \times 10^{-7} \text{ m}$$

70. **(B)**

The energy of a photon is directly proportional to its frequency

$$E = hf.$$

Thus, answer (A) is incorrect when compared to (B). All light travels at the same speed in a vacuum, which eliminates (C) and (D). A 2 eV photon has a higher wavelength than a 10 eV photon; therefore, (E) is also incorrect. Where wavelength is determined by

$$c = \lambda f,$$

c = speed of light and λ = wavelength.

DETAILED EXPLANATIONS OF ANSWERS

TEST 1

Section II

1. (a)
    The energy of a photon is given by the formula

    $E_p = hc / \lambda,$

where h is planks constant and c is the speed of light. Thus,

$E_p = 6.63 \times 10^{-34}$ J s $(3.00 \times 10^8$ m/s$) / 3.00 \times 10^{-7}$ m

$E_p = 6.63 \times 10^{-19}$ J

1. (b)
    The equation for the photoelectric effect says

    $E_k = E_p - W,$

where E_k is the energy of the electron ejected from the metal and W is the work function of the metal. The kinetic energy of the electron is

$E_k = 1/2 \ mv^2$

$= 1/2 \ (9.11 \times 10^{-31}$ kg$) (3.00 \times 10^5$ m/s$)^2$

$E_k = 4.10 \times 10^{-20}$ J

Thus, substituting into the equation for the photoelectric effect

4.10×10^{-20} J $= 6.63 \times 10^{-19}$ J $- W$

or

$W = 6.22 \times 10^{-19}$ J.

2. (a)
    The moment of inertia of a solid cylinder is given by

    $I = 1/2 \ mr^2;$

torque is given by

$$\tau = I\alpha$$

or

$$\tau = Fr = mgr$$

(as you can see from the figure). Putting this all together

$$mgr = 1/2mr^2\,\alpha$$

$$\alpha = 2\ g/r = 2(9.8\ \text{m/s}^2)/0.2\ \text{m}$$

$$= 98\ \text{rad/s}^2$$

F = mg

r

mg

2.   (b)

When the 3 m string unwraps, the cylinder travels 15 radians. Using this formula

$$\Delta\emptyset = 1/2\ \alpha\Delta t^2$$

$$15\ \text{rad} = 1/2\ (98\ \text{rad/s}^2)\ \Delta t^2$$

$$\Delta t = 0.55\ \text{s}$$

3.   (a)

The energy released will come from the loss in mass when Uranium gives off the alpha particle.

$$238.0508\ \text{amu} - (234.0436\ \text{amu} + 4.0026\ \text{amu})$$

or

$$.0046\ \text{amu}$$

but

$$1\ \text{amu} = 1.7 \times 10^{-27}\ \text{kg}$$

so

$$.0046\ \text{amu} = 7.8 \times 10^{-30}\ \text{kg}$$

Using Einstein's equation, $E = mc^2$,

$$E = 7.8 \times 10^{-30}\ \text{kg}\ (3 \times 10^8\ \text{m/s})^2 = 7 \times 10^{-13}\ \text{J}$$

3.   (b)

The energy for a gamma ray is

$E = hc/\lambda$

$E = 6.6 \times 10^{-34} \text{ J s } (3 \times 10^8 \text{ m/s}) / 2.5 \times 10^{-11} \text{ m}$

$E = 7.92 \times 10^{-15} \text{ J}$

4. (a)
The momentum of the astronaut standing still in space is zero so the momentum of the astronaut, and the propellant, after it is fired, has to be equal in magnitude but opposite in direction.

$90 \text{ kg } (0 \text{ m/s}) = 3 \text{ kg } (- 15 \text{ m/s}) + 87 \text{ kg } v$

$3 \text{ kg } (15\text{m/s}) = 87 \text{ kg } v$

$v = 0.52 \text{ m/s}$

4. (b)
For the first 5 s he will go from 0 to 0.52 m/s for an average velocity of 0.26 m/s. We know that $V = \Delta x / \Delta t$ so

$\Delta x = 1.3 \text{ m.}$

The remaining 48.7 m will be covered at a constant speed of 0.52 m/sec so

$0.52 \text{ m/s} = 48.7 \text{ m } / \Delta t$

$\Delta t = 93.6 \text{ s}$

for a total of 98.6 s.

5. The best combination has two eight ohm resistors in parallel to make an equivalent resistance of 4 ohms and that network in series with the remaining 8 ohm resistor to make a total of 12 ohms. With the 12 V battery that 12 ohms would draw 1 amp of current.

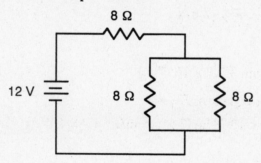

6. (a)
From the impulse formula

$F\Delta t = m\Delta v$

$210 \text{ N } (0.006 \text{ s}) = .045 \text{ kg } v$

$v = 28 \text{ m/s}$

6.   (b)

If the ball leaves the ground at a 30° angle, we need to find the vertical component of the velocity.

$v_v = \sin (30°) \ 28 \text{ m/s} = 14 \text{ m/s}$

Because it will have zero velocity at the very top of its flight, we can find the distance it will travel straight up.

$v^2 = v_0^2 + 2 A_{ave} \Delta x$

$0 \text{ m/s} = (14 \text{ m/s})^2 + (9.8 \text{ m/s}^2) \Delta x$

$\Delta x = 10 \text{ m}$

6.   (c)

To calculate the distance down range, we need to know the velocity in the horizontal direction and the time the ball will be in the air.

$v_h = \cos(30°) \ 28 \text{ m/s} = 24.3 \text{ m/s}$

$v = v_0 + A_{ave} \Delta t$

$0 \text{ m/s} = 14 \text{ m/s} + (-9.8 \text{ m/s}^2) \Delta t$

$\Delta t = 1.4 \text{ s}$

It will take 1.4 s for the ball to go up and 1.4 s for it to come down for a total of 2.8 sec. It will be traveling at a constant 24.3 m/s in the horizontal direction so

$24.3 \text{ m/s} = \Delta x / 2.8 \text{ s}$

$\Delta x = 68 \text{ m}$

ADVANCED PLACEMENT EXAMINATION IN
PHYSICS

AP Physics B
Test 2

AP PHYSICS B
TEST 2

Section I

(Answer sheets appear in the back of this book.)

TIME: 90 Minutes
70 Questions

DIRECTIONS: Each of the questions or incomplete statements below is followed by five answer choices or completions. Choose the best answer to each question.

---

1. As the wavelength of a wave increases, the amount of diffraction the wave experiences in going around a barrier

   (A) increases.   (B) decreases.

   (C) remains the same.   (D) cancels.

   (E) interferes.

2. The nonuniform bar shown below is 5 meters long. It is denser near one end than near the other. It has a fixed pivot at 2.3 m from the heavy end. If the weight of the bar is 73.3 newtons and a 20 newton weight at 0.5 m from the light end will establish rotational equilibrium, what is the location of the bar's center of mass?

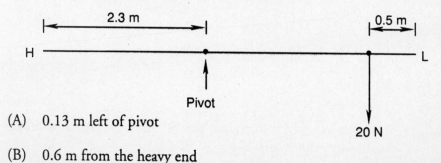

   (A)   0.13 m left of pivot

   (B)   0.6 m from the heavy end

(C)   1.7 m from the heavy end

(D)   2.5 m from the light end

(E)   2.9 m from the heavy end

3.   Polarization is a wave phenomenon which applies only to

(A)   sound.   (B)   light.

(C)   radio waves.   (D)   transverse waves.

(E)   longitudinal waves.

4.   In a breeder reactor, a Uranium 238 nucleus absorbs a neutron and becomes Uranium $^{239}_{92}$U. Uranium 239 undergoes a transmutation which produces a fissionable Plutonium 239 nucleus, $^{239}_{94}$Pu. This transmutation is a result of

(A)   the emission of an alpha particle.

(B)   the emission of 2 alpha particles.

(C)   the emission of a beta particle.

(D)   the emission of 2 beta particles.

(E)   the emission of 2 positrons.

5.   If an object is moving in circular motion due to centripetal force, F, and the radius of its circular motion is then doubled, the new force then becomes

(A) $2F$.   (B) F.

(C) $F/2$.   (D) F^2.

(E) $1/F$.

6.   A convex lens which converges parallel light rays creates an image which is real when the object is

(A)   at the focal length of the lens.

(B)   beyond the focal length of the lens.

(C)   on the same side of the lens as the image.

(D)   between the focal length of the lens and the lens.

(E)   virtual.

7.   Given that the half-life of Iodine 131 is 8 days, what was the mass of an original sample if 10 grams of I-131 remain after 72 days of observation?

(A)   80 grams   (B)   90 grams

(C)   720 grams   (D)   5120 grams

(E)   5760 grams

8.   The index of refraction for an unknown substance is 1.2. The critical angle for total internal reflection to occur in the substance if going from the substance to air is found by

(A) $\sin (1.2) = \theta$.   (B) $\sin (.8) = \theta$.

(C) $\sin \theta = 1.2$.   (D) $\sin \theta = .8$.

(E) $1/\sin (1.2) = \theta$.

9.   Which of the following statements are true under the Laws of Photo-electric Emission?

I.   The kinetic energy of photoelectrons is independent of incident light intensity.

II.   Surfaces have characteristic cut-off frequencies below which emission will stop.

III. The rate of emission is directly proportional to the frequency of incident light.

IV.   Maximum kinetic energy of photoelectrons increases as the frequency of light increases.

(A) I and III   (B) I, II, and III

(C) I, II, and IV   (D) II, III, and IV

(E) I, II, III, and IV

10. In a Hydrogen atom, an electron in any excited state which returns to ground state will emit ultraviolet line spectra found in the

(A) Balmer series.   (B) Bohr series.

(C) Lyman series.   (D) Paschen series.

(E) Planck series.

11. What amount of current passes through the 15 Ω resistor?

(A) 0.125 amps

(B) 0.417 amps

(C) 2.4 amps

(D) 8.0 amps

(E) 10.0 amps

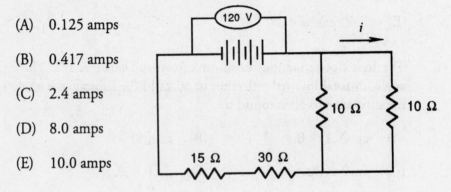

12. The moon is in a nearly circular orbit above the earth's atmosphere. Which statement is true?

(A) It is in equilibrium and has no net force.

(B) It has constant velocity.

(C) It continues to use up its energy rapidly like a spaceship and is falling back to earth.

(D) It is accelerating toward the earth.

(E) Its acceleration is in the same direction as its velocity.

13. A mass is suspended on a spring. The reaction force to the force of gravity from the earth acting on the mass is the force exerted by the

    (A) mass on the earth.   (B) mass on the spring.

    (C) spring on the mass.   (D) spring on the earth.

    (E) earth on the mass.

14. A magnet is dropped through an aluminum ring with the north pole of the magnet entering the ring first. What will be true of the induced magnetic field of the ring as the magnet passes through the ring?

    (A) There is no induced current in the ring so there is no induced magnetic field.

    (B) It will change from north up to north down.

    (C) It will change from south up to south down.

    (D) It will be constant with north up.

    (E) It will be constant with south up.

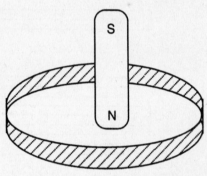

15. According to the following diagram, if a magnetic field is directed into this paper and a negatively charged particle is moving from left to right across it, there will be a force on the particle which pushes it.

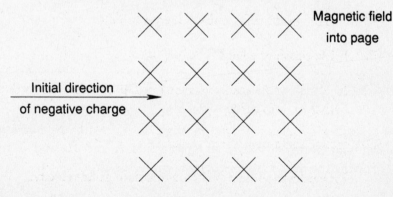

(A)   into the page.

(B)   out from the page.

(C)   toward the bottom of the page.

(D)   toward the top of the page.

(E)   from left to right across the page.

16.   Which of the following diagrams show the direction of a magnetic field about a conducting wire?

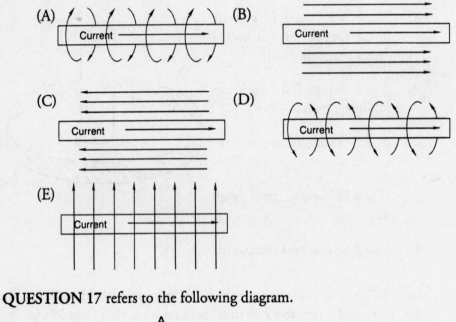

QUESTION 17 refers to the following diagram.

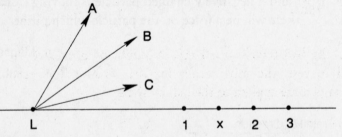

17.   Projectile *B* is launched at an angle of 45° with the horizontal, and lands at point *x*. Where did projectiles A and C land if they were launched with the same velocity as projectile *B*?

(A)   Between *L* and *x*   (B)   Between *x* and 3

(C)   Between *x* and 2   (D)   Between 2 and 3

(E)   Cannot be determined.

18.   If the switch in this circuit is closed, what will be the change in power?

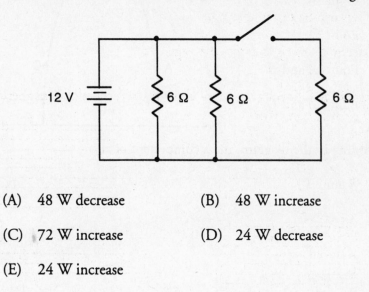

(A)   48 W decrease   (B)   48 W increase

(C)   72 W increase   (D)   24 W decrease

(E)   24 W increase

19.   A boy weighing 20 kg riding on a 10 kg cart travelling at 3 m/s jumped
      off in such a way that he landed on the ground with no horizontal
      speed. What was the change of speed of the cart?

(A)   1 m/s   (B)   2 m/s

(C)   3 m/s   (D)   6 m/s

(E)   9 m/s

20.   A .1 kg ball travelling 20 m/s is caught by a catcher. In bringing the
      ball to rest, the mitt recoils for .01 second. The absolute value of
      average force applied to the ball by the glove is

(A)   20 N.   (B)   100 N.

(C)   200 N.   (D)   1000 N.

(E)   2000 N.

21. A ball is thrown upwards from the ground and follows the path shown in the diagram. At which point does the ball have the greatest speed?

    (A) Point *A*

    (B) Point *B*

    (C) Point *C*

    (D) Points *A* and *B*

    (E) Points *A* and *C*

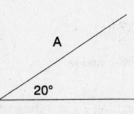

22. According to the diagram, the *x* component of *A* is

    (A) *A* tan 20°.

    (B) *A* cos 20°.

    (C) *A* sin 20°.

    (D) 0.

    (E) *A*.

QUESTION 23 refers to the following diagram, passage, and choices. An object is fired horizontally from the top of a building *A* and follows a free-fall trajectory as shown (to *B*). Neglecting air friction, consider the five vectors shown.

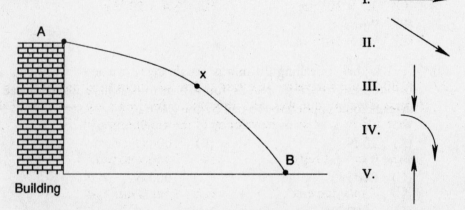

23. Which vector best represents the direction of the object's velocity at *x*?

    (A) I   (B) II

(C) III (D) IV

(E) V

24. A wave leaves one medium in which it travels 6 m/s and has a wavelength of 2 m and enters a second medium in which the wavelength is
3 m. The wave speed in the second wave is

(A) 1.5 m/s. (B) 5 m/s.

(C) 6 m/s. (D) 9 m/s.

(E) 18 m/s.

25. A load resistance of 5 kΩ can carry a maximum current of 10 amps.
What is the power that is dissipated across the load resistance?

(A) 50 kW (B) 500 W

(C) 50,000 W (D) 500,000 W

(E) 500,000 kW

26. An electron microscope produces electrons with an energy of 70 keV.
What is the wavelength of these electrons?

(A) 8.3×10^{21} m (B) 5.6×10^{-8} m

(C) 1.7×10^{19} m (D) 8.4×10^{-13} m

(E) 1.8×10^{-11} m

27. A 30 kg mass traveling due east at 5 m/s collides head on with a 15 kg
mass traveling due west at 9 m/s. If the first mass leaves the event due
west at 3 m/s, what is the velocity of the second mass?

(A) 0 m/s (at rest) (B) 5 m/s due west

(C) 7 m/s due east (D) 13 m/s due east

(E) 25 m/s due east

28. What voltage is necessary to produce a 300 μC charge or a 4 μF capacitor?

    (A) 0.013 V   (B) 4 V

    (C) 75 V   (D) 300 V

    (E) 1200 V

29. An object weighing 100 N at the earth's surface is moved to a distance of 3 earth radii from the surface of the earth. Its new weight will be

    (A) 25 N.   (B) 33.3 N.

    (C) 11.1 N.   (D) 6.25 N.

    (E) 400 N.

30. Which of the following will cause the period of a pendulum to be doubled?

    (A) Doubling the length

    (B) Doubling the mass

    (C) Doubling the acceleration of gravity

    (D) Increasing the mass by a factor of 4

    (E) Increasing the length by a factor of 4

31. When the frequency of a forced vibration approaches the natural frequency of a particular vibrating object, the vibration in the object increases its

    (A) pitch.   (B) frequency.

    (C) wavelength.   (D) speed.

    (E) amplitude.

32. Which of the following statements are accurate according to Rutherford's alpha particle scattering experiment?

    I.   Thin foils deflect a majority of alpha particles.

    II.   Thin foils deflect very few alpha particles.

    III. Scattering patterns lead to an atom model of uniform charge distribution.

    IV.   Scattering patterns lead to an atom model with concentrated positive charge.

    (A) I   (B) II

    (C) I and III   (D) I and IV

    (E) II and IV

33. You have three identical neutral hollow metal spheres. You charge the first, then touch it to the second. Now touch the second to the third. Finally, touch the third to the first. What is the fraction of the original charge now on sphere one, two, and three?

    (A) 1/4, 1/2, 1/4   (B) 3/8, 2/8, 3/8

    (C) 1/3, 1/3, 1/3   (D) 3/8, 1/4, 1/4

    (E) 1/4, 1/4, 1/8

34. A parallel plate capacitor is connected to a fixed voltage. If a dielectric material is introduced between the plates, which of the following will result?

    (A) Charge decreases and capacitance increases

    (B) Charge and capacitance decrease

    (C) Charge increases and capacitance decreases

    (D) Charge and capacitance increase

    (E) Charge and capacitance are not changed

35. Two 4 μF parallel plate capacitors are connected in parallel across a 12 V battery. What is the total amount of charge stored in the two capacitors?

(A) 48 μC   (B) 96 μC

(C) 0.3 μC   (D) 24 μC

(E) 0.6 μC

36. Which of the following diagrams best represents the most intense electric field created by two opposite charges?

(A)   (B)

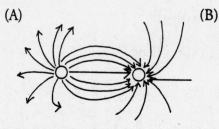   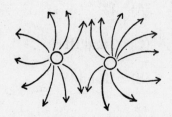

(C)   (D)

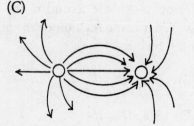   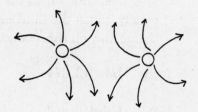

(E)

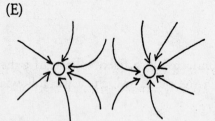

37. Two small charged pith balls separated by a distance *D* repel each other with a force *F*. If the distance between them is doubled, the force of repulsion will be

(A) 1/4 *F*.   (B) 1/2 *F*.

(C) .707 *F*.   (D) 1.4 *F*.

(E) 4 *F*.

38. If a segment, the distance between two nodes in a standing wave, is 20 cm long, the wavelength of the original travelling wave used to create the standing wave is

    (A) 10 cm.   (B) 20 cm.

    (C) 30 cm.   (D) 40 cm.

    (E) 50 cm.

39. The diagram shows 3 point charges, each 1 meter apart. The best indication of the net force on the +1 charge is

$$0 + 1$$
$$+ 2\ 0 \qquad\qquad 0 + 2$$

    (A) to the right.   (B) to the left.

    (C) straight down.   (D) straight up.

    (E) down and to the right.

40. The potential energy change a unit charge experiences in moving from one point to another is called the

    (A) voltage.   (B) current.

    (C) resistance.   (D) field.

    (E) charge.

41. A 1.0 kg pendulum is released at a height of 3.2 m vertically from a reference level. Assuming $g = 10$ m/s^2, and neglecting air resistance, at the bottom of its swing its speed will be

    (A) 8 m/s.   (B) 6 m/s.

    (C) 4 m/s.   (D) 2 m/s.

    (E) 1 m/s.

42. If you increase the intensity of light striking a photosensitive piece of metal, which of the following will be true?

(A) Electrons with a greater maximum kinetic energy will be ejected.

(B) It will take less time for the first electron to be ejected.

(C) More electrons will be ejected.

(D) The threshold energy will be less.

(E) All of the above.

43. According to the Ideal Gas Law, the behavior of gases is related to the Ideal Gas Constant, *R*. Thus, the dimensions of a possible value of *R* can be

(A) (Liter)(atm)/(mol)(°C).   (B) (Liter)(atm)/(mol)(K).

(C) (mol)(atm)/(Liter)(K).   (D) (mol)(atm)/(Liter)(°C).

(E) (Liter)(atm)/(grams)(K).

44. If you double the temperature of a mixture of H_2 and N_2 gas, which of the following will be true concerning the average kinetic energy and average velocity of each of the two gases?

(A) Molecules of N_2 and H_2 will have the same average velocity and average kinetic energy.

(B) Both will have the same average velocity but molecules of N_2 will have a higher average kinetic energy than molecules of H_2.

(C) Both will have the same average velocity but molecules of H_2 will have a higher average kinetic energy than molecules of N_2.

(D) Both will have the same average kinetic energy but molecules of N_2 will have a higher average velocity than molecules of H_2.

(E) Both will have the same average kinetic energy but molecules of H_2 will have a higher average velocity than molecules of N_2.

45. Why does a marble table feel cooler to the touch than a wooden table top?

(A) Because the marble table never absorbs enough heat to reach room temperature.

(B) Because the heat conductivity of marble is higher than wood, heat flows more readily from your fingers.

(C) Because the heat conductivity of marble is higher than wood, heat flows more readily into your fingers.

(D) Because the heat conductivity of wood is higher than marble, heat flows more readily from your fingers.

(E) Because the heat conductivity of wood is higher than marble, heat flows more readily into your fingers.

46. Which of the following phenomena are impossible according to the 2nd Law of Thermodynamics?

I. Complete conversion of heat from a single thermal reservoir into mechanical work.

II. Reduction of temperature to absolute zero, 0K.

III. The total entropy of an isolated system can decrease.

IV. The total entropy of an isolated system can increase.

(A) I and III   (B) I and IV

(C) II and III   (D) I, II, and III

(E) I, II, and IV

47. A 2.5 m long piece of wire with a radius of 0.65 mm has a resistance of 2 Ω. If the length and the radius of the wire are doubled, what will be the new resistance?

(A) 16 Ω (B) 8 Ω

(C) 4 Ω (D) 2 Ω

(E) 1 Ω

48. Which of the following graphs best represents the work done during the expansion of a gas under constant temperature?

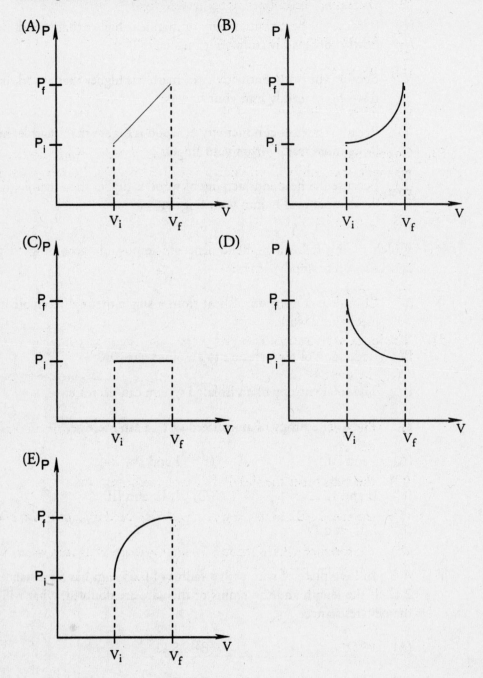

49. Which of the following procedures will increase the maximum kinetic energy of a photoelectron during photoemission?

(A)   Increasing the intensity of incident light

(B)   Increasing the frequency of incident light

(C)   Using a metal with a higher cut-off frequency

(D)   Both (A) and (B)

(E)   Both (A) and (C)

50.   Copper has a work function of 48 eV. What wavelength of the electro-magnetic spectrum will produce photoelectrons with the lowest kinetic energy?

(A) 4.1×10^{-26} m   (B) 9.5×10^{-25} m

(C) 2.6×10^{-7} m   (D) 1.3×10^{-6} m

(E) 5.8×10^{-7} m

51.   The index of refraction, *n*, of material is the relationship of

(A)   the speed of light in the material to the speed of light in a vacuum, *v/c.*

(B)   the speed of light in a vacuum to the speed of light in the material, *c/v.*

(C)   the mass times the speed of light squared, mc^2.

(D)   the speed of light in the material to the speed of light in air, v/v_a.

(E)   the speed of light in the material to the speed of light in water, v/v_w.

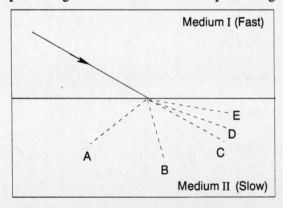

52. Which ray in the diagram shown on the previous page best predicts the new direction of the wave in medium II, a medium in which the velocity of the wave is slower than in medium I?

(A)   (B)

(C)   (D)

(E)

QUESTION 53 refers to the following before and after diagram. Mass *m* at rest splits into two parts—one with a mass 2/3*m* and one with mass 1/3*m*. After the split, the part with mass 1/3*m* moves to the right with a velocity *v*.

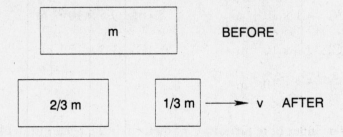

53. The velocity of 2/3*m* part after the split is

(A) 1/3 *v*.   (B) 1/2 *v*.

(C) 2/3 *v*.   (D) 2 *v*.

(E) 3 *v*.

54. An explorer leaves earth in a spacecraft traveling 99.9% the speed of light. If he travels one light year then returns, how long was his trip to an earth observer?

(A) Instantaneous

(B) One year

(C) Between one and two years

(D) Two years

(E) More than two years

55. Which of the following statements is true under Einstein's Theory of Relativity?

    (A) As energy increases, the speed of light increases and mass is constant.

    (B) As energy increases, mass increases and the speed of light is constant.

    (C) As energy increases, the speed of light decreases and mass is constant.

    (D) As energy increases, mass decreases and the speed of light is constant.

    (E) As energy increases, the speed of light and mass will increase.

56. Through this reaction

    $$_6C^{12} + _1H^2 - _7N^{13}$$

    what else is produced?

    (A) β^+ (B) $_1H^1$

    (C) $_0n^1$ (D) α

    (E) γ

57. If two objects have the same momentum, but different masses, which of these is possible?

    (A) The one with less mass has more kinetic energy.

    (B) The one with more mass requires more impulse to bring it to that momentum from rest.

    (C) The same work is done to each to accelerate it from rest.

    (D) They each have the same velocity.

    (E) None of the above.

58. A 5 kg cart accelerates at 3 m/s² for 4 seconds. After this time, what is its kinetic energy?

    (A) 22.5 J   (B) 60 J

    (C) 180 J   (D) 360 J

    (E) 720 J

59. The force needed to allow the 100 N block to go down the incline at constant speed.

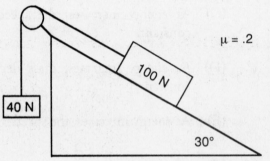

    I.   7.3 newtons down the incline

    II.   greater than 7.3 newtons down the incline

    III. between 7.3 newtons down and 27.3 newtons up the incline

    IV.   27.3 newtons up the incline

    V.   greater than 27.3 newtons up the incline

    (A) I   (B) II

    (C) III   (D) IV

    (E) V

60. A box weighing 200 newtons is lifted 2.0 meters by pushing it up a ramp with a force of 350 newtons. If 76% of the work applied is used to move the box and 24% of the work applied is used to overcome the friction, what is the length of the ramp?

    (A) 2.85 meters   (B) 8.7 meters

    (C) 9.2 meters   (D) 11.4 meters

    (E) 15.0 meters

61. The wheel of an automobile spinning at 180 rev/min begins to experience a 10 rad/sec² angular acceleration. What is the angular velocity of the wheel after 5 seconds?

    (A) 182 rev/min   (B) 230 rev/min

    (C) 275 rev/min   (D) 477 rev/min

    (E) 657 rev/min

QUESTION 62 refers to the following figures.

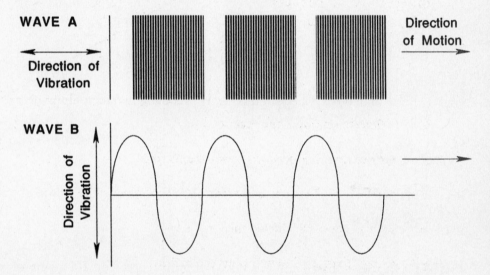

62. If the wavelength of wave *B* is doubled and its velocity remains constant, its period *T* will

    (A) remain constant.   (B) double.

    (C) decrease by 1/2.   (D) increase by 4 times.

    (E) None of the above.

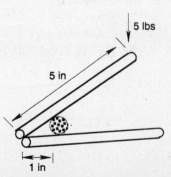

63. If a force of 5 pounds is applied 5 inches from the hinge of a nutcracker, the resistance offered by a nut placed one inch from the hinge is

(A) 15 lbs.   (B) 20 lbs.

(C) 25 lbs.   (D) 30 lbs.

(E) 50 lbs.

64. A radioactive sample with a half-life of 12.25 days registers 480 counts/ min on a Geiger counter. What counting rate would you expect to obtain 49 days later?

(A) 120 counts/min   (B) 90 counts/min

(C) 60 counts/min   (D) 30 counts/min

(E) 15 counts/min

65. $_{83}Bi^{214}$ undergoes a beta minus decay. Its daughter then alpha decays. What remains?

(A) $_{84}Po^{214}$ (B) $_{82}Pb^{210}$

(C) $_{80}Hg^{210}$ (D) $_{86}Rn^{210}$

(E) $_{83}Bi^{209}$

QUESTION 66 is based on the below heating curve for 10 grams of a substance.

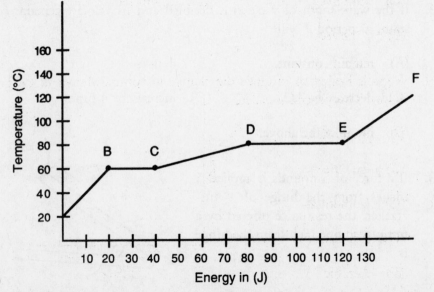

66. The heat of vaporization is

    (A)   2 joules/gram.   (B)   4 joules/gram.

    (C)   8 joules/gram.   (D)   20 joules/gram.

    (E)   40 joules/gram.

67. Absolute temperature is best described as a measure of the

    (A)   speed of molecules.

    (B)   mass of molecules.

    (C)   pressure between molecules.

    (D)   number of molecules.

    (E)   average translational kinetic energy of molecules.

68. A constant net force of 25 N is exerted on a 50 kg cart for 4 seconds. At the end of the 4 seconds the net force goes to 0 N. If the cart starts from rest, what will be the velocity of the cart after a total of 6 seconds has passed?

    (A)   1.0 m/sec   (B)   1.5 m/sec

    (C)   2.0 m/sec   (D)   2.5 m/sec

    (E)   3.0 m/sec

69. A gas is heated to produce the change in volume shown in the graph below. This process is called

    (A)   Isochoric

    (B)   Isobaric

    (C)   Isothermal

    (D)   Adiabatic

    (E)   Aerobic

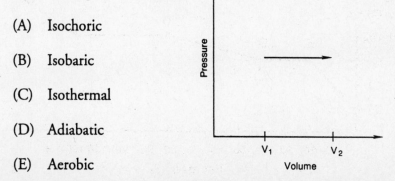

70. For waves of frequency, f, wavelength, λ, and velocity, v, propagated in a certain medium, if the frequency is doubled, then

    (A) λ is doubled and v remains the same.

    (B) λ is doubled and v is halved.

    (C) λ is the same and v is doubled.

    (D) λ is the same and v is halved.

    (E) λ is halved and v is the same.

AP PHYSICS B
TEST 2

Section II

TIME: 90 Minutes
6 Free Response Questions

DIRECTIONS: Carefully read each question and then make sure to answer *each part* of the question. You must show your work.

---

1. The diagram below shows a lever lifting a resistance weight of 2000 newtons. The weight is lifted 2 meters off the ground when the effort arm is pushed down 6 meters. The effort force required is 750 newtons.

    (a) Calculate the work done in pushing down the effort arm and the work done in lifting the weight.

    (b) Calculate the efficiency of this lever.

    (c) If 10 seconds is required to lift the weight to 2 meters, how much power was used? Establish whether power used refers to power *expended* (by 750 N force) or power *received by the box*.

2. A nonuniform bar 4 meters long has a weight of 70 newtons. The bar is on a fixed pivot at its center of mass which is 1 meter from the heavy end. If a 300 newton weight is placed 0.4 meters left of the center of mass and a 100 newton weight is placed 1.0 meters right of the center of mass,

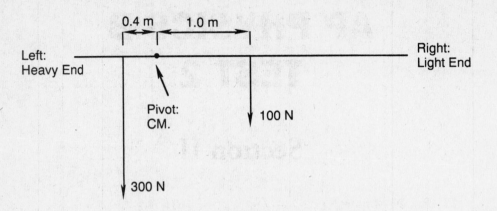

(a) what are the clockwise and counterclockwise torque values?

(b) what is the magnitude and the direction of the net torque?

(c) where must a 200 newton weight be placed to establish rotational equilibrium?

3. Given that the specific heats of ice, water, and steam are 0.485 cal/g°C, 1.0 cal/g°C, and 0.5 cal/g°C respectively; and that the heat of fusion for H_2O is 80 cal/g and the heat of vaporization for H_2O is 540 cal/g, examine the following situation. Fourteen grams of ice at $-10°C$ is heated until it has been changed to steam at 120°C.

(a) What amount of heat is needed to melt the ice at 0°C?

(b) What amount of heat has been absorbed by the process when the water just reaches 100°C?

(c) What is the heat required to vaporize the water and bring the vapor to 120°C?

4. Examine the circuit shown on the following page and answer the questions.

(a) What is the total resistance of the circuit?

(b) What is the resistance of R?

(c) Calculate the current for each branch of the circuit.

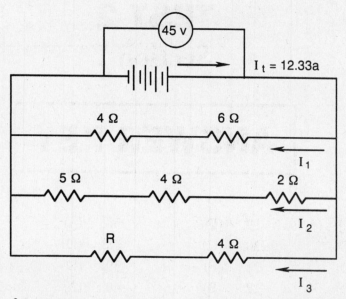

5. A mass of Oxygen gas, O_2, occupies a volume of 15 liters at a temperature of 293 Kelvin under 0.715 atm pressure.

    (a) Calculate the new volume occupied by this mass of oxygen at STP. (273K and 1.0 atm).

    (b) Assuming the oxygen behaves as an ideal gas and noting that the universal gas constant is 0.0821 L atm/mol K, how many grams of oxygen occupy this new volume at STP? (The atomic mass of Oxygen is 16 amu.)

    (c) If this mass of oxygen is now heated to 350K, what pressure is needed to maintain the same volume occupied at STP?

6. Polonium 218, $^{218}_{84}Po$, undergoes radioactive decay to form Lead 214, $^{214}_{82}Pb$. If the half-life of Polonium 218 is 3 minutes,

    (a) what decay particle is emitted during this process?

    (b) what equation represents this transmutation?

    (c) what amount of Polonium 218 remains after a 500 gram sample decays for 15 minutes?

    (d) how much time will have elapsed when only 4 grams of Polonium 218 remain?

TEST 2
Section I

1.	(A)	19.	(D)	37.	(A)	55.	(B)
2.	(C)	20.	(C)	38.	(D)	56.	(C)
3.	(D)	21.	(E)	39.	(D)	57.	(A)
4.	(D)	22.	(B)	40.	(A)	58.	(D)
5.	(C)	23.	(B)	41.	(A)	59.	(A)
6.	(B)	24.	(D)	42.	(C)	60.	(E)
7.	(D)	25.	(D)	43.	(B)	61.	(E)
8.	(D)	26.	(E)	44.	(E)	62.	(B)
9.	(C)	27.	(C)	45.	(B)	63.	(C)
10.	(C)	28.	(C)	46.	(D)	64.	(D)
11.	(C)	29.	(D)	47.	(E)	65.	(B)
12.	(D)	30.	(E)	48.	(D)	66.	(B)
13.	(A)	31.	(E)	49.	(B)	67.	(E)
14.	(B)	32.	(E)	50.	(C)	68.	(C)
15.	(C)	33.	(B)	51.	(B)	69.	(B)
16.	(D)	34.	(D)	52.	(B)	70.	(E)
17.	(A)	35.	(B)	53	(B)		
18.	(E)	36.	(A)	54.	(E)		

DETAILED EXPLANATIONS
OF ANSWERS

TEST 2

Section I

1.   **(A)**
     Diffraction is a wavelength-dependent phenomenon, directly dependent on wavelength. As wavelength increases, diffraction increases (e.g., for sound, low tones [long waves] go around corners [diffract] better than high tones). Choices (B) and (C) are contrary to (A) and must be eliminated. Cancellation and interferences are other wave phenomena not pertinent to the question, thus eliminating (D) and (E).

2.   **(C)**
     Torque in a rotational system is equal to the force applied times the distance from pivot. The 20 newton weight produces a clockwise torque of 20 N × 2.2 m = 44 Nm. The torque necessary to establish equilibrium is 44 Nm counterclockwise. Thus,

$$d \times 73.3 \text{ N} = 44 \text{ Nm and } 44/73.3 = 0.6 \text{ m}.$$

In order to produce counterclockwise torque, the center of mass must be left of the pivot 0.6 m. This gives a value of 1.7 m from the heavy end. (A) is incorrect. Generated by using 0.5 for d instead of 2.2. (B) is incorrect, obtained by forgetting that 0.6 m is from pivot, not from the end. (D) is incorrect. Any force 2.5 from the light end will create more clockwise torque. (E) is incorrect. This force would also be right of pivot and produce more clockwise torque.

3.   **(D)**
     Polarization occurs in transverse waves, not longitudinal waves, eliminating (E). Sound is a longitudinal wave eliminating (A). While polarization does occur in light and radiowaves, (B) and (C), it does not occur exclusively in either. Since the question includes the word "only," we can eliminate (B) and (C) since choosing either of them would eliminate the other and be incorrect.

4.   **(D)**
In order to produce Plutonium 239 from Uranium 239, there must be a gain of 2 protons and no mass change. Beta emission carries no mass and has a −1 proton number. Beta particles, theoretically, are emitted when a neutron transforms into a proton. Thus, the number of nucleons is constant and the charge is increased by one for each beta. (A) and (B) are incorrect because each alpha carries 4 mass units out of the nucleus, 2 of which are protons. (C) is incorrect because one beta would only increase the atomic number to 93, Neptunium. (E) is incorrect because positrons will decrease the atomic number.

5.   **(C)**
Since

$$F = mv^2 / R,$$

if R is doubled, the equation becomes

$$mv^2 / 2R \text{ and/or } (mv^2 / R) / 2 = F / 2.$$

6.   **(B)**
The thin lens equation,

1/object distance + 1/image distance = 1/focal length,

will produce a positive image distance (a real image) if the object distance is greater than the focal length for a converging lens. When the object distance is the focal length, 1/image distance must be zero and hence an image is produced at infinity (meaning never), eliminating (A). When the image is on the same side of the lens as the object, it is not a real image, it is virtual. This eliminates both (C) and (E). The image is virtual when the object is between the focal length and the lens, eliminating choice (D).

7.   **(D)**
Since the half-life of I-131 is 8 days, 72 days is equivalent to 9 half-lives. This means that the original sample mass has been divided in half 9 times. Reversing the time line, the original mass can be found by beginning with 10 grams and doubling this value 9 times. Thus, the original mass is 5120 grams. (A) is incorrect, generated by 8 × 10. (B) is incorrect, generated by 9 half-lives × 10. (C) is incorrect, generated by 72 × 10. (E) is incorrect, generated by 8 × 10 × 72.

8.   **(D)**
Since you are going from substance to air,

$$\sin i = 1/n,$$

or $\quad$ sin $\theta = 1/(6/5)$,

or $\quad$ sin $\theta = 5/6 = .8$.

You do not take the sin of the index, which is why (A) and (B) are incorrect. It is not the reciprocal of the sin of 6/5, which is why (E) is incorrect. And you do not set

$\quad$ sin $\theta = (6/5)/1$,

which is why (C) is incorrect.

9. **(C)**

Statement I is the second law of photoelectric emission. II is also true. The third law of photoelectric emission states energy is a function of frequency, not intensity. The lowest frequency which produces photoelectrons is the cut-off frequency. IV is the statement of the third law of photoelectric emission. (A), (B), (D), and (E) are incorrect because they exclude one or more true statements and/or contain statement III which is false under the first law of photoelectric emission. The first law states that the rate of emission is directly proportional to the intensity of incident light.

10. **(C)**

The Lyman series is the spectra produced in the ultraviolet range. (A) is incorrect. The Balmer series is the spectra produced in the visible range. (B) is incorrect. Bohr studied the electron emission spectra, but there is no series with his name. (D) is incorrect. The Paschen series is the spectra produced in the visible range. (E) is incorrect. There is no spectra series with Planck's name.

11. **(C)**

By Ohms's law,

$\quad i = V/R.$

If applied to the total circuit, then

$\quad i = 120/50 = 2.4$ amps.

(A) is incorrect. This is a random number within the range of possible selections. (B) is incorrect, generated by R/V rather than V/R. (D) is incorrect, generated by 120/15 rather than 120/50. (E) is incorrect. This is a random number within the range of possible selections.

12. **(D)**

The gravitational force between the earth and the moon produces a centripetal acceleration. Since the moon is not moving in a straight line, there must be a net force, eliminating (A). Since it is changing direction, it does not have a constant velocity (though it has a near constant speed) eliminating (B). Though there may be insignificant energy losses, *Conservation of Angular Momentum and Energy* are dominant factors and do not allow the moon to slow down appreciably or fall back to the earth, thus eliminating choice (C). Its velocity is always tangent to its path at any moment while its acceleration is always directed toward the earth, nearly perpendicular to its path at any moment, thus choice (E) is incorrect.

13. **(A)**

In Newton's Third Law, action/reaction pairs must apply their equal and opposite forces on each other. Thus, if the earth pulls on the mass, the mass must pull on the earth as a reaction. There are other action/reaction pairs here as well, e.g., spring on mass/mass on spring, but these are not the object of the question.

14. **(B)**

Lenz's law says that in a situation like this the induced field will oppose the field of the magnet. If the north pole of the magnet enters first then the ring will have an induced magnetic field with the north pole up to oppose the motion of the magnet. As the magnet falls through the induced north will be down so that it attracts the south pole of the magnet as it leaves the ring.

15. **(C)**

The left-hand rule which governs negative particles indicates that the magnetic field, the direction of motion of the charge and the force on the charge are mutually perpendicular. With your left hand, point your finger into the page (magnetic field), and point your thumb toward the right side of the paper (direction of charge); your palm then points in the direction of the force on the charge.

The right-hand rule can also be used and you reverse the direction of the force because the charge is negative.

16. **(D)**

Ampere's rule for straight conductors states that if the wire is grasped in the right hand with the thumb in the direction of current, then the magnetic field circles the wire in the direction of the fingers. (B), (C), and (E) are incorrect because they show straight fields, not circular. (A) is incorrect because the field shown is the opposite direction given by Ampere's law.

17. **(A)**

Projectiles travel the maximum attainable horizontal distance when launched at 45 degrees. Since *B* traveled to location *x* when launched at 45 degrees, all other projectiles launched with the same velocity will travel distances between *L* and *x*.

18. **(E)**

The power used by a circuit is given by

$$P = Vi$$

To find the power we must first calculate the current before and after we close the switch. To calculate the current we must calculate the equivalent resistance of the circuits. With two resistors in parallel we have

$$1/R = 1/6\ \Omega + 1/6\ \Omega$$

$$R = 3\ \Omega$$

from Ohm's law

$$V = iR \text{ or } 12\ V = i(3\ \Omega)$$

$$i = 4 \text{ amps}$$

Thus,

$$P = Vi \text{ or } P = 12\ V\ (4 \text{ amps})$$

$$P = 48 \text{ watts}$$

When the switch is closed

$$1/Rt = 1/6\ \Omega + 1/6\ \Omega + 1/6\ \Omega$$

$$R = 2\ \Omega$$

So

$$V = iR \text{ or } 12\ V = i\ (2\ \Omega)$$

$$i = 6 \text{ amps}$$

$$P = Vi = 12\ V\ (6 \text{ amps}) = 72 \text{ watts}$$

The change in power is from 48 watts to 72 watts or an increase of 24 watts.

19. **(D)**

Conservation of momentum requires that the forward momentum lost by the boy be gained by the cart. Thus,

$$3 \text{ m/s} \times 20 \text{ kg} = 60 \text{ kg m/s}$$

must be gained by the cart. And 60 kg m/s divided by the mass of the cart, 10 kg, necessitates a change in speed of 6 m/s. Since a change of speed was asked for, one need not add the original cart speed of 3 m/s to the 6 m/s.

20. **(C)**
Impulse, $F\Delta t$ is calculated by determining the change of an object's momentum, $M\Delta V$. Therefore,

$$F = M\Delta V / \Delta t = .1 \text{ kg} \times (0 \text{ m/s} - 20 \text{ m/s}) / .01 \text{ s} = -200 \text{ N}$$

and its absolute value is 200 N.

21. **(E)**
When the ball is at Point A the force of gravity has had less time to slow the ball down than at Point B. When the ball is at Point C it has been accelerated for the same length of time by the force of gravity as it was decelerated by gravity from Point A to Point B. Therefore the velocity at Point A and Point C is the same magnitude and reaches a maximum.

22. **(B)**
In calculating the x component by dropping a perpendicular to the x axis and creating a right triangle and using the cosine function such that

$$\text{cosine } 20 = x / A,$$

you may then solve for x and get

$$x = A \cos 20.$$

23. **(B)**
The direction of the velocity vector is indicated by the direction of a tangent line to its trajectory at that point x. Thus, (B) is correct. A tangent line is not curved as in (D).

24. **(D)**
As a wave passes the boundary between two media, its frequency must remain unchanged. Therefore,

$$V_1 / X_1 = V_2 / X_2$$

and substituting, we find $V_2 = 9$ m/s where V is wave speed and X is wavelength.

25. **(D)**
Electrical power is defined as

$$P = i^2 R,$$

thus power is

$$(10 \text{ amps})^2 \, 5 \text{ k}\Omega = 500 \text{ kW.}$$

Since 500 kW is not given as a selection, it is converted to watts by multiply-

(b)   Draw and label all the forces on block *B*.

(c)   What is the minimum coefficient of static friction (μ_s) necessary to allow the system to remain at rest?

(d)   Assume that there is no friction between block *A* and the horizontal surface. Determine the acceleration of the system.

2.   A force acting on a mass 5 kg over an interval of time is described by the equation

$$F = 7t^3 - 2t + 4,$$

where *F* is measured in newtons and *t* in seconds. The mass is at rest at $t = 0$.

(a)   Find the change in momentum of the mass for the interval $t = 0$ to $t = 5$ seconds.

(b)   Determine the speed of the mass at the end of the 5 seconds in part (a).

(c)   What is the instantaneous acceleration of the mass at $t = 5$ seconds?

3.   A bomb is released from a plane diving at an angle of 55° with the vertical. The altitude is 750 m. The bomb hits the ground 6.0 s after being released.

(a)   What is the speed of the plane?

(b)   How far did the bomb travel horizontally during its flight?

(c)   What are the horizontal and vertical components of its velocity just before striking its target?

TEST 3
Section I – Mechanics

ANSWER KEY

1.	(B)	10.	(E)	19.	(D)	28.	(B)
2.	(C)	11.	(D)	20.	(E)	29.	(E)
3.	(A)	12.	(E)	21.	(C)	30.	(B)
4.	(D)	13.	(E)	22.	(A)	31.	(B)
5.	(B)	14.	(D)	23.	(B)	32.	(A)
6.	(A)	15.	(B)	24.	(C)	33.	(C)
7.	(B)	16.	(B)	25.	(D)	34.	(B)
8.	(D)	17.	(D)	26.	(C)	35.	(D)
9.	(D)	18.	(C)	27.	(C)		

DETAILED EXPLANATIONS OF ANSWERS

TEST 3

Section I – Mechanics

1. **(B)**

Use the diameter to find the radius

$$r = \frac{d}{2} = \frac{4}{2} = 2 \text{ m}.$$

Now, Newton's second law for rotation gives

$$\Sigma\tau = rF = rT = I\alpha$$

$$\alpha = \frac{rT}{I} = \frac{(2)(40)}{10} = 8\frac{\text{rad}}{s^2}$$

$$\theta = \theta_0 + \omega_0\tau + \frac{1}{2}\alpha\tau^2$$

$$s = r\theta = \frac{1}{2}\alpha r\tau^2 = \frac{1}{2}(8)(2)(3)^2$$

$$= 72.0 \text{ m}.$$

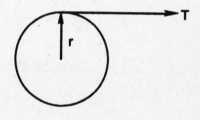

2. **(C)**

Using the general forms of the equations for the x- and y-coordinates of the center of mass we find

$$x\text{(coordinate)} = \frac{m_1x_1 + m_2x_2 + m_3x_3}{m_1 + m_2 + m_3}$$

$$y\text{(coordinate)} = \frac{m_1y_1 + m_2y_2 + m_3y_3}{m_1 + m_2 + m_3}.$$

Since all the particles have a mass of m,

$$x = [(0)m + (3)m + (0)m] / (3m) = 1$$

$$y = [(0)m + (4)m + (3)m] / (3m) = 7/3.$$

Therefore, the center of mass is located at $(1, 7/3)$.

3.　**(A)**

Work done by the external agent is:

$$W = \int_0^x F \cdot dx$$

$$= \int_0^x kx \, dx$$

$$= \frac{1}{2} kx^2 \Big|_0^{x_0}$$

$$= \frac{1}{2} kx^2.$$

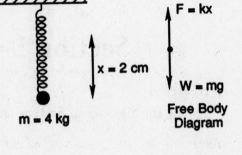

F = kx

x = 2 cm

W = mg

m = 4 kg

Free Body Diagram

In the free body diagram for the hanging mass, the downward gravitational force is balanced by the upward spring force.

$$F = mg = kx$$

$$k = \frac{mg}{x} = \frac{4(9.8)}{.02}$$

$$= 1960 \text{ N} / \text{m}$$

$$W = \frac{1}{2} kx^2$$

$$= \frac{1}{2} (1960)(0.4)^2$$

$$= 1.57 \text{ J}.$$

4.　**(D)**

The moment of inertia

$$I = \int r^2 \, dm$$

$$= \frac{1}{2} mr^2$$

for a right circular cylinder. Then by conservation of energy

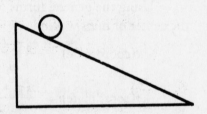

$$mgh = \frac{1}{2} mv^2 + \frac{1}{2} I\omega^2, \quad v = r\omega$$

$$= \frac{1}{2} mv^2 + \frac{1}{4} mr^2 \frac{v^2}{r^2}$$

$$mgh = \frac{3}{4} mv^2$$

$$v_R = 2\sqrt{\frac{gh}{3}}.$$

For normal translational motion

$$v_T = \sqrt{2gh}.$$

Hence,

$$\frac{v_R}{v_T} = \frac{2}{\sqrt{3}} \times \frac{1}{\sqrt{2}}$$

$$= \sqrt{\frac{2}{3}}.$$

5.   **(B)**

Since there is no external work done on the system, linear momentum is conserved,

$$\Sigma p_0 = \Sigma p_f.$$

Assuming that the positive direction is to the right

$$mv_0 + M(0) = (m + m')v_f + (M - m')v'_f.$$

where m = mass of bullet

m' = mass of "chunk"

M = mass of apple

v_0 = initial velocity of bullet

v_f = final velocity of [bullet + "chunk"]

v'_f = final velocity of [apple − "chunk"].

Substituting the values into this equation yields

(0.002 kg) (200 m/s)

$= [(0.002 + 0.002)\text{kg}] \ (190 \ \text{m/s}) + [(0.100 - 0.002)\text{kg}] \ v'_f$

0.4 kg m/s = (0.76 kg m/s) + (0.098 kg) v'_f

$v'_f = -3.67$ m/s or 3.67 m/s to the left.

6.   **(A)**

Kepler's second law is that the area swept out per unit time by a radius vector from the sun to a planet is constant. By the usual triangle area rule

$$dA = \frac{1}{2} r \ rd\theta.$$

Hence,

$$\frac{dA}{dt} = \frac{1}{2} r^2 \omega$$

$$= \frac{L}{2m}.$$

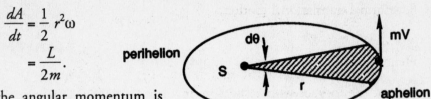

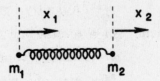

Since the angular momentum is $L = I\omega = mr^2\omega$, thus,

$$L = \text{constant}$$

$$mv_{ap}2a = mv_{pe}\, a$$

$$v_{pe}\,/\,v_{ap} = 2.$$

7.   **(B)**
In general

$$x' = \frac{dy}{dx} \quad \text{and} \quad y' = \frac{dy}{dt}.$$

x_1 and x_2 are the separation of the two masses from their equilibrium positions along the respective axis parallel to their path of motion.

$$m_1 x''_1 = -kx \quad \text{where} \quad x = x_1 - x_2$$

$$m_2 x''_2 = -kx$$

Note: x, the total compression or stretching of the spring, is equal to the algebraic difference of x_1 and x_2. Subtract the two equations to get

$$m(x''_1 - x''_2) = -2kx.$$

Since $m_1 = m_2 = m$ and $x''_1 - x''_2 = x''$

$$mx'' + 2kx = 0, \quad x'' + \frac{2k}{m}x = 0$$

$$\omega_0^2 = \frac{2k}{m} \Rightarrow \omega_0 = \sqrt{\frac{2k}{m}}.$$

8.   **(D)**
Including air resistance, the sum of the forces acting on the object are:

$$(-mg) + F_{\text{drag}} = ma \text{ at terminal velocity}$$

$$(-mg) + F_{\text{drag}} = m(0) \ F_{\text{drag}} = mg.$$

Solving this equation for the terminal velocity yields

$F_{drag} = Cv^2 = \dot{m}g \Rightarrow [(mg) / C]^{0.5} = v_{terminal}.$

9. **(D)**

Since the system is in equilibrium, the sum of the torques with respect to any point must be zero. By choosing the point of the beam to the wall as the reference, we can write:

$$\Sigma\tau = 0, \quad \tau = rF\sin\alpha$$

$$(500)\,(2)\sin(90°) + (200)\,(5)\sin(90°)$$

$$-\,(10)\,(T)\sin(120°) = 0.$$

Therefore, $T = 231$ N is the desired tension.

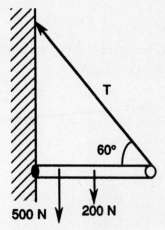

10. **(E)**

This problem is very similar to motion in a constant gravitational field. By the definition of electric field:

$$F = qE = -eE = ma$$

$$\Rightarrow \quad a = -eE/m$$

$$= -(1.6 \times 10^{-19})\,(100) / (9.1 \times 10^{-31})$$

$$= -1.76 \times 10^{13} \text{ m/s}^2.$$

Then from kinematics

$$v_y = v_{oy} + at$$

$$0 = v_o \sin\theta + at$$

$$t = -v_o \sin\theta/a$$

$$T = -2\,v_o \sin\theta \,/\, a$$

$$= -2\,(4 \times 10^5)\,(\sin 30°) / (-1.76 \times 10^{13})$$

$$= 2.3 \times 10^{-8} \text{ s}$$

$$= 23 \text{ ns.}$$

since the time of flight is twice the time to reach the apex.

11. **(D)**

Lissajous figures are generated from the coupled harmonic equations

$$\begin{cases} x'' + \omega_x^2 x = 0 \\ y'' + \omega_y^2 y = 0 \end{cases}$$

with solution

$$x = A \cos (\omega_x t + \alpha)$$

$$y = B \cos (\omega_y t + \beta).$$

The figure is thus a parametric plot $(x(t), y(t))$. Let $\delta = \beta - \alpha$ be the phase difference. Then

$$A = B, \omega_y = 2\omega_x, \delta = \pi/2$$

gives the "butterfly." Also

$$\delta = \pm \pi/2, \omega_y = \omega_x$$

gives an ellipse, and

$$\delta = 0 \quad \text{or} \quad \pm \pi \text{ with } \omega_y = \omega_x$$

is a line.

12. **(E)**

A conservative force is a force such that

$$\oint \mathbf{F} \cdot d\mathbf{r} = 0 \quad \text{or} \quad \nabla \times \mathbf{F} = 0.$$

These are equivalent conditions since

$$\nabla \times \mathbf{F} = 0$$

$$\int \nabla \times \mathbf{F} \cdot d\mathbf{a} = \oint \mathbf{F} \cdot d\mathbf{r}$$

by Stoke's theorem.

$$\oint \mathbf{F} \cdot d\mathbf{r} = 0$$

Stoke's theorem relates the surface integral of the curl to a line integral of the original vector field.

13. **(E)**

If v' is the velocity of the combined system of the pendulum and the bullet right after the collision, then according to the conservation of linear momentum

$$mv = (m + M)v'.$$

From the conservation of energy,

$$^1/_2(m + M)v'^2 = (m + M) gy.$$

Some energy has been lost during the collision and converted to heat.

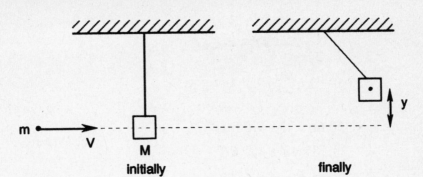

initially   finally

$$v = \frac{M+m}{m} v' = \frac{M+m}{m} \sqrt{2gy}$$

$$= \frac{2.010}{.010} \sqrt{2(9.8)(.20)}$$

$$= 398 \text{ m/s.}$$

14. **(D)**

Use Newton's second law

$$F = ma$$

and the centripetal acceleration

$$a = \frac{v^2}{r}$$

to get

$$F = \frac{mv^2}{r}$$

$$= \frac{4(6)^2}{0.8} = 180 \text{ N}$$

$$F = -180 \text{ N } \mathbf{r}.$$

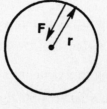

15. **(B)**

The total time T is equal to the time t that it takes for the coin to reach the bottom and the time $t*$ that it takes for the sound waves to travel back to the ground level.

$$d = \frac{1}{2} gt^2$$

$$T = t + t^*, \quad t^* = \frac{d}{v}$$

$$d = \frac{1}{2} g \left(T - \frac{d}{v} \right)^2$$

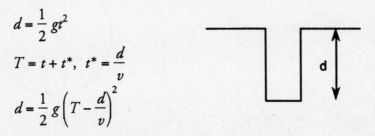

$$\frac{1}{2}gT^2 + \frac{1}{2}g\frac{d^2}{v^2} - gT\frac{d}{v} - d = 0$$

$$d^2 - d\left(\frac{2v^2}{g} + 2vT\right) + v^2T^2 = 0,$$

$$v = 330 \text{ m/s} \quad g = 9.8 \text{ m/s}^2$$

$$d^2 - 23,583.4d + 461,679.5 = 0$$

$$d = \frac{-b \pm \sqrt{b^2 - 4ac}}{2a} = \frac{23,583.4 - 23,544.2}{2}$$

$$= 19.6 \text{ m}.$$

16. **(B)**

Since the system is in equilibrium, Newton's second law shows that

$$F_{net} \;=\; Ma = M(0) = 0 \Rightarrow$$

$$F_x \;=\; (-T_B \cos 20°) + (T_A \cos 50°) = 0 \tag{1}$$

$$F_y \;=\; (T_A \sin 50°) + (T_B \sin 30°) + (-Mg) = 0 \tag{2}$$

and by solving for T_A in terms of T_B in equation (1),

$$T_A = T_B (\cos 20°/\cos 50°).$$

By substituting this value into equation (2) we find

$$[T_B (\cos 20°/\cos 50°)] \sin 50° + T_B \sin 20° = Mg.$$

Solving this equation for T_B shows $T_B = 0.684\, Mg$.

Therefore, $T_B < Mg$.

17. **(D)**

An object propelled horizontally at distance r from the center of the earth into a circular orbit feels a force

$$F = \frac{GmM}{r^2} = \frac{mv^2}{r}.$$

Hence,

$$v^2 = \frac{GM}{r} \quad \text{and} \quad v = \sqrt{\frac{GM}{r}} = r\omega.$$

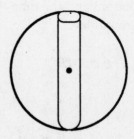

The linear frequency is then

$$v = \frac{\omega}{2\pi} = \frac{1}{2\pi}\sqrt{\frac{GM}{r^3}}$$

and thus the orbital period is

$$T_r = \frac{1}{v}$$

$$= 2\sqrt{\frac{r^3}{GM_E}}.$$

It is interesting to note that this is the same as the period of an object dropped from distance $r = r_E$ and falling through a hole in the earth (see above figure) to execute simple harmonic motion.

18. **(C)**

$$\theta_0 = 45°$$

$$\alpha = 4 \text{rad} / s^2 \times \frac{180°}{\pi \text{ rad}}$$

$$= 720 / \pi \text{ deg} / s^2$$

Now

$$\theta = \theta_0 + \omega_0 t + \frac{1}{2}\alpha t^2$$

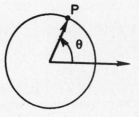

is one of the basic rotational kinematics equations.

$$\theta = 45° + \frac{360}{\pi}t^2$$

$$= 45° + 114.6° \, t^2$$

19. **(D)**

Drawing the forces acting on the body and resolving them into their *x*- and *y*-components shows that if the body is just beginning to slide it has attained the maximum static friction

$$f s_{max} = \mu_s N,$$

where N is the normal force, and μ_s is the coefficient of static friction between the surfaces.

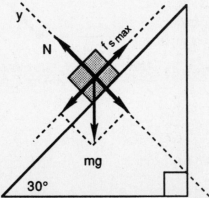

Assuming equilibrium,

$$\Sigma F_x = 0; \quad \Sigma F_y = 0$$

$$N = mg \cos 30° \quad \text{and} \quad [f_s]_{max} = mg \sin 30° \Rightarrow$$

$$\mu_s \, mg \cos 30° = mg \sin 30° \quad \mu_s = (mg \sin 30°) / (mg \cos 30°)$$

$$\mu_s = \tan 30° = 0.577 \text{ (no units)}.$$

20. **(E)**

Gauss' law for gravitation is

$$\nabla \cdot \mathbf{g} = -4\pi \, G\rho,$$

where G is the universal constant of gravitation. Applying the divergence theorem, we get

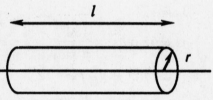

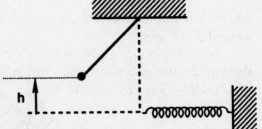

$$\oint \gamma \cdot d\alpha = -4\pi G m_{in}.$$

For an infinite line mass, the mass density is $\lambda = m/l$. Use a Gaussian cylinder for integration to get

$$\oint \mathbf{g} \cdot d\mathbf{a} = -4\pi \, G\lambda l$$

$$-g \, 2\pi \, rl = -4\pi \, G\lambda l$$

or $\mathbf{g} = -(2\lambda G / r) \, \mathbf{r}.$

21. **(C)**

By conservation of energy

$$mgh = \frac{1}{2} \, mv^2 \quad \text{or}$$

$$v = \sqrt{2gh}$$

is the pendulum bob velocity just before it hits the spring.

The conservative force is

$$F = -kx - bx^3$$

so that

$$U = -\int F dx = \frac{1}{2} \, kx^2 + \frac{1}{4} \, bx^4.$$

Again by conservation of energy

$$\frac{1}{2}\,mv^2 = mgh = \frac{1}{2}\,kx^2 + \frac{1}{4}\,bx^4.$$

Rearranging

$$\left(x^2 + \frac{k}{b}\right)^2 = \frac{4mgh}{b} + \frac{k^2}{b^2}$$

or

$$x = \left(\sqrt{\frac{4mgh}{b} + \frac{k^2}{b^2}} - \frac{k}{b}\right)^{1/2}.$$

22. **(A)**

With standard kinematics, we get

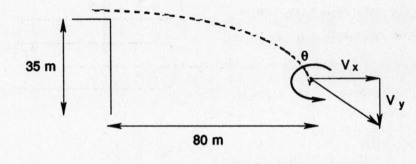

$$y = \frac{1}{2}\,gt^2,\quad t = \sqrt{2y/g} = \sqrt{80/9.8} = 2.86\,s$$

$$x = v_x t,\quad v_x = \frac{x}{t} = \frac{80}{2.86} = 28.0\ \text{m/s}$$

$$v_y^2 - v_0^2 = 2a(y - y_0)$$

$$v_y = -\sqrt{2gy} = -\sqrt{2(9.8)\,(40)} = -28.0\ \text{m/s}$$

$$\theta = A\tan\left(\frac{v_y}{v_x}\right) = 315°.$$

23. **(B)**

Since the pulley's mass is being considered and there is no slippage of the cord on the pulley, once the system is released to move freely the pulley must undergo a net torque

$$\tau = \mathbf{r} \times \mathbf{F}.$$

If the tensions were equal, the net torque would be zero. If the system is given no initial torque, upon release the pulley will rotate in the clockwise direction. This shows that the net torque is clockwise

$$T_A < T_B.$$

24. **(C)**

This is the standard Atwood's machine problem with $m_1 > m_2$. The two free body diagrams are shown here.

By Newton's second law

$$m_1 g - T = m_1 a \text{ and } T - m_2 g = m_2 a.$$

Solving the second equation

$$T = m_2 a + m_2 g$$

and substituting in the first:

$$m_1 g - m_2 a - m_2 g = m_1 a$$

$$(m_1 - m_2)g = (m_1 + m_2)a$$

$$a = (m_1 - m_2)g / (m_1 + m_2).$$

For $m_1 = 4m$ and $m_2 = m$, we obtain

$$a = \frac{3}{5} g.$$

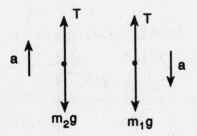

25. **(D)**

The given position vector is:

$$r = (3t + 5t^3)\mathbf{x} \quad \text{or} \quad x = 3t + 5t^3$$

$$v = \frac{dx}{dt} = 3 + 15t^2$$

$$a = \frac{dv}{dt} = 30t \Rightarrow F = ma = 60t$$

since $m = 2\,kg$ is given. The power is

$$P = \mathbf{F} \cdot \mathbf{v} = 180t + 900t^3.$$

The work is then

$$W = \int_0^1 P \, dt = \int_0^1 (180t + 900t^3) \, dt$$

$$= 90t^2 + 225t^4 \big|_0^1 = 315 \text{ J}.$$

26. **(C)**

The acceleration versus time graph provides the change in velocity necessary to compute the change in momentum. The area under the graph gives the change in velocity $[a \, \Delta \, t]$ and the graph provides the acceleration directly

$$a = 2 \text{ m/s}^2$$

$$\text{Area} = (2 \text{ m/s}^2)(5 \text{ s}) = 10 \text{ m/s} = \Delta v$$

and   impulse $= \Delta$ momentum $(\Delta p) = F \Delta t =$ (mass area)

$$\Rightarrow \Delta p = (1 \text{ kg})(10 \text{ m/s}) = 10 \text{ kg m/s}.$$

27. **(C)**
From the conservation of angular momentum,

$$(\Sigma L)_0 = (\Sigma L)_f$$

$$I_0 \omega_0 = (I_0 + I_1) \omega_f$$

$$\omega_f = \frac{I_0 \omega_0}{I_0 + I_1}.$$

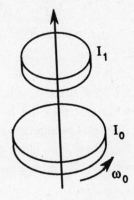

28. **(B)**
The force may be found from the derivative of the potential.

$$V = -\frac{Gmm'}{r}(1 - ae^{-r/\lambda})$$

$$\frac{dV}{dr} = \frac{Gmm'}{r^2}(1 - ae^{-r/\lambda}) - \frac{Gmm'}{r}\frac{a}{\lambda}e^{-r/\lambda}$$

$$= \frac{Gmm'}{r^2}\left(1 - ae^{-r/\lambda}\left(1 + \frac{r}{\lambda}\right)\right) \qquad \frac{r}{\lambda} \ll 1$$

$$F = -\frac{dV}{dr}\Big|_{r \ll \lambda} = -\frac{Gmm'}{r^2}(1 - a).$$

29. **(E)**
Using the free body diagram and $\Sigma F = 0$, we get

$$T_1 = mg = 2(9.8) = 19.6 \text{ N}.$$

A second free body diagram is drawn where the strings meet.

$$T_{3y} = T_1 = 19.6 \text{ N}$$

$$T_3 = T_{3y} / \sin(30°)$$

$$= 39.2 \text{ N}$$

$$T_2 = T_{3x} = T_3 \cos(30°) = 33.9 \text{ N}$$

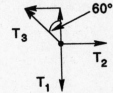

$T_1 = mg = 2(9.8) = 19.6 \text{ N}$

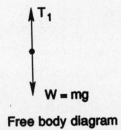

Free body diagram

30. **(B)**

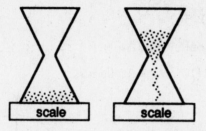

Let the initial weight be W_0 then when the hourglass is inverted, the weight must be less than W_0 while the sand is in the air.

As the sand strikes the bottom of the hourglass, it delivers impulsive forces to the scale. The effect is that the scale's measure of weight increases to a value greater than W_0. Therefore, (B) is the correct answer. However, the weight decreases to W_0 after all of the sand has fallen.

31. **(B)**

$$F = \frac{Gm_1m_2}{r^2} = \frac{(6.672 \times 10^{-8})m^2}{1^2} = 1$$

$$m = 3.87 \times 10^3 \text{ g}$$
$$= 3.87 \text{ kg}.$$

In this convenient gravitational system of units, one could take $G = 1$.

32. **(A)**

This is the standard pendulum problem, but in an effective local gravitational field

$$g_e = g + \frac{1}{2}g$$

$$= \frac{3}{2}g.$$

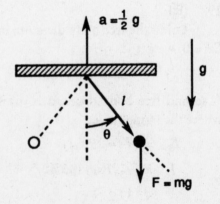

By Newton's second law for rotational motion,

$$\Sigma\tau = I\alpha$$

$$-mg_e l \sin\theta = I\theta''$$

$$= ml^2\theta''$$

Thus, $\theta'' + \frac{g_e}{l}\sin\theta = 0,$

is the equation of motion. For $\theta \ll 1$, a Taylor expansion gives $\sin \theta \approx \theta$.

Thus, $\theta'' + \omega_0^2 \theta = 0$,

where $\omega_0 = \sqrt{\dfrac{g_l}{l}} = \sqrt{\dfrac{3g}{2l}}$

is the angular frequency. Also,

$$v_0 = \frac{\omega_0}{2\pi} = \frac{1}{2\pi}\sqrt{\frac{3g}{2l}}$$

is the linear frequency. In other words, the problem may be solved by substituting g_e for g.

33. **(C)**

The basic simple harmonic motion equation is

$$x = A \cos(\omega t + \delta)$$

$$A = 16 \text{ cm}, \; T = 2 \text{ s}.$$

The linear frequency is then

$$v = 1/T \text{ or } v = {}^1/_2 \text{ Hz}.$$

Hence, $\omega = 2\pi v = \pi \text{ rad/s}$
is the angular frequency. Hence, at $t = 0$:

$$-16 = 16 \cos(+\delta)$$

$$\delta = \pi \text{ rad}.$$

Therefore,

$$x = 16 \cos(\pi t + \pi).$$

34. **(B)**

Use basic kinematics.

$$v^2 - v_0 = 2a(x - x_0)$$
$$v = \sqrt{2ax}$$
$$= \sqrt{2(9.8)\,200}$$
$$62.61 \text{ m/s}$$
$$v^2 - v_0^2 = 2a(x - x_0)$$
$$0^2 - 62.61^2 = 2a(0.5 - 2)$$
$$a = 1307 \text{ m/s}^2$$
$$a = 133 \, g$$

using $g = 9.8 \text{ m/s}^2$.

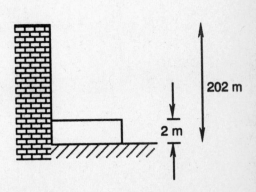

202 m

2 m

35. **(D)**

The net total force exerted on the chain (by both the surface and gravitation) at any time is equal to its mass times the acceleration of its center of mass.

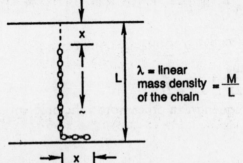

λ = linear
mass density $= \dfrac{M}{L}$
of the chain

To find the equation of motion of the center of mass, according to the figure, we can write (all the distances are evaluated with respect to the hanging point):

$$x_{cm} = \frac{\Sigma mx}{\Sigma m} = \frac{(x\lambda)L + (L-x)\lambda\left(x + \dfrac{L-x}{2}\right)}{L\lambda}$$

$$= x + \frac{L^2 - x^2}{2L}$$

$$\Rightarrow x'_{cm} = x' - \frac{xx'}{L}$$

$$x''_{cm} = x'' - \frac{xx'' + x'^2}{L} \Rightarrow Mx''_{cm} = Mg - N = M\left(x'' - \frac{xx'' + x'^2}{L}\right)$$

N: the normal force of the surface.

But $x'' = g$ since the chain is falling freely and also we have:

$$x'^2 = 2gx$$

(equation of motion with constant acceleration). So we have

$$N = \frac{M}{L}(xg + 2gx) = \frac{3M}{L}gx.$$

DETAILED EXPLANATIONS OF ANSWERS

TEST 3

Section II – Mechanics

1. (a)

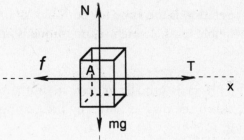

1. (b)

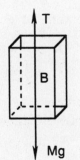

1. (c)

Resolving the vectors into the *x*- and *y*-components yields the following conditions to achieve translational equilibrium. The tension of the string (T) is equal for both blocks since the pulley simply changes the direction of the force.

$$F_x = T + (-f_s) = 0; \quad F_y = N + (-mg) = 0$$

and $\quad F_x = 0; \quad F_y = T + (-mg)$ therefore $T = Mg$

since the maximum $f_s = \mu N = \mu mg$

$$T = \mu mg = Mg \quad \mu = (Mg) / (mg) = M/m.$$

The correct answer is the minimum $\mu = [M/m]$.

1. (d)

Without friction the system will accelerate, but not at g as most students predict. Using Newton's second law for each block we find that

$$F_{net} = ma.$$

For block A:

$$T = ma.$$

For block B:

$$Mg - T = Ma \qquad Mg - (ma) = Ma$$
$$Mg = Ma + ma = (M + m)a$$
$$a = Mg/(M + a).$$

Note: The acceleration is the same for both blocks since the pulley is frictionless and of negligible mass. Therefore, no torque is present.

2. (a)

Since the object is initially at rest, its initial momentum is zero. The impulse imparted to the mass is found by integrating the force equation with respect to time:

$$F = ma \qquad F = m \, dv/dt \qquad \int F \, dt = \int m \, dv$$
$$\text{Impulse [J]} = \Delta \text{ momentum } (\Delta p) = \int F \, dt$$
$$\int 7t^3 - 2t + 4 \, dt = (7/4)t^4 - t^2 + 4t = \Delta p$$
$$\Rightarrow \Delta p = [(7/4)(5^4)] - (5^2) + (4)(5) = 1{,}089 \text{ N s.}$$

2. (b)

$$p = m\Delta v \Rightarrow (\Delta p)/m = v_f - v_0,$$

where $v_0 = 0$

$$v_f = (1{,}089 \text{ kg m/s})/(5 \text{ kg}) = 218 \text{ m/s.}$$

2. (c)

$$F = m \, dv/dt$$
$$\Rightarrow dv/dt = F/m$$

for $t = 5$ seconds.

$$F/m = [[7(5^3)] - (2)(5) + 4]/(5) = 174 \text{ m/s}^2.$$

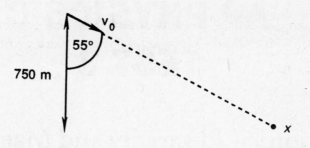

3. (a)

Using basic kinematic equations for motion with constant acceleration in the $x - y$ plane.

$$y = v_{y_0} t + 1/2\, a_y\, t^2 \quad a_y = g = 9.8 \text{ m/s}^2$$

$$750 = (v_0 \cos 55)\, 6 + 1/2\, (9.8)\, (6)^2$$

$$v_0 = 166.7 \text{ m/s.}$$

3. (b)

$$x = x_0 + v_{x_0}\, t + 1/2\, a_x\, t^2$$

but $\quad x_0 = a_x = 0$

and $\quad v_{x_0} = v_0 \sin 55$

$$x = 166.7\, (\sin 55)\, 6$$

$$= 819.3 \text{ m.}$$

3. (c)

Since there is no acceleration in the horizontal direction, $v_x = v_{x_0}$

$$v_x = 166.7\, (\sin 55)$$

$$v_x = 136.6 \text{ m/s}$$

$$v_y = v_{y_0} + a_y\, t$$

$$= (166.7)\, (\cos 55) + 9.8\, (6)$$

$$v_y = 154.4 \text{ m/s}$$

AP PHYSICS C
TEST 3

Section I – Electricity and Magnetism

TIME: 45 Minutes
        35 Questions

DIRECTIONS: Each of the questions or incomplete statements below is followed by five answer choices or completions. Choose the best answer to each question.

---

36. A wire 100 cm in length carries a current of 1.0 amp in a region where a uniform magnetic field has a magnitude of 100 Tesla in the x-direction. Calculate the magnetic force on the wire if $\theta = 45°$ is the angle between the wire and the x-axis.

    (A)   70.7 z N   (B)   141.4 z N

    (C)   – 141.4 z N   (D)   – 70.7 z N

    (E)   0 since I is not parallel to B

37. Gauss' law may be used to derive Coulomb's law. Let k_E be the constant in Coulomb's law. Furthermore, Ampere's law may be used to derive the force per unit length between two currents. Let k_B be the constant in this magnetic Coulomb law. What is the ratio k_B / k_E?

    (A) c (B) $2\mu_0 \varepsilon_0$

    (C) $2c$ (D) $\mu_0 \varepsilon_0$

    (E) c^2

38. What is the magnetic field at the center of a circular ring of radius r that carries current I?

(A) $\mu_0 I / 2r$

(B) $\mu_0 I / 2\pi r$

(C) $\mu_0 I / r$

(D) $\mu_0 I / \pi r$

(E) It is equal to zero.

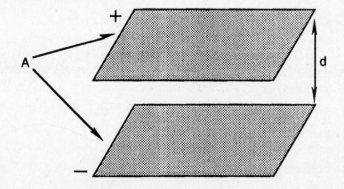

QUESTIONS 39 AND 40 refer to a parallel-plate capacitor with a plate separation of d and surface area A.

39. If the potential difference between the plates is V and the distance between the plates is d, the potential energy of the capacitor is

(A) $[\varepsilon_0 A V^2] / 2$.

(B) $[\varepsilon_0 A V^2] / 2d$.

(C) $[\varepsilon_0 A V^2] / d$.

(D) $[\varepsilon_0 A V] / 2d$.

(E) $[\varepsilon_0 A V] / d$.

40. The plates are now separated an additional distance Δd. The work required to separate the plates is equal to

(A) $\left[\dfrac{\varepsilon_0 A V^2}{2}\right]\left[\dfrac{\Delta d}{d^2 + d\Delta d}\right]$.

(B) $\left[\dfrac{\varepsilon_0 A V^2}{2}\right]\left[-\dfrac{\Delta d}{d^2 + d\Delta d}\right]$.

(C) $\left[\dfrac{\varepsilon_0 A V^2}{2}\right]\left[\dfrac{\Delta d}{d+\Delta d}\right].$ (D) $\left[\dfrac{\varepsilon_0 A V^2}{2}\right]\left[\dfrac{\Delta d}{d+\Delta d}\right].$

(E) $\left[\dfrac{\varepsilon_0 A V^2}{2}\right]\left[\dfrac{\Delta d^2}{d^2+d\Delta d}\right].$

41. What is the gravitational field of an infinite line mass of linear mass density λ?

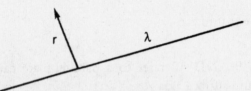

(A) $-(\lambda G/r)\,\mathbf{r}$ (B) $-(2\lambda G/r^2)\,\mathbf{r}$

(C) $(\lambda G/r)\,\mathbf{r}$ (D) $-(\lambda G/r^2)\,\mathbf{r}$

(E) $-(2\lambda G/r)\,\mathbf{r}$

42. Area of sphere $A = 4\pi r^2$

Area of sphere $B = 4\pi R^2$

A point charge P is shown with two Gaussian surfaces A and B of radii r and $R = 2r$. Which statement best describes this system?

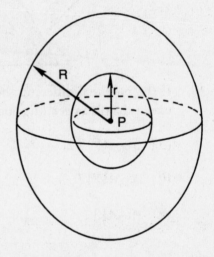

(A) Twice the electric flux passes through area B than through area A.

(B) One-half the electric flux passes through area B than through area A.

(C) One-fourth the electric flux passes through area B than through area A.

(D) Four times the electric flux passes through area *B* than through area *A*.

(E) The electric flux through each area is the same.

43. Charges q_1 and q_2 are isolated and fixed in space. The amount of work necessary to bring q_3 from infinity to point *C* is

(A) 0 J.

(B) 9.9 J.

(C) 99.0 J.

(D) 990 J.

(E) 9990 J.

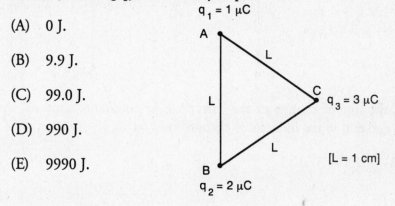

44. Figure out the total electric potential energy of a *single* spherical object of uniform charge density ρ, total charge *Q*, and radius *R*. Let $K = 1/4\,\pi\varepsilon_0$ as usual.

(A) 0

(B) kQ^2/R

(C) $1/2\ kQ^2/R$

(D) $3/5\ kQ^2/R$

(E) $2/3\ kQ^2/R$

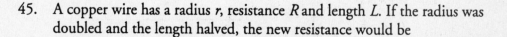

45. A copper wire has a radius *r*, resistance *R* and length *L*. If the radius was doubled and the length halved, the new resistance would be

(A) 1/8 *R*.　　　　　(B) 1/4 *R*.

(C) *R*.　　　　　(D) 4*R*.

(E) 8*R*.

46. Consider the problem of four infinite charged planes situated as shown. Find the electric field in the region $|x| < a/2$.

    (A) $\sigma / 2\,\varepsilon_0\,x$

    (B) $-\sigma / 2\,\varepsilon_0\,x$

    (C) $2\sigma / \varepsilon_0\,x$

    (D) $-2\sigma / \varepsilon_0\,x$

    (E) 0

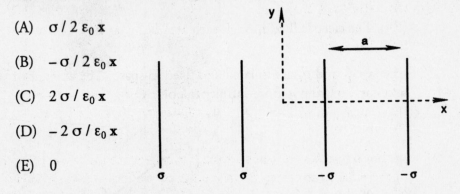

47. If the rate of change of the current in an inductor is tripled, the induced emf in the inductor is changed by a factor of

    (A) 1/9.   (B) 1/3.

    (C) 1.   (D) 3.

    (E) 9.

48. A capacitor is constructed from two rectangular metal plates of area A separated by a distance d. Suppose that one-half of the space between the plates is filled by a dielectric κ_1 and the other half by a dielectric κ_2. Find the capacitance in terms of the free space capacitance C_0.

    (A) $2\kappa_1 \kappa_2\, C_0 / (\kappa_1 + \kappa_2)$

    (B) $(\kappa_1 + \kappa_2)\, C_0$

    (C) C_0

    (D) $(\kappa_1 + \kappa_2)\, C_0 / 2$

    (E) $\kappa_1 \kappa_2\, C_0 / (\kappa_1 + \kappa_2)$

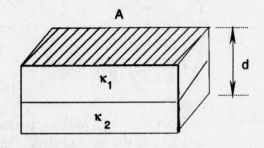

49. Two parallel conductors separated by a distance $r = 10$ cm carry currents $I_1 = 1.5$ amps and $I_2 = 2.0$ amps in the same direction as shown below. What is the force per unit length exerted on the second conductor by the first?

(A) $(-\mu_0 I_1 I_2 / 2\pi x)$ **x**

(B) $(\mu_0 I_1 I_2 / 2\pi x)$ **x**

(C) $(\mu_0 I_1 I_2 / \pi x)$ **x**

(D) $(-\mu_0 I_1 I_2 / \pi x)$ **x**

(E) $(\mu_0 \pi I_1 I_2 / x)$ **x**

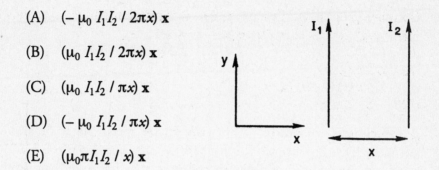

50. In the circuit shown, when switch 1 is closed, the instantaneous current in the circuit (assuming the resistance of the inductor to be negligible) is

    (A) zero.

    (B) V/R.

    (C) V/L.

    (D) $(V/L)\ dt$.

    (E) $(V/R)\ dt$.

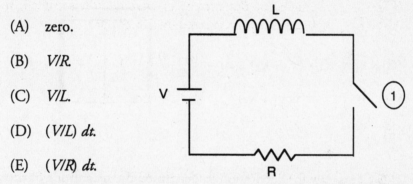

51. Use Ampere's law to derive for the magnetic field of a toroid (N turns each carrying current I) of inner radius a and outer radius b at a distance r midway between a and b.

    (A) $\mu_0 NI / 2\pi (a + b)$

    (B) $\mu_0 NI / \pi (a + b)$

    (C) $\mu_0 NI / \pi b$

    (D) $\mu_0 I / \pi (a + b)$

    (E) $4 \mu_0 NI / \pi (a + b)$

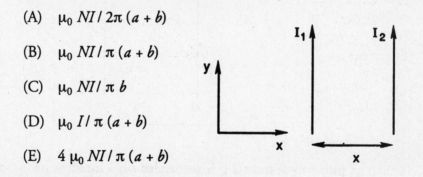

52. A rod 20 cm long has a total charge $q = -75\ \mu C$. Find the electric field along the axis of the rod 10 cm from one end.

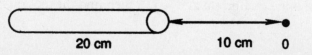

20 cm   **10 cm**   0

(A) $-5.50 \times 10^5 \ N/C \mathbf{x}$ (B) $-2.25 \times 10^5 \ N/C \mathbf{x}$

(C) 0 N/C   (D) $2.25 \times 10^5 \ N/C \mathbf{x}$

(E) 5.50×10^5 N/C $\mathbf{x}$

53. A capacitor is constructed from two square metal plates of area L^2 separated by a distance d. One-half of the space between the plates is filled with a substance of dielectric constant (κ_1). The other half is filled with another substance with constant (κ_2). Calculate the capacitance of the device assuming that the free space capacitance is C_0.

(A) $.5 \ C_0 \ \kappa_1 \ \kappa_2 \ / \ (\kappa_1 + \kappa_2)$

(B) $(\kappa_1 + \kappa_2) \ C_0$

(C) $\kappa_1 \ \kappa_2 \ C_0 \ / \ (\kappa_1 + \kappa_2)$

(D) $2 \ \kappa_1 \ \kappa_2 \ C_0 \ / \ (\kappa_1 + \kappa_2)$

(E) $(\kappa_1 + \kappa_2) \ C_0 \ / \ 2$

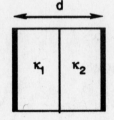

54. Use Gauss' law for gravitation to determine the magnitude of the gravitational field for two infinite sheets of mass density σ in regions I and III.

(A) $4\pi G\sigma$

(B) $2\pi G\sigma$

(C) $\pi G\sigma$

(D) $2\pi G\sigma / \varepsilon_0$

(E) 0

55. A charged pith ball of mass 2 g is suspended on a massless string in an electric field

$$E = (3x + 4y) \times 10^5 \ \text{N/C}.$$

If the ball is in equilibrium at $\theta = 57°$, then find the tension in the string.

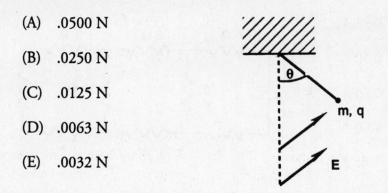

(A) .0500 N

(B) .0250 N

(C) .0125 N

(D) .0063 N

(E) .0032 N

56. Determine the electric potential of the infinite sheet of charge shown below for $x > 0$. Let the charge density be σ and the x-direction be to the right.

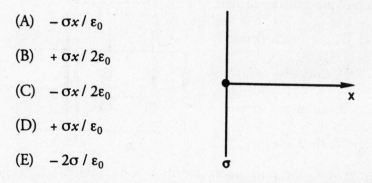

(A) $- \sigma x / \varepsilon_0$

(B) $+ \sigma x / 2\varepsilon_0$

(C) $- \sigma x / 2\varepsilon_0$

(D) $+ \sigma x / \varepsilon_0$

(E) $- 2\sigma / \varepsilon_0$

57. In the circuit shown, the battery has an emf and internal resistance r. The meter reads 12.0 volts when the switch is open. When the switch is closed, the steady-state reading on the voltmeter is 11.6 volts. The resistance of the wires and switch are negligible. $R_{meter} = \infty$. What is the internal resistance (r) of the battery?

(A) 0.69 ohms

(B) 0.90 ohms

(C) 1.5 ohms

(D) 4.8 ohms

(E) 5.2 ohms

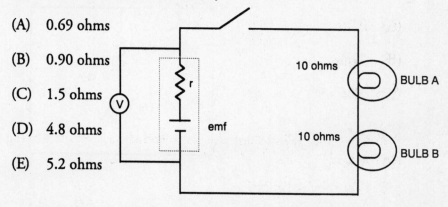

58. Consider the circuit shown below. Calculate the effective resistance of the circuit and use this knowledge to find the current in the 4Ω resistor.

(A)   0.25 A

(B)   0.50 A

(C)   0.75 A

(D)   1.00 A

(E)   1.25 A

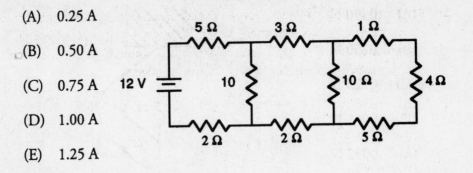

59. Consider that a sliding conductive bar closes the circuit shown below and moves to the right with a speed $v = 4$ m/s. If $l = 1.5$ m, $R = 12\Omega$, and $B = 5$ T, then find the magnitude of the induced power and the direction of the induced current.

(A)   75 W, counterclockwise

(B)   75 W, clockwise

(C)   2.5 W, counterclockwise

(D)   2.5 W, clockwise

(E)   0 W, there is no current flow

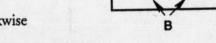

60. In the circuit below, switch 1 is closed until the capacitor is fully charged. Then, switch 1 is opened and switch 2 is closed. Immediately after switch 2 is closed the instantaneous current through the resistance R is

(A)   0.

(B) V/R.

(C) R/V.

(D) CV.

(E) CR.

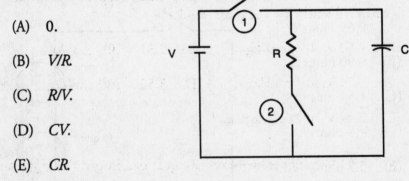

61. A beam of singly ionized boron is accelerated through a potential difference of 4 kilovolts and then passed through a mass spectrometer with
magnetic field $B = 0.5$ Tesla. What is the radius R through which the
boron is bent? Note $A = 10.0129$ amu for boron.

   (A)   5.76 cm   (B)   2.88 cm

   (C)   8.64 cm   (D)   11.52 cm

   (E)   14.40 cm

62. Two wires are bent into semicircles of radius a as shown. If the upper
half has resistance $2R\,\Omega$ and the lower half has resistance $R\,\Omega$, then find
the magnetic field at the center of the circle in terms of the current I.

   (A) $-(\mu_0\, I\, /\, 12a)\, z$

   (B) $(\mu_0\, I\, /\, 12a)\, z$

   (C) $-(\mu_0\, I\, /\, 6a)\, z$

   (D) $(\mu_0\, I\, /\, 4a)\, z$

   (E) $-(\mu_0\, I\, /\, 4a)\, z$

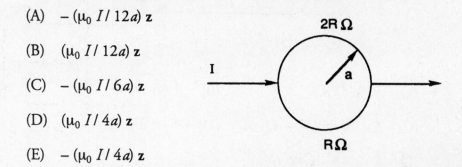

63. Suppose that the parameters in J.J. Thomson's *e/m* apparatus are: path
length of deflecting plates = 5 cm, plate separation = 1.5 cm, potential
between deflecting plates = 50 volts, and deflection of the beam when
the magnetic field is off = 1.25 mm. Further suppose that no deflection
is observed when $B = 1.2$ gauss. Find *e/m*.

   (A) 4.62×10^{11} coul/kg   (B) 2.31×10^{11} coul/kg

   (C) 1.76×10^{11} coul/kg   (D) 3.52×10^{11} coul/kg

   (E) 2.04×10^{11} coul/kg

64. Which of the following Maxwell equations imply that there are no
magnetic monopoles?

   (A) $\nabla \cdot E = \dfrac{\rho}{\varepsilon_0}$ (B) $\nabla \cdot B = 0$

(C) $\nabla \times E = -\dfrac{\partial B}{\partial T}$

(D) $\nabla \times B = \mu_0 J + \mu_0 \varepsilon_0 \dfrac{\partial E}{\partial T}$

(E)   Magnetic monopoles have recently been found.

65.   A resistor is made from a hollow cylinder of length l, inner radius a, and outer radius b. The region $a < r < b$ is filled with material of resistivity ρ. Find the resistance R of this component.

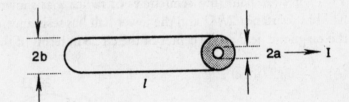

(A) $R = \rho \, l / \pi \, b^2$
(B) $R = \rho \, l / \pi \, a^2$

(C) $R = \rho \, l / \pi \, (b^2 - a^2)$
(D) $R = \pi \, b^2 \rho / l$

(E) $R = \pi \, (b^2 - a^2) \, \rho / l$

66.   Consider a circuit that consists of four resistors (each with $R = 1 \, M\Omega$), a capacitor ($C = 1 \, \mu F$), and a battery ($V = 10 \, MV$) as shown. If the capacitor is fully charged and then the battery is removed, find the current at $t = 0.5$ s as the capacitor discharges.

(A)   40 A

(B)   20 A

(C)   24.3 A

(D)   14.7 A

(E)   5.4 A

TEST 3
Section I – Mechanics

$$\boxed{\textbf{ANSWER KEY}}$$

1.	(B)	10.	(E)	19.	(D)	28.	(B)
2.	(C)	11.	(D)	20.	(E)	29.	(E)
3.	(A)	12.	(E)	21.	(C)	30.	(B)
4.	(D)	13.	(E)	22.	(A)	31.	(B)
5.	(B)	14.	(D)	23.	(B)	32.	(A)
6.	(A)	15.	(B)	24.	(C)	33.	(C)
7.	(B)	16.	(B)	25.	(D)	34.	(B)
8.	(D)	17.	(D)	26.	(C)	35.	(D)
9.	(D)	18.	(C)	27.	(C)		

$$F_{\text{drag}} = Cv^2 = mg \Rightarrow [(mg) / C]^{0.5} = v_{\text{terminal}}.$$

9. **(D)**

Since the system is in equilibrium, the sum of the torques with respect to any point must be zero. By choosing the point of the beam to the wall as the reference, we can write:

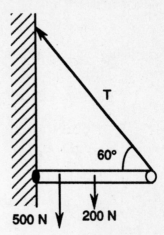

$$\Sigma\tau = 0, \quad \tau = rF\sin\alpha$$

$$(500)\,(2)\sin(90°) + (200)\,(5)\sin(90°)$$

$$-\,(10)\,(T)\sin(120°) = 0.$$

Therefore, $T = 231$ N is the desired tension.

10. **(E)**

This problem is very similar to motion in a constant gravitational field. By the definition of electric field:

$$F = qE = -\,eE = ma$$

$$\Rightarrow \quad a = -\,eE/m$$

$$= -\,(1.6 \times 10^{-19})\,(100) / (9.1 \times 10^{-31})$$

$$= -\,1.76 \times 10^{13} \text{ m/s}^2.$$

Then from kinematics

$$v_y = v_{oy} + at$$

$$0 = v_o \sin\theta + at$$

$$t = -\,v_o \sin\theta/a$$

$$T = -\,2\,v_o \sin\theta / a$$

$$= -\,2\,(4 \times 10^5)\,(\sin 30°) / (-\,1.76 \times 10^{13})$$

$$= 2.3 \times 10^{-8} \text{ s}$$

$$= 23 \text{ ns}.$$

since the time of flight is twice the time to reach the apex.

11. **(D)**

Lissajous figures are generated from the coupled harmonic equations

$$\begin{cases} x'' + \omega_x^2 x = 0 \\ y'' + \omega_y^2 y = 0 \end{cases}$$

$$\frac{1}{2}gT^2 + \frac{1}{2}g\frac{d^2}{v^2} - gT\frac{d}{v} - d = 0$$

$$d^2 - d\left(\frac{2v^2}{g} + 2vT\right) + v^2T^2 = 0,$$

$$v = 330 \text{ m/s} \quad g = 9.8 \text{ m/s}^2$$

$$d^2 - 23{,}583.4d + 461{,}679.5 = 0$$

$$d = \frac{-b \pm \sqrt{b^2 - 4ac}}{2a} = \frac{23{,}583.4 - 23{,}544.2}{2}$$

$$= 19.6 \text{ m}.$$

16. **(B)**

Since the system is in equilibrium, Newton's second law shows that

$$F_{net} = Ma = M(0) = 0 \Rightarrow$$

$$F_x = (- T_B \cos 20°) + (T_A \cos 50°) = 0 \tag{1}$$

$$F_y = (T_A \sin 50°) + (T_B \sin 30°) + (- Mg) = 0 \tag{2}$$

and by solving for T_A in terms of T_B in equation (1),

$$T_A = T_B (\cos 20°/\cos 50°).$$

By substituting this value into equation (2) we find

$$[T_B (\cos 20°/\cos 50°)] \sin 50° + T_B \sin 20° = Mg.$$

Solving this equation for T_B shows $T_B = 0.684 \, Mg$.

Therefore, $T_B < Mg$.

17. **(D)**

An object propelled horizontally at distance r from the center of the earth into a circular orbit feels a force

$$F = \frac{GmM}{r^2} = \frac{mv^2}{r}.$$

Hence,

$$v^2 = \frac{GM}{r} \quad \text{and} \quad v = \sqrt{\frac{GM}{r}} = r\omega.$$

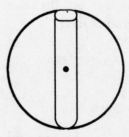

The linear frequency is then

$$v = \frac{\omega}{2\pi} = \frac{1}{2\pi}\sqrt{\frac{GM}{r^3}}$$

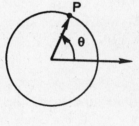

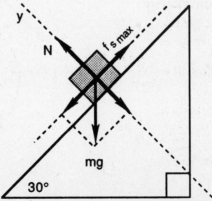

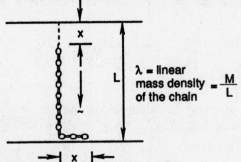

61. A beam of singly ionized boron is accelerated through a potential difference of 4 kilovolts and then passed through a mass spectrometer with magnetic field $B = 0.5$ Tesla. What is the radius R through which the boron is bent? Note $A = 10.0129$ amu for boron.

(A)   5.76 cm   (B)   2.88 cm

(C)   8.64 cm   (D)   11.52 cm

(E)   14.40 cm

62. Two wires are bent into semicircles of radius a as shown. If the upper half has resistance $2R\,\Omega$ and the lower half has resistance $R\,\Omega$, then find the magnetic field at the center of the circle in terms of the current I.

(A) $-(\mu_0\,I\,/\,12a)\,\mathbf{z}$

(B) $(\mu_0\,I\,/\,12a)\,\mathbf{z}$

(C) $-(\mu_0\,I\,/\,6a)\,\mathbf{z}$

(D) $(\mu_0\,I\,/\,4a)\,\mathbf{z}$

(E) $-(\mu_0\,I\,/\,4a)\,\mathbf{z}$

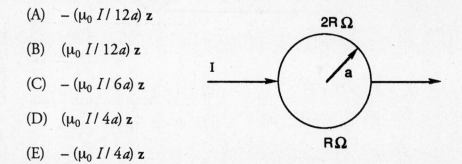

63. Suppose that the parameters in J.J. Thomson's e/m apparatus are: path length of deflecting plates = 5 cm, plate separation = 1.5 cm, potential between deflecting plates = 50 volts, and deflection of the beam when the magnetic field is off = 1.25 mm. Further suppose that no deflection is observed when $B = 1.2$ gauss. Find e/m.

(A) 4.62×10^{11} coul/kg   (B) 2.31×10^{11} coul/kg

(C) 1.76×10^{11} coul/kg   (D) 3.52×10^{11} coul/kg

(E) 2.04×10^{11} coul/kg

64. Which of the following Maxwell equations imply that there are no magnetic monopoles?

(A) $\nabla \cdot \mathbf{E} = \dfrac{\rho}{\varepsilon_0}$ (B) $\nabla \cdot \mathbf{B} = 0$

67. For the circuit shown, find the amount of current that passes through the 5 Ω resistor.

(A)   0.873 A

(B)   0.127 A

(C)   0.346 A

(D)   0.254 A

(E)   0.654 A

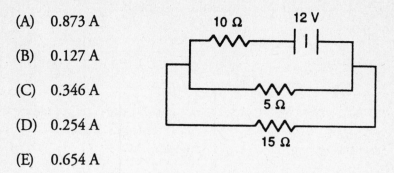

68. Consider a series RL circuit with $R = 10\ \Omega$, $L = 10\ \mu H$, and $V = 30$ volts. Suppose that $I = 0$ at $t = 0$. Find the energy stored in the inductor as $t \rightarrow \infty$.

(A) 9.0×10^{-5} J   (B)   90 J

(C)   45 J   (D) 4.5×10^{-5} J

(E) 1.5×10^{-5} J

69. What must the speed of the sliding bar be when the current in the resistor is 0.5 amp given that $B = 1\ T$, $R = 2\ \Omega$, and $w = .5$ m.

(A)   2 m/s

(B)   4 m/s

(C)   1 m/s

(D)   3 m/s

(E)   5 m/s

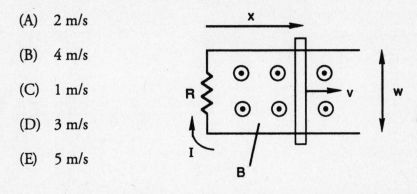

70. Two infinite nonconducting sheets of charge are parallel to each other. Each sheet has a positive uniform charge density σ. Calculate the value of the electric field to the right of the two sheets.

(A) 0

(B) $\dfrac{\sigma}{2\varepsilon_0}\mathbf{x}$

(C) $-\dfrac{\sigma}{2\varepsilon_0}\mathbf{x}$

(D) $-\dfrac{\sigma}{\varepsilon_0}\mathbf{x}$

(E) $\dfrac{\sigma}{\varepsilon_0}\mathbf{x}$

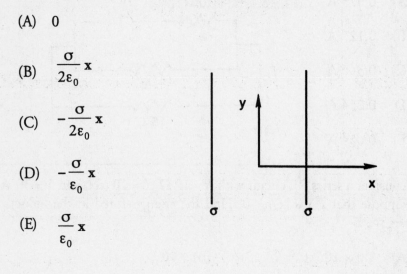

AP PHYSICS C
TEST 3

Section II – Electricity and Magnetism

TIME: 45 Minutes
3 Questions

DIRECTIONS: Allow 10 to 15 minutes of time per question.

---

1.   Three point charges are in a triangular configuration as shown below.

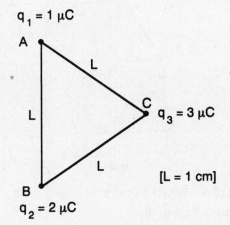

$q_1 = 1\ \mu C$

$q_3 = 3\ \mu C$

$q_2 = 2\ \mu C$

[L = 1 cm]

(a)   Assuming that all three charges were brought to their respective positions from infinity, determine the work required to achieve this system.

(b)   Find the electrical potential energy of the system.

2.   A parallel-plate capacitor possesses a plate surface area of A and a plate separation of d. The potential difference between the plates is V. The permittivity of free space is ε_0.

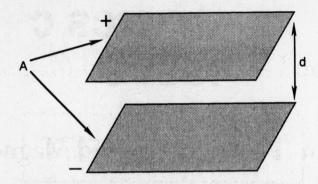

(a) Assuming there is a vacuum between the plates, determine the capacitance.

(b) A dielectric κ is now placed between the plates. Find the capacitance of this configuration.

(c) Two new dielectric of values κ_1 and κ_2 are placed between the plates as shown. Find the new capacitance of this system.

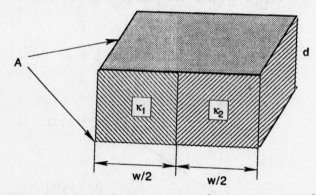

3. The L-R circuit shown below is in steady state. Assume the resistance of the inductor is negligible.

(a) Determine the current through the circuit.

(b) Find the time constant for this circuit. The switch is positioned so that the circuit is in the configuration shown below.

(c) Sketch the graph of instantaneous current (i) versus time (t) for the time $t = 0$ to steady state.

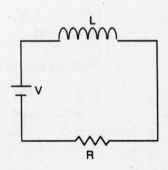

TEST 3
Section I – Electricity and Magnetism

36. (D)	45. (A)	54. (A)	63. (B)
37. (B)	46. (C)	55. (C)	64. (B)
38. (A)	47. (D)	56. (C)	65. (C)
39. (B)	48. (A)	57. (A)	66. (E)
40. (B)	49. (A)	58. (A)	67. (E)
41. (E)	50. (A)	59. (A)	68. (D)
42. (E)	51. (B)	60. (B)	69. (A)
43. (B)	52. (B)	61. (A)	70. (E)
44. (D)	53. (D)	62. (B)	

DETAILED EXPLANATIONS OF ANSWERS

TEST 3

Section I – Electricity and Magnetism

36. **(D)**

$$F = ILB \sin \theta$$

$$= (1)(1)(100)\left(\frac{1}{\sqrt{2}}\right)$$

$$= 70.7 \text{ Newtons}$$

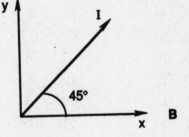

The direction of F is $-z$ (right-hand rule).

37. **(B)**

Derivation of Coulomb's law from Gauss' law:

$$\nabla \cdot E = \rho / \varepsilon_0$$

$$\oint \nabla \cdot E \, dV = \oint E \cdot d\mathbf{a}$$

by the divergence theorem.

$$\oint E \cdot d\mathbf{a} = \oint \rho \, dV / \varepsilon_0.$$

For a point charge

$$E \cdot 4\pi r^2 = q / \varepsilon_0$$

$$E = q / 4\pi\varepsilon_0 r^2$$

for a charge $q = q_1$

$$E_1 = q_1 / 4\pi\varepsilon_0 r^2$$

$$F = q_2 E_1 = q_1 q_2 / 4\pi\varepsilon_0 r^2 = k_E q_1 q_2 / r^2$$

for the force on another charge q_2 due to q_1.

Using Ampere's law:

$$\nabla \times B = \mu_0 \mathbf{j}$$

$$\int \nabla \times \mathbf{B} \cdot d\mathbf{a} = \oint \mathbf{B} \cdot d\mathbf{l}$$

by Stoke's theorem.

$$\int \mathbf{B} \cdot d\mathbf{a} = \mu_0 \int \mathbf{j} \cdot d\mathbf{a}$$

For a line current

$$2\pi\, r\, B = \mu_0\, I$$
$$B = \mu_0\, I \,/\, 2\pi\, r$$
$$B_1 = \mu_0\, I_1 \,/\, 2\pi\, r.$$

For a current $I = I_1$.

The Lorentz force is

$$\mathbf{F} = q_2\, \mathbf{v} \times \mathbf{B} = I_2\, \mathbf{l} \times \mathbf{B}$$
$$F / l = \mu_0\, I_1\, I_2 \,/\, 2\pi\, r = k_B\, I_1\, I_2 \,/\, r.$$

Hence:
$$\frac{k_B}{k_E} = \frac{\mu_0}{2\pi}\, 4\pi\varepsilon_0$$

$$= 2\mu_0\varepsilon_0.$$

38. **(A)**
Use

$$d\mathbf{B} = \frac{\mu_0}{4\pi} \cdot \frac{I d\mathbf{l} \times \mathbf{r}}{r^2}$$

the Biot-Savart Law where **r** is the unit radial vector. Only the z component of B is non-zero at the origin.

$$(d\mathbf{l} \times \mathbf{r})_z = r\,d\theta$$
$$B_z = \left(\frac{\mu_0 I}{4\pi}\right)\int_0^{2\pi} \frac{d\theta}{r} = \frac{\mu_0 I}{2r}$$

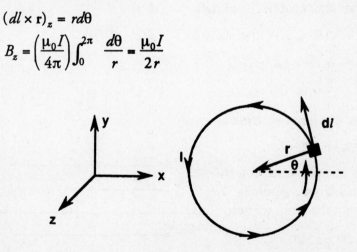

39. **(B)**

Using the relationship between capacitance, plate separation (d), and permittivity (ε_0)

$$C = \varepsilon_0 \, A/d.$$

The work necessary to charge a capacitor from zero to a final charge of Q (assuming a constant potential of V) is

$$dW = Vdq \quad \int dW = \int Vdq$$
$$= V \int dq$$
$$= \int (q/c) \, dq$$
$$= (1/C) \int q \, dq$$
$$= (1/C) \, (q^2) \, / \, 2$$
$$= (Q^2) \, / \, (2C) = [(CV)^2] \, / \, [2C]$$
$$= 1/2 \, CV^2.$$

The potential energy $(U) = W = (1/2) \, (\varepsilon_0 \, A/d) \, V^2$.

40. **(B)**

Assuming that the total work done on the system is equal to the change in the electric potential energy of the capacitor,

$$W = U = U_f - U_0 = [1/2 \, C' \, V^2] - [1/2 \, CV^2],$$

where C' is the new capacitance with a plate separation of $(d + \Delta d)$.

$$U = [1/2 \, (\varepsilon_0 \, A/(d + \Delta d)) \, V^2] - [1/2 \, (\varepsilon_0 \, A/d) \, V^2]$$
$$= (1/2 \, \varepsilon_0 \, AV^2) \, [((d + \Delta d)^{-1}) - (d^{-1})]$$
$$= (1/2 \, \varepsilon_0 \, AV^2) \, [(d - d - \Delta d) \, / \, (d \, (d + \Delta d))]$$
$$= \varepsilon_0 \, AV^2 \, / \, 2 \, [- \Delta d / \, (d^2 + d\Delta d)]$$

41. **(E)**

Gauss' law for gravitation is

$$\nabla \cdot g = -4\pi G\rho,$$

where G is the universal constant of gravitation. Applying the divergence theorem, we get

$$\oint \gamma \cdot d\alpha = -4\pi Gm_{in}.$$

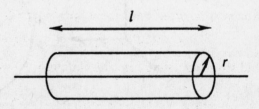

For an infinite line mass, the

mass density is $\lambda = m/l$. Use a Gaussian cylinder for integration to get

$$\oint \mathbf{g} \cdot d\mathbf{a} = -4\pi G \lambda l$$

$$-g 2\pi r l = -4\pi G \lambda l$$

or $\qquad \mathbf{g} = -(2\lambda G / r)\, \mathbf{r}.$

42. (E)

The total surface area of each sphere is proportional to the square of the radius. Since $R = 2r$, the area of Gaussian surface B is

$$4\pi (2r)^2.$$

This is 2^2, or 4 times the surface area of Gaussian surface A.

But, all of the lines of electric flux [Φ] must pass through both surfaces; therefore,

$$\Phi_A = \Phi_B.$$

43. (B)

Using infinity as the zero potential reference, choose any one of the charges and bring it from infinity to its present position. Since there are no other charges assumed to be present, no work is done. Choosing q_1 as the initial charge,

$$W_1 = -\int F_E \, dx = 0.$$

Bringing q_2 from infinity requires work since there is an increasing repulsive force between the two charges

$$W_2 = -\int_\infty^L F \, dx = (k\, q_1\, q_2) / L.$$

(Where $k = 1/4\pi\varepsilon_0$)

Bringing q_3 from infinity requires working against both q_1 and q_2. The total work done is equal to the work done against each charge

$$W_3 = [(k\, q_1\, q_3) / L] + [(k\, q_2\, q_3)) / L].$$

So the total work done is the sum of the work done for each charge

$$W_T = (k / L)\, [(q_1\, q_2) + (q_1\, q_3) + (q_2\, q_3)].$$

Substituting values into the equation:

$$((9 \times 10^9\, \text{Nm}^2/\, C^2)/(0.01\text{m}))[((2 \times 10^{-12})+(6 \times 10^{-12}) + (3 \times 10^{-12}))C^2]$$

$$= 9.9 \text{ Joules}.$$

44. **(D)**

Consider the electric potential energy between the spherical shell of differential charge

$$dq = 4\pi r^2 dr\rho$$

and the central charge

$$q = \frac{4}{3}\pi r^3 \rho.$$

The differential potential energy is

$$dU = kqdq/r$$

$$= 16\pi^2 k\rho^2 r^4 \, dr / 3.$$

The spherical charge distribution is total electric potential energy is then

$$U = \frac{16\pi^2 k\rho^2}{3}\int_0^R r^4 dr$$

$$= \frac{16}{15}\pi^2 k\rho^2 R^5.$$

Since

$$Q = \int \rho d^3 r = \frac{4}{3}\pi R^3 \rho,$$

we arrange to get

$$U = \frac{3}{5}kQ^2 / R.$$

45. **(A)**

Under normal temperature conditions, the resistance of a wire is dependent on several factors. The decrease in length means less work necessary to move a charge the length of the wire,

$$R \propto L.$$

The increase in diameter means an increase in cross-sectional area or as d increases, R decreases,

$$R \propto 1/A,$$

where A is the cross-sectional area of the wire

$$[A = \pi R^2].$$

The type of material determines the conductivity of the wire. The reciprocal of the conductivity is the resistivity [ρ].

The resistance of the wire is calculated by the equation

$$R = \rho(L/A)$$

$$\Rightarrow R' / R = [(L/2) / (\pi(2r)^2] / [L/(\pi r^2)] = 1/8$$

so the new resistance is $1/8R$ or $R/8$.

46. **(C)**

For an infinite charged plane

$$\int \mathbf{E} \cdot d\mathbf{a} = q / \varepsilon_0$$

by Gauss' law or Maxwell's first equation:

$$EA + EA = \sigma \cdot A / \varepsilon_0$$

$$E = \sigma / 2\varepsilon_0.$$

In between the planes where $-a/2 < x < a/2$, there are four identical contributions

$$\mathbf{E} = 4\,\sigma/2\varepsilon_0\,\mathbf{x} = 2\,\sigma/\varepsilon_0\,\mathbf{x}.$$

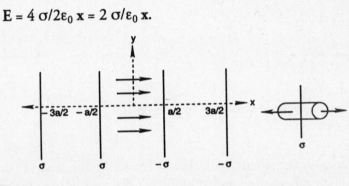

47. **(D)**

The induced emf in an inductor is defined by the equation

$$\varepsilon = -L\,di/dt.$$

Since a changing current creates a changing magnetic field which tries to counter any current change in that circuit (which is the basis of the concept self-inductance), the two circuit parameters are directly related. If the current is tripled, the induced emf [ε] is tripled.

48. **(A)**

In vacuum,

$$C_0 = \varepsilon_0\,A/d.$$

In a dielectric,

$$C = \kappa\,\varepsilon_0\,A/d.$$

Here we really have two capacitors in series:

$$C_1 = \frac{\kappa_1\varepsilon_0 A}{d/2}, \quad C_2 = \frac{\kappa_2\varepsilon_0 A}{d/2}.$$

The rule for adding capacitance in series is:

$$C = C_1 C_2 / (C_1 + C_2).$$

Hence, $= \kappa_1 \kappa_2 (2 \, \varepsilon_0 \, A/d)^2 / (\kappa_1 + \kappa_2) (2 \, \varepsilon_0 \, A/d)$

$= 2 \, \kappa_1 \, \kappa_2 \, C_0 / (\kappa_1 + \kappa_2).$

49. **(A)**

$$B_1 = \frac{\mu_0 I_1}{2\pi x}$$

is the magnetic field produced by I_1 at distance $r = x$. The force I_1 exerts on I_2 is given by:

$$F_2 = I_2 \, LB_1.$$

Force per unit length =

$$\frac{F_2}{L} = \frac{\mu_0 I_1 I_2}{2\pi x}$$

in the $- x$-direction.

The force is attractive between like currents.

50. **(A)**

At time $t = 0$, the circuit is affected by the self-inductance (L) of the coil (inductor) which generates a counter emf that tries to moderate the change in current in the circuit such that

$$\varepsilon = - L \, di/dt \text{ therefore } V - (L \, di/dt) - iR = 0$$

from Kirchoff's voltage law.

Rearranging this equation and integrating yields the classic equation for instantaneous current $i(t)$

$$i(t) = (V/R) (1 - e^{-(R/L)t}).$$

This problem can be solved by (a) plugging in zero for time and finding that the current is zero.

51. **(B)**

We use Ampere's law

$$\oint \mathbf{B} \cdot dl = \mu_0 I_{in}$$

and take the Amperean path as a circle of radius r. Hence,

$$B(2\pi r) = \mu_0 NI$$

$$B = \frac{\mu_0}{2\pi} \frac{NI}{r} \qquad r = \frac{a+b}{2}$$

$$B = \frac{\mu_0 NI}{\pi(a+b)}.$$

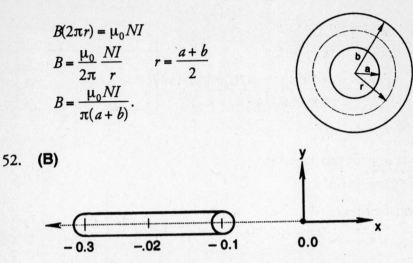

52. **(B)**

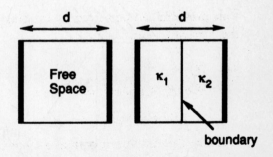

The given charge is

$$q = -75\,\mu\,C.$$

Therefore, the linear charge density is

$$\lambda = \frac{q}{l} = \frac{-75 \times 10^{-6}}{.20} = -3.7\mu C/\,m.$$

Now calculate the electric field

$$E = \int \frac{dq}{4\pi\varepsilon_0 r^2}\mathbf{r} = \frac{1}{4\pi\varepsilon_0}\int_{-.30}^{-.10} \frac{\lambda dx}{x^2}(-\mathbf{x})$$

$$= \frac{-\lambda}{4\pi\varepsilon_0}\left(\frac{1}{.10} - \frac{1}{.30}\right)\mathbf{x}$$

$$= -2.25 \times 10^5\,N/C\,\mathbf{x}.$$

Substituting

$$\varepsilon_0 = 8.85 \times 10^{-12}.$$

53. **(D)**

$$C_0 = \frac{\varepsilon_0 L^2}{d}$$

D is continuous across boundary where

$$D = \kappa_0\kappa_1 E_1 = \kappa_0\kappa_2 E_2 = \frac{q}{L^2}$$

$$V = E_1\frac{d}{2} + E_2\frac{d}{2}$$

$$V = \frac{d}{2\kappa_0}\left(\frac{1}{\kappa_1} + \frac{1}{\kappa_2}\right)\frac{q}{L^2}$$

$$C = \frac{q}{V} = \frac{2\kappa_0 L^2}{d}\left(\frac{\kappa_1\kappa_2}{\kappa_1 + \kappa_2}\right) = \frac{2C_0\kappa_1\kappa_2}{\kappa_1 + \kappa_2}.$$

54. **(A)**

Gauss' law for gravitation is

$$\nabla \cdot \mathbf{g} = -4\pi G\rho$$

in differential form or

$$\oint \mathbf{g} \cdot d\mathbf{a} = -4\pi G m_{in}$$

in integral form. For a single infinite sheet of mass density $\sigma = m / A$ use a Gaussian pillbox as in the figure. Then

$$\oint \mathbf{g} \cdot d\mathbf{a} = -4\pi G m_{in}$$

$$-gA - gA = -4\pi G\sigma A$$

$$2gA = 4\pi G\sigma A$$

$$g = 2\pi G\sigma.$$

For two sheets, the field will be $4\pi G\sigma$ in magnitude in regions I and III and zero in region II.

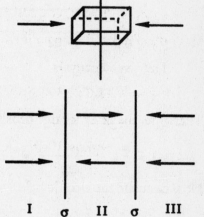

I   σ   II   σ   III

55. **(C)**

We are given that

$$m = 2g,$$

$$E = (3x + 4y) \times 10^5 \text{ N/C},$$

and $\theta = 33°$.

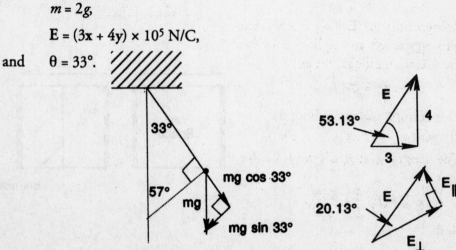

The angle **E** makes with respect to the horizontal is found from

$$\tan \theta = \frac{E_y}{E_x}$$

$$= \frac{4}{3}$$

$$\Rightarrow \theta = 58.13°.$$

We resolve **E** into parallel and perpendicular components:

$$E_{\parallel} = 5 \times 10^5 \sin 20.13 = 1.72 \times 10^5 \text{ N/C}$$

$$E_{\perp} = 5 \times 10^5 \cos 20.13 = 4.70 \times 10^5 \text{ N/C}$$

Since the pith ball is in equilibrium

$$qE_{\perp} = mg \sin \theta$$

$$q = (.002)(9.8) \sin (33°) / 5 \times 10^5 \cos (20.13°)$$

$$= 2.27 \times 10^{-8} \text{ C}$$

$$T = mg \cos \theta - qE_{\parallel}$$

$$= (.002)(9.8) \cos (33°) - (2.27 \times 10^{-8})(1.72 \times 10^5)$$

$$= 0.0125 \text{ N}.$$

56. **(C)**
The electric field of an infinite sheet of surface charge may be found from Gauss' law.

$$\nabla \cdot \mathbf{E} = \rho / \varepsilon_0$$

$$\oint \mathbf{E} \cdot d\mathbf{a} = q_{in} / \varepsilon_0.$$

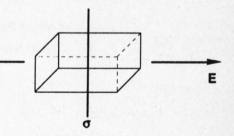

Recognizing the **E** · $d\mathbf{a}$ is only non-zero on the left and right side faces of the Gaussian pillbox, we get

$$EA + EA = \sigma A / \varepsilon_0$$

or $\quad E = \begin{cases} \sigma / 2\varepsilon_0 x, & x > 0 \\ -\sigma / 2\varepsilon_0 x, & x < 0 \end{cases}.$

The electric potential must be such that

$$\mathbf{E} = -\nabla V = -\frac{\partial V}{\partial x} x$$

thus

$$V = -\int \mathbf{E} \cdot d\mathbf{r} = -\int E \, dx$$
$$= -\sigma x / 2\varepsilon_0$$

for $x > 0$ as desired.

57. **(A)**

The key to solving this problem is to determine the current (I) of the equivalent circuit shown below.

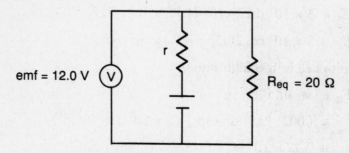

By adding the resistance of the two bulbs in series the circuit is easier to analyze. When the switch is closed and the circuit is in steady state, *all* the current in the circuit travels through R_{eq} and r. The voltage drop across r is

$$(12.0 - 11.6) \text{ volts} = 0.4 \text{ volts} = Ir.$$

For the equivalent resistance of the two bulbs [R_{eq}] the potential difference is the same as the meter since they are in parallel; therefore by Ohm's law

$$I = V/R = (11.6 \text{ volts}) / (20 \text{ ohms}) = 0.58 \text{ ampere}.$$

So, the internal resistance of the battery is

$$r = V_r / I = (0.4 \text{ } V) / (0.58 A) = 0.69 \text{ ohms}.$$

58. **(A)**

$$R_{\text{eff}} = 12 \text{ } \Omega$$
$$I = V/R = 12 \text{ } V / 12 \text{ } \Omega$$

Now working backward the $I = 1$ A splits first into

$$I_1 = I_2 = {}^1/_2 \text{ } A$$

and then I_2 splits into

$$I_3 = I_4 = {}^1/_4 \text{ } A,$$

which equals the current in the 4Ω resistor.

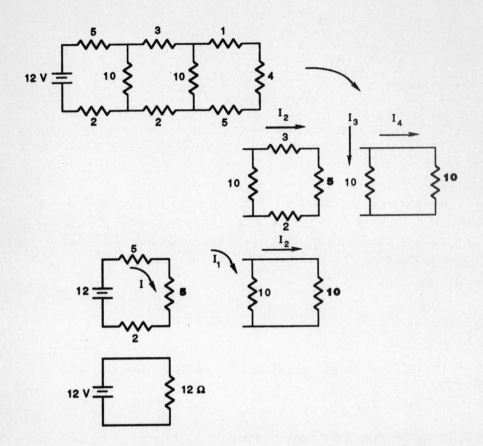

59. **(A)**

We must use Faraday's law:

$$\nabla \times E = -\partial B/\partial t$$

$$V = \int E \cdot d1 = -\frac{\partial \Phi}{\partial t},$$

where

$$\Phi = \int B \cdot da = Blx$$

$$V = -Blv \text{ and } V = RI \Rightarrow I = V/R = Blv/R.$$

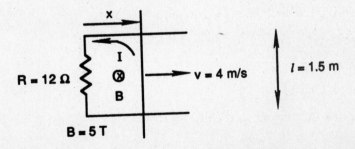

The power is

$$P = VI$$

$$= (Blv)^2 / R$$

$$= (5 \cdot 1.5 \cdot 4)^2 / 12 = 75 \text{ W.}$$

Furthermore, I must be *counterclockwise* by Lentz's law to counteract the increase of magnetic flux due to the motion of the bar.

60. **(B)**

At time $t = 0$, the capacitor is fully charged and the potential across the capacitor is V (or Q/C). When switch 1 is open and switch 2 is closed, the resistor R is in series with capacitor C and the instantaneous voltage across R is equal to that of C,

$$V_R = V_C = V,$$

$$I = V/R.$$

61. **(A)**

The potential energy is transformed into kinetic energy

$$\frac{1}{2} mv^2 = qV_0.$$

The centripetal force is the magnetic force

$$\frac{mv^2}{R} = qvB \Rightarrow v = q\frac{BR}{m}.$$

Thus

$$\frac{q}{m} = v^2 / 2V_0 = (qBr/m)^2 / 2V_0$$

$$q/m = 2V_0 / B^2 R^2$$

$$R = \sqrt{2V_0 m / B^2 q}$$

$$= \sqrt{2(4000)(10.0129)(1.66 \times 10^{-27}) / (.5^2 \cdot 1.602 \times 10^{-19})}$$

$$= 0.0576 \text{ m}$$

$$= 5.76 \text{ cm.}$$

62. **(B)**

$$d\mathbf{B} = \frac{\mu_0}{4\pi} \frac{I}{r^2} dl \times \mathbf{r}$$

$$\mathbf{B}_1 = \frac{\mu_0}{4\pi} \frac{I_1}{d^2} \int dl(-\mathbf{z})$$

$$= \frac{\mu_0 I_1}{4\pi d^2}\, \pi az$$

$$= -\frac{\mu_0 I_1}{4 d^2}\, z$$

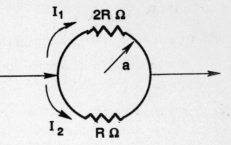

Similarly, $B_2 = \frac{\mu_0}{4a}\, z$.

Now reduce the series resistor:

$$\frac{1}{R_T} = \frac{1}{R} + \frac{1}{2R} = \frac{3}{2R}, \quad R_T = \frac{2}{3}R$$

$$V = R_T I = \frac{2}{3}RI$$

$$I_1 = \frac{V}{R_1}, \quad I_1 = \frac{V}{2R} = \frac{1}{3}I, \; I_2 = \frac{V}{R} = \frac{2}{3}I$$

$$B = B_1 + B_2 = \frac{\mu_0}{4a}\, z\, (I_2 - I_1) = \frac{\mu_0 I}{12a}\, z.$$

63. **(B)**

In the Thomson experiment, the electric force balances the magnetic force

$$eE = eVB.$$

Thus, $v = E/B$.

In the absence of B, the deflection is

$$s = \frac{1}{2}\, at^2$$

$$= \frac{1}{2}\frac{eE}{m}\left(\frac{l}{V}\right)^2$$

$$s = \frac{1}{2}\frac{eE}{m}\frac{l^2 B^2}{E^2} = \frac{1}{2}\frac{e}{m}\frac{l^2 B^2}{V/d}.$$

Hence, $\frac{e}{m} = 2(1.25 \times 10^{-3})(50/1.5 \times 10^{-2})/(5 \times 10^{-2})^2(1.2 \times 10^{-4})^2$

$$= 2.31 \times 10^{11}\,\text{coul}/\text{kg}.$$

64. **(B)**

$$\nabla \cdot \mathbf{B} = 0$$

implies that there are no magnetic monopoles. If there were, then we would have

$$\nabla \cdot \mathbf{B} = \rho_B$$

with ρ_B a positive or negative magnetic charge density.

It is identical to its integral form which is analogous to Gauss' law for magnetism:

$$\oint \mathbf{B} \cdot d\mathbf{a} = Q_B$$

but we know that the result of the integral is always zero and we cannot have a magnetic monopole.

65. **(C)**

Now the current density is

$$j = I/A = I/\pi(b^2 - a^2)$$

and by Ohm's law

$$j = \sigma E = \frac{1}{\rho} E = \frac{1}{\rho} \frac{V}{l},$$

where s is the conductivity and r is the resistivity. Hence,

$$\frac{1}{\rho} \frac{V}{l} = \frac{I}{\pi(b^2 - a^2)}.$$

Finally,

$$R = V/I = \rho l/\pi(b^2 - a^2).$$

66. **(E)**

The law for parallel resistors is

$$\frac{1}{R_t} = \Sigma \frac{1}{R}.$$

Hence,

$$\frac{1}{R_T} = \frac{4}{R}$$

$$R_T = \frac{1}{4} R = \frac{1}{4} M\Omega.$$

The reduced circuit is a basic RC circuit. From Kirchoff's law

$$-RI - \frac{Q}{C} = 0 \quad \text{or} \quad Q' + \frac{Q}{\tau} = 0$$

with $\tau = RC$ as the time constant. The solution is

$$Q = Q_0 e^{-t/\tau}$$

$$\tau = RC = \frac{1}{4} \times 10^6 \times 1 \times 10^{-6} = \frac{1}{4} s$$

$$I = I_0 e^{-t/\tau}$$

$$I_0 = \frac{V}{R} = 10 \times 10^6 / \frac{1}{4} \times 10^6 = 40 \text{ A}$$

$$= 40 e^{-.5/.25}$$

$$= 5.41 \text{ A}.$$

67. **(E)**

The bottom two resistors are parallel.

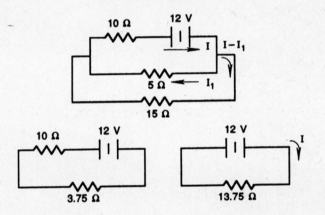

Thus,

$$R = \frac{R_1 R_2}{R_1 + R_2} = \frac{15(5)}{15 + 5} = 3.75\,\Omega.$$

The last two resistors now add up since they are in series:

$$R = R_1 + R_2$$

$$= 10 + 3.75$$

$$= 13.75\ \Omega.$$

The current in the reduced circuit is then

$$I = V/R = 12/13.75 = .873 \text{ A}.$$

Applying Kirchoff's voltage law to the second circuit, we get:

$$12\ V = 5I_1 + 10I = 5I_1 + 8.73$$

thus, $I_1 = 3.27/5 = 0.654 \text{ A}.$

68. **(D)**

   Kirchoff's law tells us that

   $$V - RI - LI' = 0.$$

   Differentiating, we get

   $$I'' + \frac{I'}{\tau} = 0 \quad \text{where} \quad \tau = \frac{L}{R}$$

   is the time constant of the circuit. The solution is

   $$I = \frac{V}{R}(1 - e^{-t/\tau}), \quad \tau = \frac{L}{R}.$$

   Hence,

   $$I_\infty = \frac{V}{R} = \frac{30}{10} = 3\,A$$

   $$U_\infty = \frac{1}{2}LI_\infty^2$$

   $$= \frac{1}{2}(10 \times 10^{-6}\,H)(3A)^2$$

   $$= 4.5 \times 10^{-5}\,J.$$

69. **(A)**

   By Faraday's law or Maxwell's second equation:

   $$\nabla \times E = -\frac{\partial B}{\partial t}$$

   $$\oint E \cdot d\mathbf{r} = -\frac{d\phi_B}{dt}.$$

   Thus, the induced voltage is

   $$V = \frac{d}{dt}\int B \cdot d\mathbf{a}$$

   $$= \frac{d}{dt}B \times w$$

   $$= Bwv.$$

   By Kirchoff's law

   $$V = RI.$$

   Thus, $\quad Bwv = RI$

   $$v = RI / Bw$$

   $$= (2\,\Omega)(0.5\,A) / (1\,T)(0.5\,m)$$

   $$= 2\,m/s.$$

70. **(E)**

$$\nabla \cdot E = \frac{\rho}{\varepsilon_0}$$

According to superposition principle, we can evaluate the electric field produced by each sheet separately and then add them up, because the presence of each sheet does not have any effect on the charge of the other. Therefore, to find the electric field or one of the sheets we can write:

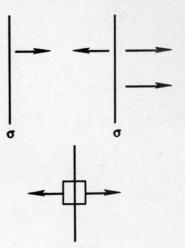

$$\oint E \cdot d A = \frac{q}{\varepsilon_0}$$

$$2EA = \frac{\sigma S}{\varepsilon_0}.$$

Using a Gaussian pillbox

$$E = \frac{\sigma}{2\varepsilon_0}.$$

Thus, $\quad E_{tot} = \frac{\sigma}{\varepsilon_0} x$

to the right of the sheets.

DETAILED EXPLANATIONS OF ANSWERS

TEST 3

Section II – Electricity and Magnetism

1. (a)

Since the zero potential level is assumed to be at infinity, the work done to move charge q from infinity to a distance R from charge q' is the integral

$$-\int F\, dR = \int (kqq')/R^2\ dR = (kqq')/R.$$

This is independent of the path and when used with a group of charges, the total work is the sum of the work done to move each charge from infinity to the desired position. It does not matter which charge is initially moved.

So the total work done is

$(kq_1q_2/R) + (kq_2q_3/R) + (kq_1q_3/R) =$ total work done

$= [k/R]\ [(q_1q_2) + (q_2q_3) + (q_1q_3)]$

$= [(9 \times 10^9\ \text{Nm}^2/C^2)/(0.01\ \text{m})]\ [(2 \times 10^{-6}\ C) + (6 \times 10^{-6}\ C)$

$\quad + (3 \times 10^{-6}\ C)]$

$= 9.9 \times 10^6\ \text{J}.$

1. (b)

The potential energy of the system is equal to the work done to change their position. It is the same answer as (a) which is 9.9×10^6 J.

2. (a)

The capacitance is defined by the equation

$C = \varepsilon_0\ A/d.$

2. (b)

The introduction of the new dielectric medium changes the net field between the plates. The dielectric is polarized due to the plate field and a counter field is produced, thereby weakening the net field and decreasing the potential difference between the plates. The resulting increase in capacitance is the factor κ, the dielectric constant, therefore

$$C_{new} = \kappa C_0 = k \varepsilon_0 \, A/d.$$

2. (c)

Each portion of the dielectric material "sees" one-half the surface area of each plate, but they both experience the same electric field (assuming that the field is constant),

potential $(V) = Ed$

for both materials. This configuration is similar to having two capacitors of plate area $A/2$ and distance d, but possessing two different dielectrics, and connecting them in parallel.

$$C_{new} = C_1 + C_2 = [\kappa_1 \varepsilon_0 \, A/(2d)] + [\kappa_2 \varepsilon_0 \, A/(2d)]$$

$$C_{new} = \varepsilon_0 \, A/(2d) \, [\kappa_1 + \kappa_2]$$

3. (a)

Since the sum of the voltages around the circuit equal zero

$$V - [L \, (di/dt)] - iR = 0,$$

where $- L(di/dt)$ is the self-induced emf of the inductor and (iR) is the voltage drop across the resistor. The lowercase (i) represents the instantaneous current at any time t.

But, since the circuit is in steady-state, the current is constant

$$di/dt = 0$$

and the circuit is purely resistive in nature,

$$V = iR.$$

3. (b)

The time constant is the time at which the current is 63% of V/R, or when

$$(1 - e^{-Rt/L}) = 0.63 \Rightarrow Rt/L = 1$$

or $\quad t = L/R.$

3. (c)

The integral of the equation shows that as the circuit reaches steady-state, di/dt approaches zero and the circuit reaches the final current of V/R.

Rewriting this equation and integrating gives an exponential function relating the time, inductance, and resistance to the current in the circuit at time t.

$$[(V/R) - i] \, dt = (L/R) \, di \Rightarrow di \, / \, [(V/R) - i] = (R/L) dt$$

integrating these two equalities yields the solution

$$\ln (V/R - i) = (R/L)t + C,$$

where C is the constant of integration which can be found by analyzing the circuit at $t = 0$. The current at $t = 0$ is V/R which fits the general form

$$i(t) = V/R \, [1 - e^{-Rt/L}].$$

As t increases, $i(t)$ becomes closer and closer to V/R, or it simply becomes purely resistive as di/dt approaches zero.

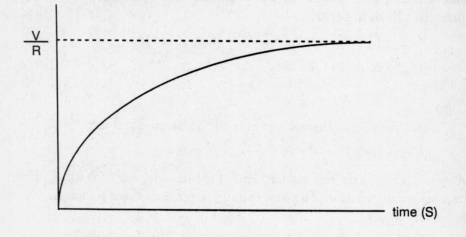

Advanced Placement Examination in
PHYSICS B — Test 1

1. Ⓐ Ⓑ Ⓒ Ⓓ Ⓔ
2. Ⓐ Ⓑ Ⓒ Ⓓ Ⓔ
3. Ⓐ Ⓑ Ⓒ Ⓓ Ⓔ
4. Ⓐ Ⓑ Ⓒ Ⓓ Ⓔ
5. Ⓐ Ⓑ Ⓒ Ⓓ Ⓔ
6. Ⓐ Ⓑ Ⓒ Ⓓ Ⓔ
7. Ⓐ Ⓑ Ⓒ Ⓓ Ⓔ
8. Ⓐ Ⓑ Ⓒ Ⓓ Ⓔ
9. Ⓐ Ⓑ Ⓒ Ⓓ Ⓔ
10. Ⓐ Ⓑ Ⓒ Ⓓ Ⓔ
11. Ⓐ Ⓑ Ⓒ Ⓓ Ⓔ
12. Ⓐ Ⓑ Ⓒ Ⓓ Ⓔ
13. Ⓐ Ⓑ Ⓒ Ⓓ Ⓔ
14. Ⓐ Ⓑ Ⓒ Ⓓ Ⓔ
15. Ⓐ Ⓑ Ⓒ Ⓓ Ⓔ
16. Ⓐ Ⓑ Ⓒ Ⓓ Ⓔ
17. Ⓐ Ⓑ Ⓒ Ⓓ Ⓔ
18. Ⓐ Ⓑ Ⓒ Ⓓ Ⓔ
19. Ⓐ Ⓑ Ⓒ Ⓓ Ⓔ
20. Ⓐ Ⓑ Ⓒ Ⓓ Ⓔ
21. Ⓐ Ⓑ Ⓒ Ⓓ Ⓔ
22. Ⓐ Ⓑ Ⓒ Ⓓ Ⓔ
23. Ⓐ Ⓑ Ⓒ Ⓓ Ⓔ

24. Ⓐ Ⓑ Ⓒ Ⓓ Ⓔ
25. Ⓐ Ⓑ Ⓒ Ⓓ Ⓔ
26. Ⓐ Ⓑ Ⓒ Ⓓ Ⓔ
27. Ⓐ Ⓑ Ⓒ Ⓓ Ⓔ
28. Ⓐ Ⓑ Ⓒ Ⓓ Ⓔ
29. Ⓐ Ⓑ Ⓒ Ⓓ Ⓔ
30. Ⓐ Ⓑ Ⓒ Ⓓ Ⓔ
31. Ⓐ Ⓑ Ⓒ Ⓓ Ⓔ
32. Ⓐ Ⓑ Ⓒ Ⓓ Ⓔ
33. Ⓐ Ⓑ Ⓒ Ⓓ Ⓔ
34. Ⓐ Ⓑ Ⓒ Ⓓ Ⓔ
35. Ⓐ Ⓑ Ⓒ Ⓓ Ⓔ
36. Ⓐ Ⓑ Ⓒ Ⓓ Ⓔ
37. Ⓐ Ⓑ Ⓒ Ⓓ Ⓔ
38. Ⓐ Ⓑ Ⓒ Ⓓ Ⓔ
39. Ⓐ Ⓑ Ⓒ Ⓓ Ⓔ
40. Ⓐ Ⓑ Ⓒ Ⓓ Ⓔ
41. Ⓐ Ⓑ Ⓒ Ⓓ Ⓔ
42. Ⓐ Ⓑ Ⓒ Ⓓ Ⓔ
43. Ⓐ Ⓑ Ⓒ Ⓓ Ⓔ
44. Ⓐ Ⓑ Ⓒ Ⓓ Ⓔ
45. Ⓐ Ⓑ Ⓒ Ⓓ Ⓔ
46. Ⓐ Ⓑ Ⓒ Ⓓ Ⓔ
47. Ⓐ Ⓑ Ⓒ Ⓓ Ⓔ

48. Ⓐ Ⓑ Ⓒ Ⓓ Ⓔ
49. Ⓐ Ⓑ Ⓒ Ⓓ Ⓔ
50. Ⓐ Ⓑ Ⓒ Ⓓ Ⓔ
51. Ⓐ Ⓑ Ⓒ Ⓓ Ⓔ
52. Ⓐ Ⓑ Ⓒ Ⓓ Ⓔ
53. Ⓐ Ⓑ Ⓒ Ⓓ Ⓔ
54. Ⓐ Ⓑ Ⓒ Ⓓ Ⓔ
55. Ⓐ Ⓑ Ⓒ Ⓓ Ⓔ
56. Ⓐ Ⓑ Ⓒ Ⓓ Ⓔ
57. Ⓐ Ⓑ Ⓒ Ⓓ Ⓔ
58. Ⓐ Ⓑ Ⓒ Ⓓ Ⓔ
59. Ⓐ Ⓑ Ⓒ Ⓓ Ⓔ
60. Ⓐ Ⓑ Ⓒ Ⓓ Ⓔ
61. Ⓐ Ⓑ Ⓒ Ⓓ Ⓔ
62. Ⓐ Ⓑ Ⓒ Ⓓ Ⓔ
63. Ⓐ Ⓑ Ⓒ Ⓓ Ⓔ
64. Ⓐ Ⓑ Ⓒ Ⓓ Ⓔ
65. Ⓐ Ⓑ Ⓒ Ⓓ Ⓔ
66. Ⓐ Ⓑ Ⓒ Ⓓ Ⓔ
67. Ⓐ Ⓑ Ⓒ Ⓓ Ⓔ
68. Ⓐ Ⓑ Ⓒ Ⓓ Ⓔ
69. Ⓐ Ⓑ Ⓒ Ⓓ Ⓔ
70. Ⓐ Ⓑ Ⓒ Ⓓ Ⓔ

Advanced Placement Examination in
PHYSICS B — Test 2

1. (A) (B) (C) (D) (E)
2. (A) (B) (C) (D) (E)
3. (A) (B) (C) (D) (E)
4. (A) (B) (C) (D) (E)
5. (A) (B) (C) (D) (E)
6. (A) (B) (C) (D) (E)
7. (A) (B) (C) (D) (E)
8. (A) (B) (C) (D) (E)
9. (A) (B) (C) (D) (E)
10. (A) (B) (C) (D) (E)
11. (A) (B) (C) (D) (E)
12. (A) (B) (C) (D) (E)
13. (A) (B) (C) (D) (E)
14. (A) (B) (C) (D) (E)
15. (A) (B) (C) (D) (E)
16. (A) (B) (C) (D) (E)
17. (A) (B) (C) (D) (E)
18. (A) (B) (C) (D) (E)
19. (A) (B) (C) (D) (E)
20. (A) (B) (C) (D) (E)
21. (A) (B) (C) (D) (E)
22. (A) (B) (C) (D) (E)
23. (A) (B) (C) (D) (E)

24. (A) (B) (C) (D) (E)
25. (A) (B) (C) (D) (E)
26. (A) (B) (C) (D) (E)
27. (A) (B) (C) (D) (E)
28. (A) (B) (C) (D) (E)
29. (A) (B) (C) (D) (E)
30. (A) (B) (C) (D) (E)
31. (A) (B) (C) (D) (E)
32. (A) (B) (C) (D) (E)
33. (A) (B) (C) (D) (E)
34. (A) (B) (C) (D) (E)
35. (A) (B) (C) (D) (E)
36. (A) (B) (C) (D) (E)
37. (A) (B) (C) (D) (E)
38. (A) (B) (C) (D) (E)
39. (A) (B) (C) (D) (E)
40. (A) (B) (C) (D) (E)
41. (A) (B) (C) (D) (E)
42. (A) (B) (C) (D) (E)
43. (A) (B) (C) (D) (E)
44. (A) (B) (C) (D) (E)
45. (A) (B) (C) (D) (E)
46. (A) (B) (C) (D) (E)
47. (A) (B) (C) (D) (E)

48. (A) (B) (C) (D) (E)
49. (A) (B) (C) (D) (E)
50. (A) (B) (C) (D) (E)
51. (A) (B) (C) (D) (E)
52. (A) (B) (C) (D) (E)
53. (A) (B) (C) (D) (E)
54. (A) (B) (C) (D) (E)
55. (A) (B) (C) (D) (E)
56. (A) (B) (C) (D) (E)
57. (A) (B) (C) (D) (E)
58. (A) (B) (C) (D) (E)
59. (A) (B) (C) (D) (E)
60. (A) (B) (C) (D) (E)
61. (A) (B) (C) (D) (E)
62. (A) (B) (C) (D) (E)
63. (A) (B) (C) (D) (E)
64. (A) (B) (C) (D) (E)
65. (A) (B) (C) (D) (E)
66. (A) (B) (C) (D) (E)
67. (A) (B) (C) (D) (E)
68. (A) (B) (C) (D) (E)
69. (A) (B) (C) (D) (E)
70. (A) (B) (C) (D) (E)

Advanced Placement Examination in
PHYSICS C — Test 3

MECHANICS

1. Ⓐ Ⓑ Ⓒ Ⓓ Ⓔ
2. Ⓐ Ⓑ Ⓒ Ⓓ Ⓔ
3. Ⓐ Ⓑ Ⓒ Ⓓ Ⓔ
4. Ⓐ Ⓑ Ⓒ Ⓓ Ⓔ
5. Ⓐ Ⓑ Ⓒ Ⓓ Ⓔ
6. Ⓐ Ⓑ Ⓒ Ⓓ Ⓔ
7. Ⓐ Ⓑ Ⓒ Ⓓ Ⓔ
8. Ⓐ Ⓑ Ⓒ Ⓓ Ⓔ
9. Ⓐ Ⓑ Ⓒ Ⓓ Ⓔ
10. Ⓐ Ⓑ Ⓒ Ⓓ Ⓔ
11. Ⓐ Ⓑ Ⓒ Ⓓ Ⓔ
12. Ⓐ Ⓑ Ⓒ Ⓓ Ⓔ

13. Ⓐ Ⓑ Ⓒ Ⓓ Ⓔ
14. Ⓐ Ⓑ Ⓒ Ⓓ Ⓔ
15. Ⓐ Ⓑ Ⓒ Ⓓ Ⓔ
16. Ⓐ Ⓑ Ⓒ Ⓓ Ⓔ
17. Ⓐ Ⓑ Ⓒ Ⓓ Ⓔ
18. Ⓐ Ⓑ Ⓒ Ⓓ Ⓔ
19. Ⓐ Ⓑ Ⓒ Ⓓ Ⓔ
20. Ⓐ Ⓑ Ⓒ Ⓓ Ⓔ
21. Ⓐ Ⓑ Ⓒ Ⓓ Ⓔ
22. Ⓐ Ⓑ Ⓒ Ⓓ Ⓔ
23. Ⓐ Ⓑ Ⓒ Ⓓ Ⓔ

24. Ⓐ Ⓑ Ⓒ Ⓓ Ⓔ
25. Ⓐ Ⓑ Ⓒ Ⓓ Ⓔ
26. Ⓐ Ⓑ Ⓒ Ⓓ Ⓔ
27. Ⓐ Ⓑ Ⓒ Ⓓ Ⓔ
28. Ⓐ Ⓑ Ⓒ Ⓓ Ⓔ
29. Ⓐ Ⓑ Ⓒ Ⓓ Ⓔ
30. Ⓐ Ⓑ Ⓒ Ⓓ Ⓔ
31. Ⓐ Ⓑ Ⓒ Ⓓ Ⓔ
32. Ⓐ Ⓑ Ⓒ Ⓓ Ⓔ
33. Ⓐ Ⓑ Ⓒ Ⓓ Ⓔ
34. Ⓐ Ⓑ Ⓒ Ⓓ Ⓔ
35. Ⓐ Ⓑ Ⓒ Ⓓ Ⓔ

ELECTRICITY AND MAGNETISM

36. Ⓐ Ⓑ Ⓒ Ⓓ Ⓔ
37. Ⓐ Ⓑ Ⓒ Ⓓ Ⓔ
38. Ⓐ Ⓑ Ⓒ Ⓓ Ⓔ
39. Ⓐ Ⓑ Ⓒ Ⓓ Ⓔ
40. Ⓐ Ⓑ Ⓒ Ⓓ Ⓔ
41. Ⓐ Ⓑ Ⓒ Ⓓ Ⓔ
42. Ⓐ Ⓑ Ⓒ Ⓓ Ⓔ
43. Ⓐ Ⓑ Ⓒ Ⓓ Ⓔ
44. Ⓐ Ⓑ Ⓒ Ⓓ Ⓔ
45. Ⓐ Ⓑ Ⓒ Ⓓ Ⓔ
46. Ⓐ Ⓑ Ⓒ Ⓓ Ⓔ
47. Ⓐ Ⓑ Ⓒ Ⓓ Ⓔ

48. Ⓐ Ⓑ Ⓒ Ⓓ Ⓔ
49. Ⓐ Ⓑ Ⓒ Ⓓ Ⓔ
50. Ⓐ Ⓑ Ⓒ Ⓓ Ⓔ
51. Ⓐ Ⓑ Ⓒ Ⓓ Ⓔ
52. Ⓐ Ⓑ Ⓒ Ⓓ Ⓔ
53. Ⓐ Ⓑ Ⓒ Ⓓ Ⓔ
54. Ⓐ Ⓑ Ⓒ Ⓓ Ⓔ
55. Ⓐ Ⓑ Ⓒ Ⓓ Ⓔ
56. Ⓐ Ⓑ Ⓒ Ⓓ Ⓔ
57. Ⓐ Ⓑ Ⓒ Ⓓ Ⓔ
58. Ⓐ Ⓑ Ⓒ Ⓓ Ⓔ

59. Ⓐ Ⓑ Ⓒ Ⓓ Ⓔ
60. Ⓐ Ⓑ Ⓒ Ⓓ Ⓔ
61. Ⓐ Ⓑ Ⓒ Ⓓ Ⓔ
62. Ⓐ Ⓑ Ⓒ Ⓓ Ⓔ
63. Ⓐ Ⓑ Ⓒ Ⓓ Ⓔ
64. Ⓐ Ⓑ Ⓒ Ⓓ Ⓔ
65. Ⓐ Ⓑ Ⓒ Ⓓ Ⓔ
66. Ⓐ Ⓑ Ⓒ Ⓓ Ⓔ
67. Ⓐ Ⓑ Ⓒ Ⓓ Ⓔ
68. Ⓐ Ⓑ Ⓒ Ⓓ Ⓔ
69. Ⓐ Ⓑ Ⓒ Ⓓ Ⓔ
70. Ⓐ Ⓑ Ⓒ Ⓓ Ⓔ

REA's **Problem Solvers**

The "PROBLEM SOLVERS" are comprehensive supplemental text-books designed to save time in finding solutions to problems. Each "PROBLEM SOLVER" is the first of its kind ever produced in its field. It is the product of a massive effort to illustrate almost any imaginable problem in exceptional depth, detail, and clarity. Each problem is worked out in detail with step-by-step solution, and the problems are arranged in order of complexity from elementary to advanced. Each book is fully indexed for locating problems rapidly.

Problem Solvers
CALCULUS
A Complete Solution Guide
to Any Textbook

ADVANCED CALCULUS
ALGEBRA & TRIGONOMETRY
AUTOMATIC CONTROL
   SYSTEMS/ROBOTICS
BIOLOGY
BUSINESS, MANAGEMENT, & FINANCE
CALCULUS
CHEMISTRY
COMPLEX VARIABLES
COMPUTER SCIENCE
DIFFERENTIAL EQUATIONS
ECONOMICS
ELECTRICAL MACHINES
ELECTRIC CIRCUITS
ELECTROMAGNETICS
ELECTRONIC COMMUNICATIONS
ELECTRONICS
FINITE & DISCRETE MATH
FLUID MECHANICS/DYNAMICS
GENETICS
GEOMETRY

HEAT TRANSFER
LINEAR ALGEBRA
MACHINE DESIGN
MATHEMATICS for ENGINEERS
MECHANICS
NUMERICAL ANALYSIS
OPERATIONS RESEARCH
OPTICS
ORGANIC CHEMISTRY
PHYSICAL CHEMISTRY
PHYSICS
PRE-CALCULUS
PSYCHOLOGY
STATISTICS
STRENGTH OF MATERIALS &
   MECHANICS OF SOLIDS
TECHNICAL DESIGN GRAPHICS
THERMODYNAMICS
TOPOLOGY
TRANSPORT PHENOMENA
VECTOR ANALYSIS

*If you would like more information about any of these books,
complete the coupon below and return it to us or go to your local bookstore.*

RESEARCH & EDUCATION ASSOCIATION
61 Ethel Road W. • Piscataway, New Jersey 08854
Phone: (908) 819-8880

Please send me more information about your Problem Solver Books

Name _____

Address _____

City _____ State _____ Zip _____

REA's Test Preps
The Best in Test Preparation

The REA "Test Preps" are far more comprehensive than any other test series. They contain more tests with much more extensive explanations than others on the market. Each book provides several complete practice exams, based on the most recent tests given in the particular field. Every type of question likely to be given on the exams is included. Each individual test is followed by a complete answer key. **The answers are accompanied by full and detailed explanations.** By studying each test and the explanations which follow, students will become well-prepared for the actual exam.

REA has published over 40 Test Preparation volumes in several series. They include:

Advanced Placement Exams (APs)
Biology
Calculus AB & Calculus BC
Chemistry
Computer Science
English Literature & Composition
European History
Government & Politics
Physics
Psychology
United States History

College Board Achievement Tests (CBATs)
American History
Biology
Chemistry
English Composition
French

German
Literature
Mathematics Level I, II & IIC
Physics
Spanish

Graduate Record Exams (GREs)
Biology
Chemistry
Computer Science
Economics
Engineering
GENERAL TEST
History
Literature in English
Mathematics
Physics
Political Science
Psychology

ASVAB - Armed Service Vocational Aptitude Battery Test

CBEST - California Basic Educational Skills Test
CDL - Commercial Driver's License Exam
ExCET - Exam for Certification of Educators in Texas
FE (EIT) - Fundamentals of Engineering Exam
GED - High School Equivalency Diploma Exam
GMAT - Graduate Management Admission Test
LSAT - Law School Adm. Test
MCAT - Medical College Admission Test
NTE - National Teachers Exam
SAT - Scholastic Aptitude Test
TASP - Texas Academic Skills Program
TOEFL - Test of English as a Foreign Language

RESEARCH & EDUCATION ASSOCIATION
61 Ethel Road W. • Piscataway, New Jersey 08854
Phone: (908) 819-8880

Please send me more information about your Test Prep Books

Name_____

Address_____

City _____ State _____ Zip _____